W9-BBP-986

FEB 12 '91	DATE DUE		

THE POSTPONED GENERATION

THE
POSTPONED
GENERATION

Why America's
Grown-up Kids Are
Growing Up Later

SUSAN LITTWIN

William Morrow and Company, Inc.
New York

Library of Congress Cataloging-in-Publication Data

Littwin, Susan.
  The postponed generation.

  1. Young adults—United States—Psychology.
2. Adult children—United States. 3. College graduates—
United States. 4. United States—Social conditions—
1980–   . I. Title.
HQ799.7.L58   1986   305.2′35   85–18831
ISBN 0-688-04890-0

Printed in the United States of America

First Edition

1 2 3 4 5 6 7 8 9 10

BOOK DESIGN BY RICHARD ORIOLO

Acknowledgments

This book was made possible by the many young adults who were willing to talk to me and sometimes even introduce me to their friends. They appear in the book under pseudonyms, but they know who they are and I thank them.

I would also like to thank those people who shared their knowledge and contacts: Henry Durand, Barry Reister, and Bernice Russell at Loyola Marymount; Barbara McGowan, Valerie Oppenheimer, Robert Ehrmann, Beth Beeler, Alan Hanson, and Guy Sanders at UCLA; Abby Parsons at Pitzer College, John Clarke at the University of Tennessee, Martha Greene at Barnard College, Tom Omalia at USC, Albert Cantril of the Bureau of Social Survey Research, and Lee Quarnstrom, Rik Knablein, Thomas J. Moore, Helen Slater, Helaine Sokolik, and Jerry Gaither.

I owe thanks to three writer friends: Gary Diedrichs, Delia Ephron, and John Riley. Gary read chapters, and Delia and John were office neighbors who listened to me a lot.

My editor, Pat Golbitz, deserves thanks for her good advice at the start and her acute suggestions at the end.

Deepest thanks go to my agents, Maureen and Eric Lasher. They did more than represent me and make this book happen. They were a full-service agency.

And my husband, Larry, did more than just read chapters, praise warmly, and criticize tactfully. He was in my corner the whole time.

CONTENTS

PART IV: THE CHANGING LANDSCAPE

PART I

THE HISTORICAL WRINKLE

1
The Graduate Summer

Everyone had to be out of the dorm by noon, and it looked as if the sets for about a dozen movies were being struck at once. Kids in jeans and shorts and Izod shirts were cramming stereo speakers and turntables and high-intensity lamps and cartons of odds and ends into the elevators and carrying them out to cars waiting in the red no parking zone. Jenny just had the paintings she had done for art honors—her parents had taken the rest—and she loaded the vivid canvases into a friend's station wagon. They were what she had done with her life so far and the only things in the world she really treasured, but they had already taken on the silly look of out-of-style clothes. What would she do with them?

Slowly, the wagon maneuvered out of the tangle of campus traffic, through the noon-quiet streets of the town and onto the highway. That was when Jenny started to cry. Three states later, pulling into the palm- and hibiscus-lined driveway of her parents' home, she was still crying. College was over and she hadn't the faintest idea what she wanted to do next.

She spent the summer lying in the pool on a rubber float, just like Dustin Hoffman in *The Graduate*. Her tan got deeper and darker, and then turned yellowish, but she didn't really care. Her parents would look out the window or stand awkwardly around the coping fully dressed and ask her if she didn't ever plan to do anything else. "I don't know," she'd answer languidly. "I've been under a lot of stress. I can't think." After a few weeks, she stopped answering and they stopped asking.

When her mother graduated from college twenty-five years ago, she had a teacher's job waiting. Her father—who was more ambitious for his bright, assertive daughter—kept talking about law school. He had gone straight through, working in the textile mill during the summers to pay his tuition. Jenny, of course, wouldn't have to do any of that. All she had to do was want to go. And after law school, there would be a job with the firm and then a partnership and then eventually, when Dad retired . . . "You can paint on the weekends," he'd say.

That was when Jenny would close her eyes and reach into the float pocket for another Miller Lite. A week after Labor Day, her father got her a job as a bank teller. She bought clothes and some aloe vera cream for her damaged skin and joined the nine-to-five world.

At the local branch bank, that meant other tellers who wore short skirts and heavy eye makeup and chewed gum while they tried to teach her to operate the peculiar change machines. She was inept at that, so the manager moved her to accounting, where sweet old ladies gave her things to file. "It was humiliating," she remembers. "In college, I was so special. Now, I had this shit job, and I wasn't even good at it. I realized how college hadn't prepared me for a professional job or a shit job." After a week and a half, she left in the middle of the day, walked to her father's office and phoned the bank to say that she was quitting. She worked for her father for a few months, but then they quarreled and she took off for Boston with a hundred dollars in her pocket, a B.A. in art by way of qualifications, and not the slightest notion of who she was or what she wanted to do with her life. Seven years later she is slowly finding answers.

What is special about Jenny is that her story has become so commonplace. Jenny isn't especially alienated, and she isn't on unusually bad terms with her parents. *The Graduate* summer is almost a part of college now, like the junior year in Europe or an internship with a legislator. Perhaps it is God's way of telling us that we have too many backyard pools. Yet many parents will probably recognize indoor variations on the theme. Some graduates watched soap operas or drank gin and tonics or didn't change their clothes for three months. Having had an expensive education and more advantages than any other generation on earth, they seemed confused, unfocused, and dependent.

Studies by the University of Michigan's Institute for Social Research and by the social survey research firm of Yankelovich, Skelly, and White show that young Americans feel increasingly goalless and anxious. But to each family, the situation seemed unique, a bizarre malady at a time when—according to the media—every other young person was career-oriented and fiercely pragmatic.

But the media were wrong. The eighties may have arrived smoothly enough in the newsrooms and in editors' offices. In the real lives of real young adults, the adjustment wasn't so easy. Adulthood was turning out to be a crisis of confused expectations. The crisis was more than the graduate summer. Jenny spent the next seven years moving back home and then leaving again, as she struggled to gain independence and a sense of reality. An *A* student in high school and a leader in college, she has since been in therapy, toyed with graduate school, and worked at jobs ranging from television production to pumping gas to installing telephones—her most recent and stable employment. She has put her painting on a back burner because she is unwilling to compromise or to starve. If she is like others of her generation, it may also be that she is unwilling to risk failure. Now, at twenty-nine, she is beginning to know who she is and how she wants to lead her life.

Jenny is not unique nor is her confusion limited to art majors or even college graduates. She is real, but she is a cipher for a generation of young Americans. Most of them are now in their twenties and from affluent, educated families who wanted everything for their children. The crisis they face is part of their special history. They were raised in the sixties when we were all greening and changing in various ways and—best of all—knew that we could afford to do so and believed that our children would also be able to. If we never told them that life could be tough, it was because we had forgotten it ourselves. And perhaps we were tired of the dreary, depression-era lessons about hard work and frugality and caution that we had been raised with. For our own children, life would be rich and rewarding. We encouraged them to express themselves and to fulfill themselves, believing that somehow, sheer abundance would support them. "They can paint on weekends," we thought, imagining perhaps that most of their lives would consist of weekends. And we accomplished this together, as a society. Jenny's parents believed in and lived the work ethic, but the message of high expectations was there, in the very air she breathed. It seemed to go into the pool with the chlorine and the acid, and she absorbed it osmotically: *She was special.*

So at twenty-two, she had more than expectations. She had a sense of entitlement. In *Privileged Ones*, the fifth volume in his *Children of Crisis* series, child psychiatrist Robert Coles wrote about the complicated, class-connected psychology of "narcissistic entitlement" that he found in the children of the very rich. But middle-class young Americans have managed to take on elements of the condition. Like the children born to wealth and power in Coles's study, they put great emphasis on the self, dislike answering to others, believe that things will somehow work out for the best, that their fantasies will come true, and that the world they move in will be strung with safety nets. These are reasonable beliefs for children who will inherit wealth and social position. For everyone else, they are dangerous illusions.

Many middle-class young people add special expectations of their own to this already heady brew. Some of them feel entitled to good times, expensive equipment, and the kind of homes they grew up in. Others believe their rights include instant status, important, meaningful work, and an unspoiled environment. All of them believed that they had limitless choices, arrayed like cereals on the market shelves. Comparatively speaking, Jenny had her feet on the ground. She believed that she was different from the other bank tellers and office workers, in class background and in education, yet she had enough sense of reality to question her assumption that she was heir to some unnamed throne. Others calmly state that they would like a job "with impact" or that they can't work until they find something they really love. And where Jenny used home and Daddy as a refuge whenever the outside world got too nasty, many others never even take those tentative, exploratory steps. They linger in various kinds of far more serious dependency.

For history—with what seems to be a deliberate sense of irony or a need to punish hubris—has thrown them a curve. In the sixties, when these young people were growing up, we almost believed that material scarcity was a thing of the past and that we could now focus on what Daniel Yankelovich calls the search for self-fulfillment. In the early years of school, we taught children to enjoy the *process* and not focus on the goal. Paint what you feel; it doesn't have to look like anything. We emphasized self-expression and feeling good, what in education jargon was called "the affective domain." Our children took it all seriously, ingested it, and grew in its image.

They came of age in the eighties only to find that scarcity was back, that no one cared if they could paint or run a mock constitutional convention or work on relationships or jog six miles. If they couldn't design computers or analyze the profit potential of an investment, no one wanted them. They had spent sixteen years in school being told they were wonderful. "After the first moon landing, our teacher told us that we were God's children, and that the world was ours," a twenty-five-year-old New Yorker named Sharon Pollack remembers. Now, it seems, the society had changed its promises. It wasn't just a matter of a bad economy or even a lean economy. It was a changed economy with different values and different priorities. Perhaps Sharon's teacher should have pointed out to the class just who it was who had sent that rocket up—scientists, engineers, and technicians. The ones whose talents lay in that direction were indeed God's children. And therein lies our tale.

For the rest of them, it would turn out that the expectations they grew up with weren't going to work—at least not in reality. But they lived on in fantasy and since the fantasies were so much nicer, it was reality that had to go. So our children with such high IQ's have become young adults who puzzle us with their inability to understand the most obvious facts of life. They lament that so many jobs are in the city rather than up in the mountains where the air is cleaner. Or they leave entry-level jobs because the company did not implement their ideas immediately.

It is hard enough to establish an adult identity, even in the best of times. But to do it with such a jarring conflict between expectation and reality is a stunning task. What many of today's twenty- to thirty-year-olds have elected to do is continue the identity search while avoiding reality, and that makes it exceedingly slow work. Unless they are fortunate enough to be born with the talent or inclination to go into a field where their expectations are met—such as high technology—they find themselves in their late twenties or early thirties before they have any sense of who they are or where they are going in life. I don't mean that they have arrived on the doorstep of success—just that they have seen a glimmer at the end of the tunnel. They are, in other words, a decade older than their parents were at the same stage in their lives. That they do it at all is perhaps a testament to their flexibility and resilience.

This book is about the crisis of this generation of young adults, hovering reluctantly in the passageway to maturity in a world for which they were unprepared. It is about the world they face and their infinitely varied responses to it.

2
Children of the
Children of the Sixties

This chapter is about the sixties that today's young adults grew up in. It isn't about the decade of Ken Kesey, the Chicago Seven, the Rolling Stones, the Vietnam War or the Manson murders, except indirectly. It is about the sixties that filtered through to a lot of middle-class American families who made some money and some life changes in that delusional decade.

At the turn of the sixties, when the young adults that this book is about were babies or young children, we were still an innocent enough country. We watched an incredible amount of television, danced the twist, read about a sport called surfing, and drove cars with fins. We had just elected as our President a handsome, witty war hero with a beautiful wife, and we loved their wealth and their special American elegance. They were Camelot, a liberal royal court, incorporating both our idealism and our new prosperity and burgeoning appreciation of the good life. We were putting brave young pilots into rockets and shooting them off into space, and giving them heroes' welcomes when they returned. If there was anything disquieting in our ebullient view of life then, it was the nagging, undeniable charge of racial injustice. And, in those salad days, even that produced heroes—the freedom riders, the astronauts of the conscience—as well as villains like Bull Connor.

Until halfway through, the sixties were almost a continuation of the smooth fabric of the fifties—with a few omens. The handsome, young

President had been assassinated in what we were certain was a freak crime by a lone gunman. There was a contraceptive pill that was supposed to be 100 percent effective. A music group called the Beatles appeared on the Ed Sullivan show. And Mario Savio and the Free Speech movement turned Berkeley on its ear with a militant demand for student power.

But the great upheaval of social change and liberation from just about everything was still only a whisper. In 1965, news magazine ads for office machines talked about making "your girl" more productive. Media still used the word "Negro." A University of Illinois professor was fired for suggesting that sexual intercourse between consenting, unmarried adults was all right now that effective birth control was available. And a *Newsweek* poll of college students revealed that only 24 percent of them believed that the United States should withdraw its troops from Vietnam. "Ill-disposed to shake the earth, confident in existing institutions such as banks, big corporations, the medical profession, and the scientific community," was Newsweek's description of college students in 1965.

We were optimistic almost to the point of euphoria. "No youth, not in ancient Greece, enlightened Europe, nor modern America, has ever grown up under so strong a sun. . . . Never have so many children been such complete strangers to famine, plague, want, or war. Theirs are the blessings of prosperity, theirs the spoils of peace," rhapsodized that 1965 article in *Newsweek*. "Contemporary life is changing faster than a laser beam can transmit 'Mario Savio.' Biochemists have cracked the genetic code, may soon be monkeying with evolution as poor John Scopes could never have dreamed of. Mental illness is yielding not so much to the Freudians as to the giant pharmaceutical houses. Theoretical physics is in thrilling flux," the piece continued.

But more than anything, the sixties were about money. We started getting rich after the war, and we stayed rich until the Arab oil embargo in 1973. Everyone seemed to be making money, and more noticeably, everyone was spending it. We had a passion for everything that was multicolored, disposable, or instant: Froot Loops, Trix, instant breakfast, Screaming Yellow Zonkers, Bugles, Dippy Canoes, freeze-dried coffee, instant whipped potatoes, aerosol cheese. We got Pampers for babies— a clear blessing of progress—and we also got paper clothes for adults. There were cheap, disposable beach shifts but there were also filigreed designer gowns and two-hundred-dollar coats covered with shredded paper pompoms. They didn't last because they looked odd on the body, but the mood of the time was so ebulliently experimental, so convinced that we were entitled to the good life that somebody had at least to try the wicked notion of throwing clothes away instead of taking care of them. We genuinely believed that scarcity was over.

It was a consumer culture that worshiped youth, and our children were the projections of all of our dreams. We gave them everything, feeling vastly superior to our own parents, who had less to give. For even if they had money, there were no Pampers, no Bugles, no battery-operated space men, no Barbie dolls with dozens of outfits and a matching boyfriend.

In more or less that vein, sensible American plumbing manufacturers began turning out bidets, certain that heartland housewives needed one more luxury in the bathroom. The manufacturers were wrong, perhaps because our bathrooms were too small. But they were responding accurately to the spirit of the time. For the other theme that emerged with such innocent buoyancy was sex. We had money to spend and a sense that we deserved fun, and that pill became popular as the decade ripened. Women really could be free of the fear of pregnancy. In 1964, a designer named Rudi Gernreich interpreted the new freedom with a topless bathing suit. Only three thousand of the high-rise shorts with halter straps actually sold, but they turned out to be the red-herring scandal of the sixties, angering the Vatican, the Republican party, and countless city councils, which declared them illegal at public beaches and pools.

The real threat to morality turned out to be the mini-skirt. Mary Quant, who manufactured the first of the short skirts in 1965, summed up their meaning in one word: sex. Mini-skirts made traditional undergarments— like girdles, garters, and stockings—impossible. Sturdy, serious-support bras were on their way out anyway. (Gernreich was also the designer of the "No-Bra bra.") And if women could be sexually free and even aggressive, well, it was only fair that men could drop their hard-edged machismo and grow their hair long and wear tight pants.

Freedom was everywhere, and there always seemed to be choices. The roles and the rules no longer worked, and that applied to our relationships with our children as well. If the parents were experimenting with drugs and open marriage, it seemed hypocritical and inappropriate to raise children in the old authoritarian way. We had lots of choices and we offered them lots of choices. "They were given so much power that it made them insecure and manipulative," says Dr. Leo Pirojnikoff, a Southern California psychologist. "Parents had the philosophy of 'He'll clean up his room when he's ready to have a clean room.'"

We tend to blame Dr. Spock and the child care establishment for the "permissive" rearing that came into vogue in the sixties, but they may be taking a bad rap. Most professional child care advice of the period seems remarkably sensible and unradical by today's standards. Spock himself never even opposed spanking, and anyway, he had grown fairly bored with the baby business by then and was almost completely preoccupied with the peace movement. The media stars of the child care world then were Dr. Bruno Bettelheim—a distinguished psychoanalyst and author who had a monthly column in the *Ladies' Home Journal*—and Dr. Haim Ginott, a child psychologist who had written a popular book called *Between Parent and Child*, and who frequently appeared on television talk shows. Bettelheim was conservative enough to be called "Dr. Brutalheim" by the left and to be the subject of a *New York Times Magazine* article called "Bruno Bettelheim Is Dr. No." And Ginott offered advice that was down-to-earth, funny, even authoritarian. ("I will see you in my study after dinner," he would have a father say to a child who misbehaved.)

What the child care experts did do, at least indirectly, was create the idea of the professional parent. With all of this advice available on television talk shows and in magazines and paperback books, raising children could no longer be something that you did by tradition or whim or common sense. There was a right way and a wrong way to put a child to bed, to leave him with a baby-sitter, to get him started at school, to have a friend over. Being a parent was a career, and like any career, the harder you worked, the more you gained. From that theorem came the corollary that you couldn't do enough for your children. So we found activities for them and drove them there and picked them up. We made spectacular birthday parties and planned elaborate outings. We took enough interest in their schoolwork to learn new math, to find original sources for their reports, and to type them neatly. It was nice if you had an artist friend to do the cover. It came to a point where no self-respecting fifth-grade teacher would assign work that could be done by a fifth grader, unaided by a staff of educated, highly motivated adults.

The change in the way we raised our children just seemed to come with all of the other changes. We were different, and there was no shortage of crackpot philosophies and even reasonably legitimate philosophies to reflect and validate our new attitudes. Sociologists such as Edgar Z. Friedenberg, Paul Goodman, and John Holt saw our children being crushed by the conforming values of mass society, especially as they were expressed by the schools. In fact, school became the great stage for acting out our new feelings about our children. Parents got involved in the public schools far beyond PTA meetings and bake sales to raise money for a movie projector. The community control movement begun by minority groups also created middle-class parent advisory groups in every suburban school. And middle-class parents wanted more freedom, more creativity, more "personal development" for their children. When they couldn't find it in the public schools, they started "alternative" schools, which were often variations on Summerhill, the English "free" school. Free schools had no grades, classes, curriculum, or daily schedule. "If they're in a hang-around-the-yard mood, we let them do that," a San Francisco free-school teacher told a reporter in 1966. Her pupils built rowboats and went to the beach to launch them or to mold sand castles. Even conventional nursery schools in suburban churches emphasized creativity and self-expression. Toddlers finger-painted, sculpted with cornmeal, and made collages out of eggshells and macaroni. What matters, they learned, is not what you produce, but *you*.

The public schools, prodded by manufacturers of fancy new educational equipment and a rush of young teachers (in 1966, half of the nation's teachers had less than ten years' experience) began switching to "individualized" instruction, which allowed each pupil to proceed, self-checked, at his own pace, listening perhaps to his own drummer. Grading systems were like the ones used for olives—from large to colossal—and the worst grade anyone got was *N* for "needs improvement." There were no failures.

Some of this was wonderful, much of it was inevitable, and a lot of it was delusional. It's hard to say when all the experimenting started to turn sinister. It was liberating to drop the Lastex armor of Victorian prudishness and rigid sex roles. It all seemed so harmless, and besides, it's easy to flirt with danger when you have everything. So we started to believe that we had a right to be happy, to be *ourselves* instead of cogs in the wheels of family, community, and friends' expectations. The concept was almost in the Declaration of Independence. In 1966, a book called *The World of the Formerly Married* by Morton Hunt gave it official status. Divorce was no longer a back-of-the-stairs solution for Hollywood stars, neurotic heiresses, and kids from the wrong side of the tracks who married young to get away from home. Nice, affluent suburban couples with children were getting divorced. According to Hunt, 40 percent of all broken marriages survived ten or more years, and 60 percent of divorced couples had children under eighteen. And the percentage had grown from 42 percent in 1948. Hunt's "Formerly Marrieds" (FM's was the hip name) were "a semi-secret society within a society." They had their own language, their own conventions, bars, and resorts. They had better and fancier sex than married people, experiencing what Hunt called "the erotomania of the newly divorced, an exuberant, egotistical delight in their newfound sensuality."

Divorce became hip. Charlotte Curtis, then women's editor of the *New York Times*, said it was "almost like getting in and out of taxis." Politicians found they could divorce their wives and marry younger women without being run out of office. At worst, the papers would call them "swingers." In 1966, *Harper's Bazaar* referred to divorce as "another tack of fashion." "Unless she botches it," *Bazaar* said of the divorced woman, "divorce puts her in the driver's seat. It's almost better to have loved and lost, period." And in 1967 *Newsweek*, the great chronicler of the sixties life-style, said, "Indeed, divorce may be evolving—at least in the fashion and society pages—into something of a status symbol. The stereotype of the gay New York divorcée has never seemed more in vogue. Having deposited the children at the Hewitt School, we are told, she flits from Kenneth's to Kounovsky's gym to Henri Bendel; lunch is spent at La Grenouille with the sorority, dinner on the patio with 'the new man.' " And further down in the same piece, "In the age of the pill, the sexual revolution, and the feminine mystique, the notion that happiness takes precedence over family solidarity has clearly captured the female imagination."

The *Newsweek* piece went on to observe that divorce wasn't painless and not all divorcées shopped at Bendel's. But basically, the message was that divorce was now just fine, a part of the culture. In 1967, Betty Friedan's *The Feminine Mystique* appeared, and the women's movement became a natural extension of sixties individualism. Marriage and the family were seen as oppressive institutions, and divorce became almost a moral and political imperative. To stay married in that climate was to be retrograde, a female Uncle Tom, shuffling around the master's house long after emancipation. Marriages seemed to dissolve for no known reason and divorced women—depressed, lonely, and worried about money— would still gamely insist that it was all worth it. "I'm my own person now."

The women who stayed married felt vaguely embarrassed and even they were going back to law school or opening art studios or marching, at last becoming separate individuals, rather than passive reflections of their husbands and children.

So to be a child back then was to have everything, except maybe an on-duty mother, a protected childhood, and a stable family. The once full-time professional mother suddenly lost interest and started finding herself. "When I was in junior high, my mother got involved in art and causes," says a twenty-eight-year-old woman. "She took a studio and painted and had a lot of artist friends. She was also head of a lot of committees. What I remember is that she was on the phone all the time."

It is hard to remember how crazy all of that was. Couples are still divorcing and women, more than ever, are working and having lives outside of their families. But we have institutionalized the change and we go about our lives without guilt. There is day care and after-school care and family therapy and joint custody and dozens of other buffers that make it work routinely, if not painlessly. But in the sixties, the breakup of the nuclear family—with mama at home—exploded on us.

Dr. Judith Mack, the director of counseling at the University of California, Davis, says that her department's most difficult, therapy-resistant cases come from homes where parents were so caught up in the momentum of their own lives that they hardly had time to be functioning parents. Their children were given every advantage, including continuous therapy, but what they needed were parents. "Kids like this just haven't the emotional resources to handle even campus life on their own," Mack observes.

It was often confusing. On the one hand, they were the golden youth, the children who never failed. On the other, they got to learn a lot about upheaval, firsthand. That may be one of the reasons that this generation has such a curious personality. Insecure, immature, unrealistic, at times silly, they can also be brave, resilient, loyal, uncannily insightful, and shatteringly precocious.

We believe that we have left the sixties behind, with shaggy hair and Hula-Hoops, and that we have returned to a neater, more traditional life-style. In ways we have. Education has gone "back to the basics," and we don't mind uniforms and strict requirements. Our politics are more conservative. In fact we are almost apolitical. While sixties kids searched with a fine-tooth comb for issues to protest about, eighties students will swallow real injustice whole rather than "get involved." More significantly, our values have changed. In the sixties, we were altruistic, dedicated to helping others, to saving the world whenever possible. Now doing good is doing well.

Still, we live with our history as if it were one of those rooms that were furnished piece by piece with whatever happened to be in style at the time. And much that happened in the sixties has simply been absorbed into contemporary life. Drugs are a permanent part of the culture. Most young people experiment with them, and an astonishing number use them regularly. Simply the fact that drugs are available is a powerful message all by itself. It echoes the other voices, from their parents and from the culture, the voices that say, "You don't have to suffer or struggle. Life can be painless and fun." People who live with or treat young drug abusers make one invariable observation: They don't mature while they are using. Drugs allow them to escape all struggle, and in that way they are a metaphor for the culture.

The women's movement is also still with us. Women's lives have changed even if they never had anything to do with the movement. Our sexual rules and relationships will never be rolled back to the old fifties standard. Nowadays, nice girls do, and they don't always get married, and that makes life more complicated. Young women's lives have changed radically. Being a wife and mother is no longer an acceptable (or even an affordable) goal. Women want financial independence and achievement apart from their families, and this means that their mothers probably won't serve as role models. It is a problem that also affects young men. If women won't be homemakers, men don't have to be providers, and they too are cut loose to explore other definitions of themselves. The old maps to adulthood don't work.

The wealth and sense of entitlement linger in memory as a basic standard. The hippies are gone and so are the rap groups, but we still believe that there are alternatives to the middle-class life-style and that we have a right to self-fulfillment, choice, power, even the right to transcend ordinary life.

For today's young adults, these aren't artifacts or curiosities from another era lying around; they are part of life. The sixties were a shaping force in their mind-set and expectations. The decade was their childhood, and it will come up again and again in thinking about this generation. They were the kids caught in a wrinkle of history.

3
Coming of Age in the Land of Lowered Expectations

When I first met Alexa three years ago, she was living with her mother in the house they had through two of her mother's marriages. It was a large, rambling wood and glass structure, perched on top of a steep hill, half hidden behind a fence and some untrimmed bougainvillaea, a house of big rooms with beamed ceilings and pegged wood floors. The furniture was oversized modern, plump and comfortable, and cleverly mixed with antiques. There were plants everywhere—hanging plants, potted plants on end tables and Victorian stands, and masses of them, like a miniature jungle, lining the far wall beneath an expanse of window that looked out over the hills. A big white Samoyed guarded the driveway, and an Angora cat and a Persian cat stalked the living room—all as healthy and well-cared for as the plants.

Alexa was about to graduate from college and had no job prospects. None. The papers and the evening news were filled with stories about college graduates hitting the pavements looking for work. And the companies that used to hire through the university network had let it be known that they just weren't hiring this year. The guys in her major were applying to the police and fire departments, and the women were glad that they could type. Alexa's ace in the hole was a friend of her mother's. "My mom just told me last night about some whiz kid who wants to have lunch with me. It sounds pretty promising," she said cheerfully. She didn't know exactly what it was the whiz kid did. "He's one of those people who can do anything," said Alexa, vaguely. It turned out that he was looking for a job himself.

But this house wasn't a bad place to be unemployed, and Alexa was staying put. Sprawled on a suede couch, waiting for her hair to dry, she considered her options. She would like to go out and buy something that would make her feel better or go on a trip, but that all cost money, and that's just what she didn't have. "I always thought I'd grow up, go to college, graduate, and make money. But it's not working out that way, and I'm scared."

She was scared that she wouldn't ever find the kind of job she wanted, a job in her field—journalism. And she was scared that once she left the house on the hill, she wouldn't ever live this way again. "I hate the thought of living in a cracker box in a bad neighborhood," she said, shuddering at the thought of the ugly world out there below the hill. "No matter where I lived, I would make it cute on the inside, somehow. But I don't want to live in a neighborhood that's dangerous." She had also decided that she wanted to stay close to home and her mother. "I'm sort of chicken. I've grown up around this area, and all my friends are here."

I reached her again two years later. The whiz kid's plans didn't materialize and neither did any other job prospect. While she was in college, she worked part-time as a hostess at an Italian restaurant, a job she didn't much like. "I don't like having to be nice to people when I'm in a bad mood." A year after graduation, she was still working there, putting in more hours. And she was still living at home. When her mother married again and bought another house closer to town, Alexa moved with her. The new house is also in the hills and is just as nice.

That year, the job market for college graduates was even worse than it was the year before, when she graduated. And there was another year's worth of graduates added to the labor supply. University career advisers assumed a permanent grimace. Robert Ehrmann, director of the Career Development Unit at the University of California, Los Angeles, called it the worst labor market he had seen in his twelve years on the job. The *New York Times* wrote, "This spring's college graduates are facing one of the bleakest job markets in at least two decades." And Victor Lindquist, director of placement at Northwestern University, told the *Times*, "This is the most troublesome job market for college graduates in the last twenty-five years." The *Wall Street Journal* ran a grim story, headlined "Cold, Cold World," about college graduates hunting for their first job five months after leaving campus. And the Los Angeles *Times* ran a story headed, "Entry-Level Job Prospects Poorest Since Depression." A few weeks later, they ran a photo showing about three hundred students who had spent fifteen hours in line outside the UCLA placement office just to sign up for job interviews. The job market has improved since 1983, but mainly for engineers, accountants, computer scientists, and finance majors. For the "soft" majors, like Alexa's, the prospects and the starting salaries are still bleak.

Sixteen months after graduation, Alexa landed a job as part-time copy clerk at the city's afternoon paper. It didn't take her out of the restaurant business altogether. To make ends meet, she also worked part-time at Carl's Jr. A year later—almost two and a half years after graduation—the copy clerk job became full-time. She now makes $5.13 an hour plus overtime. She runs dummies and photos to the copy desk and makes sure the syndicated bridge column and comics are on line. She took a cut in pay from the restaurant job, but she is at last in journalism. She believes she could move into her own apartment if she had to, but that seems silly. Home is so nice and she is so close to her mom. "I'm spoiled, I guess," she says without much regret.

Alexa's story is a good illustration of how her generation has been caught in a nasty pincer movement. Raised in the sixties, with material plenty and the expectation that success would be automatic, she now has to face the very different and much more unpleasant reality of the eighties.

Part of that reality is the Job Gap—the disparity between the growing number of college graduates and the shrinking number of available jobs. The term was coined by Thomas J. Moore, an enterprising reporter for the Chicago Sun-Times. Using a large computer at George Washington University, Moore analyzed the raw data from the National Longitudinal Study—an unusual federal government study of twenty-two thousand young people who were high school seniors in 1972—and checked the data against other sources of information at the Labor Department, the Census Bureau, the Education Department, and other studies.

The numbers showed what many young job seekers knew. There were almost twice as many college graduates as there were college-level jobs. And more than 40 percent of those graduates were working at jobs that didn't require a college education. Instead they were competing with high school graduates and driving job qualifications up.

As UCLA's Ehrmann put it, "All jobs are now upgraded. A typist is a word processor. A secretary is an administrative assistant. We don't have the classic media picture of Ph.D.'s driving cabs yet, but there are higher educational standards for every job." And Alexa, a glorified office girl, feels she has finally gotten a job in journalism. Her vision has adjusted to the reality of the job market. According to Moore's figures, the college-educated work force has grown by 126 percent since 1970—an increase fueled by three trends. One was the tail end of the baby boom. In 1981, there were half again as many twenty-two-year-olds as there were in 1967, and the growth rate for this age group far outstripped that of the rest of the population. The second was that more people were going to college. In 1965, twelve out of every hundred high school graduates completed college. By 1980, that figure had swelled to nineteen out of every hundred. The third change was that college-educated women of all ages were going to work instead of keeping house. In 1980, more than two thirds of the college-educated women aged twenty-five to forty-four had a job as well as a family. Ironically, the last two trends are outgrowths of the sixties culture. More kids went to college because their parents had the money, because they were special—even if their SAT's and grades weren't—and because they didn't want to be drafted. And it was feminism that sent women back to the job market—even if it was the economy that kept them there. The predictable result of these trends was that high school graduates were more likely to be unemployed. And college graduates were taking jobs that didn't require a college education. Moore defined a "college-level" job as one in which at least 30 percent of those holding the title have a college education. So engineer, teacher, and bank officer are college-level positions. Draftsman, restaurant manager, secretary, and janitor are not. The definition works, even if it does involve some circular reasoning. We may eventually find that more and more secretaries and restaurant managers are college graduates. (I would guess that about 100 percent of the copy clerks at newspapers are.) But by Moore's reckoning, 43 percent of the college class of 1979 were not holding college-level positions three years after graduation.

Using a different approach, Russell W. Rumberger of Stanford University came to a similar conclusion. In a study of "Overeducation in the U.S. Labor Market," Rumberger scored each occupation by the level of education required to perform the specific tasks of the job. He estimated that 40 percent of all college-educated workers in 1976 were overeducated for what they did.

And in 1982, Labor Department figures showed that 47 percent of college graduates twenty-four years old or younger were in non-college jobs. The situation was getting worse with the deterioration in the economy. And none of these three analyses included those who were unemployed, working part-time, going to school full-time, or keeping house. If the figures counted in those among them who would have preferred full-time, college-level work, the percentage caught in the Job Gap would probably be closer to fifty.

But Alexa, you may think, knew what she was bargaining for. The newspaper business has been depressed for more than a decade, while other job opportunities have soared. That is entirely true. At the moment, anyone qualified for a job as an electrical or systems engineer has only to stay above ground. Michigan State University's Placement Services surveyed 617 potential employers of 1984 college graduates and found an "insatiable" demand for technical graduates, who, naturally enough, also commanded the highest starting salaries. According to the Michigan figures, a 1984 graduate with a bachelor's degree in electrical engineering could expect to start at $26,643. A liberal arts major could hope for $14,179. And according to Moore's computations, 83.8 percent of math majors, 81.2 percent of engineering majors, and 77.4 percent of accounting majors were in college-level jobs three years after graduation. By contrast, only 48.4 percent of English majors, 43.9 percent of social science majors, and 38.0 percent of communications majors were doing work that required their expensive education.

The solution, then, would seem perfectly obvious. A little basic career planning is all it takes, and every college graduate can have the rosy future that was supposed to come with his or her diploma. There are a number of good, objective reasons why this isn't the case, and there are also a few reasons that have more to do with the ability of today's young adults to deal with reality. The two can't always be separated.

For one thing, it is very hard to predict what the job market will be four or five years down the road. Students are asked to declare their majors fairly early in their college careers, and their information is seldom very good. Often, it's a combination of advice from parents and teachers— who have not themselves faced the job market in decades—buzz words gleaned from newspaper articles, wisdom distilled from friends or recruiters who came to their high school, and a nice admixture of fantasy. College career advisers often have very good projections of future job markets, but remarkably few students use their school's placement office, except perhaps to get a part-time job. There does not seem to be any hard statistic about the percentage of students who actually go into the place-ment office and talk to a professional about their future job plans. But a national study of over a quarter of a million 1982 college freshmen indicates that only 5.6 percent intend to seek vocational counseling. And Kitty Arnold, who is director of career and placement services at Notre Dame and chairman of the American College Personnel Association's commission on career and placement counseling, doubts that the percent-age who do get advice is very high. "Students tend to seek advice from their academic adviser, who is a faculty member in their major. They expect him to know the job market as well as his academic field. They want a one-stop service."

Faculty members, however, may be the very worst source of advice on careers. They have no special knowledge and they often have biases.

Aside from their own love for their field, the size of their department depends on enrollment, and they are not eager to be known as a training ground for the unemployable. I first interviewed Alexa and some of her fellow journalism majors in connection with a magazine article on college students' anxiety about the future. When the piece appeared, members of the journalism department called it "too negative"—a special irony in a discipline that values accuracy and objectivity. But their sensitivity was understandable. Their program was on the line. If students stopped majoring in journalism, the department would have to start whittling away at its course offerings.

But even the best of career advisers don't always have the answers. The economy fluctuates, and students—by responding to the job market and going into "hot" fields—create an oversupply that they will suddenly feel when they graduate. These are sophisticated considerations for an eighteen-year-old. No one could tell the freshman who chose chemical engineering in 1979 that there would be an oil glut and too many chemical engineers in 1983. Nor could the nursing major possibly predict that the shortage of nurses would continue but that a restructuring of medicare payments would force hospitals to cut back on their hiring.

According to some, even the job-rich computer field may someday dry up. UCLA's Ehrmann foresees "disastrous cycles in computer employment" by the end of the decade because of changes in technology. As computers learn English, there will be less need for programmers and a steep drop in job demand on the lower end of the scale. "They can't all be systems analysts," he says, and points out that even now, demand for computer science majors has dropped slightly. "They used to get five or six offers apiece. Now they're getting two or three. Their situation may be similar to engineers' in the early seventies. They were making thirty or forty thousand a year and in great demand, and then suddenly they were laid off and couldn't find work."

(People within the computer field have infinite faith in their future. "As the hardware gets cheaper and better, more and more applications will be practical," says Rik Knablein, a systems engineer for TRW who also does campus recruiting for the company. "More computer engineers will be needed to design the systems and the software, and more people will be needed to maintain the systems." Ehrmann inadvertently supports this point. Next year, UCLA will computerize its job interview program so that students don't have to line up around the building and wait all night to sign up.)

So the ironic result is that the student who chose his major with a career in mind may be in the worst straits. Alexa majored in journalism because she had wanted to be a reporter since she was fifteen and worked on a small paper in the resort town where her father lived. Yet if she had majored in English literature or European history, she would be no worse off than she was with journalism, a practical, job-oriented major. In fact, according to Moore's analysis, communications majors (which usually means journalism) are about 10 percent less likely to get college-level jobs than English majors. Majoring in business, for instance, is a good career choice if the specialty is accounting or finance. Business administration and marketing majors, on the other hand, have turned out even less employable than the dreamers who studied art and music, English, or social sciences. On the Moore scale, only 42.9 percent of the business and marketing students were employed in college-level jobs three years after graduation, compared to 43.4 for art and music, 48.4 for English, and 43.9 for social science. The reason for their predicament is fairly obvious. Their training is too narrow for them to do much else, so if there is no room in their field, they have educated themselves into a corner.

A good illustration—of both the predicament and the decision-making process—is Evan, twenty-two and a recent graduate of Ohio State. Stocky, with neatly trimmed hair and wearing a blazer, tie, and white shirt, Evan looks very much like a young man eager to be a pillar of the community. His parents are both teachers with solid midwestern values. His older brother is a lawyer, his sister is a nurse. Both are married. He himself will probably be settled and successful before he turns thirty. His ambitions are hardly visionary. He wants a good managerial job in this heartland city and he wants to buy and renovate a Victorian house in an older section of town that he is fond of. Right now, he is finding the going a little rocky.

Evan went to college partly because it was expected of him, but mostly because of the great romance of college life and Ohio State in particular. During his first two years, "I was Joe All-American College. I lived in the dorms, I was on the planning committee, I was president of the floor in my dorm and social director. I played intramural football and softball. I went to every sporting event." His grades were about average, and his major—business—was uninspiring. "It wasn't interesting. There were too many numbers." A friend from his hometown was majoring in medical records administration. She liked the program, describing it as a mixture of business and science. It qualifies the graduate for a job as administrator of a hospital's records department, supervising the systems and the clerks. Evan tried it and liked it too and switched majors.

On the surface, it seemed like a specific, goal-oriented, realistic choice in a solid field. The sick, after all, will always be with us. No one—not parents or teachers—advised him against it. He planned to stay in Columbus after graduation because he had settled in and liked the city and most of his friends were there. He assumed there would be no trouble getting a job in this growing area. After all, his was a wide open field; he had come out of a small department, and only thirty-six campuses in the country offered the major. He was so confident that he took a month off after graduation to take a trip before looking for a job. He returned to a rude awakening. What he hadn't reckoned on was that a few others wanted to stay in Columbus, and they were all competing for a limited number of jobs. Out of sixteen who graduated that year in his major, three are still in Columbus, jobless. One got a job in town, and the other twelve spread out over the country. And, of course, there were job seekers from previous graduating classes, still in Columbus. So Evan spent the summer looking, without success, and living off his savings. "I hated it. I always thought I'd go to college and get a good job afterwards. But it didn't happen," he says, echoing so many of his peers. In August, he was offered a consulting job, overseeing the closing of a facility for the mentally retarded. It is, by definition, a temporary job, and it is far from the job he once had in mind: director of a major hospital's records department, managing clerks, supervisors, and assistant directors. "Everyone lowers their goals after graduation," he explains with a shrug. "It's devastating to the ego. You're not on top of the mountain anymore."

I don't know who told them they were on top of the mountain, but it seems to be implied in the contract his generation has with life. He and Alexa grew up almost two thousand miles away from each other and perhaps light years away in background. Yet the same themes appear in both stories, like a refrain. Both chose career-oriented majors and assumed that success came with the degree. They chose their fields rather casually. They hate the thought of relocating. And they set great store by having a stylish place to live. This is not a generation of pioneers. They are just kids with a high sense of entitlement and a not so high sense of reality.

An interesting contrast comes from Jessica, a twenty-three-year-old senior at the University of Tennessee. She was born and raised in Memphis, and her parents were professional, liberal, and a little bohemian. Jessica herself is an elegant blond woman, creamy skinned, well dressed, with a soft Southern accent and easy social sensitivity. She started college at Sophie Newcomb, a private women's school in New Orleans, and spent her freshman year going to terrific parties. She is vague about her major. It was probably math, but it may have been French or anthropology. "I got a social education," she says accurately. "New Orleans society was fascinating. It's French and archaic." As a pretty student at Newcomb, she got into all the nicest homes and even met Conrad Hilton. But even then she understood that it was basically a closed society. "They let you in while you're at Newcomb, as long as you don't marry their sons."

That led to another insight. Her grade point average was an unimpressive 2.7, and she wasn't "getting anything done. I had a fear of sliding into nowhere. It didn't matter for the others, but an education wasn't so crucial for them. They could go into somebody's family business. What mattered there was who you knew." Jessica had no network of connections to take care of her, and no family fortune to fall back on. The very worst thing she could do would be to be seduced by the life-style of New Orleans' society. So she transferred to the business school at the University of Tennessee at Knoxville and majored in marketing. She also got some part-time jobs in marketing research. But the field seemed irrational and emotional to her. "You do all this research and then the clients do what they want anyway."

After a year there, she decided she needed some time away from school. "I wanted a clearer direction. I needed to do some testing and exploring." So she went back to Memphis and got a job. Using the corporate contacts she made, she talked to executives and asked them what their hiring needs were. In effect, she interviewed them. 'We don't need marketing people," they told her. "We need people in finance." So Jessica went back to UT Knoxville and switched her major to finance. "I want my skills to be valued," she says. "My therapists said that it was because I have a big fear of rejection. I need a lot of control because I have a middle child's fear of being left out." Her fear of being left out might have been lucky and prescient. It prepared her for the job market in the eighties.

In her case, of course, the switch was easy and workable. She had an interest in the business world and ability in math. Not everyone can ask 'What do you need?" and then shape himself to fill the space. Ehrmann says, "Our worst cases are those who try to make something of themselves that they are not. For instance, the writer who becomes an accountant. Or anyone who takes a pragmatic route and goes into a highly employable field where he is mismatched. These people come back disasters, emotional and physical wrecks."

Which brings us to the plight of liberal arts majors, humanists, and well-educated generalists, who still comprise a sizeable—if shrinking— section of the college population. When today's twenty-two-year-old was growing up, these were perfectly acceptable paths to take. They even had a certain social cachet, especially in the East, where traditional liberal arts colleges are strong. Their parents and teachers encouraged it. Education, they reasoned, should train the mind, provide culture, background, and a deeper ability to enjoy life and to understand the world. Until recently, a good liberal arts education also led to employment. There was academia, the arts, government, media, public relations. Even business wanted well-rounded, well-connected people. So the bright liberal arts major didn't really have to think about careers. He just did what interested him, and assumed that the career question would fall into place in the fullness of time. Then without warning to all of the young people who had signed up for that view of things, the world began to change. As discussed earlier, there were too many of them. Then, in the mid-seventies, the economy got tighter, thanks to the Arab oil embargo, high interest rates, and two decades of inflation. The "soft" jobs—like public relations or community affairs—were the first to go in a company with a tight profit margin. Next to feel the axe was middle management. Government and public colleges and universities were hit by a taxpayer revolt and virtually stopped hiring. Law was overcrowded. So if you couldn't do something useful in a narrow and specific way, there wasn't a job. And the change, it turned out, was fairly permanent. Even as the economy recovered, companies discovered that they liked operating lean.

With the change from a "soft" to a "hard" economy came a change in values. Helping others—once an important occupation for liberal arts majors—was no longer in style. "Once," says Ehrmann, "it was okay to be aspiring and floundering. Now it's not. 'Do-gooder' is a bad word. I rarely see kids now who want to go into counseling or social work, even among minorities."

Martha Green, director of career services at Barnard College, says just as bluntly, "Our values and priorities have changed. Helping isn't a national priority anymore. Barnard women used to want to be professors, but there aren't any jobs." She points out that Barnard recently presented panel discussions on various careers. Over forty students came to a banking panel on an afternoon when rainstorms derailed the Broadway–7th Avenue subway. About a dozen showed for a social workers panel the next day, which was much dryer. "Ten years ago, we would have had the big turnout for social work," said Green. "I'm not saying that no one cares about people anymore. What I am saying is that no one is paying anyone to care about other people. In the great society, people could make money and care. People could make a living and teach other people. It isn't just that interests have changed. Responsible young men and women know they have to make a living."

But interests do change with the economy. Another career counselor said, "Go to a cocktail party and tell people you're a teacher or a social worker. They'll drop you. It's like saying you're nobody."

Many liberal arts majors have responded to the change in their situation by not facing it. The confusion they feel is vague and nameless. They don't know exactly what jobs they expected or what happened to those jobs or whom to blame. They just feel cheated. And since they don't know what the problem is, their solutions are just as haphazard. They go back to school, sometimes to get master's degrees in the very subjects that rendered them unemployable to begin with. They take menial jobs "temporarily." They travel. They develop philosophies. We will see a lot of them as this book progresses.

And those liberal arts graduates who want nice, white-collar jobs in corporate glass towers find that corporations don't want them. One personnel executive confided to a California state university administrator, "Don't send us liberal arts graduates. It's not that they lack the skills because we would just as soon train them ourselves. They just don't fit in. Their attitude is wrong. They don't dress in a businesslike way. They don't like hierarchy and procedures."

Bernice Russell, director of placement at Loyola Marymount University in Los Angeles, is a lot more optimistic, perhaps because students at a private, Catholic school like Loyola are accustomed to dress codes and rules. At Loyola, liberal arts majors are about 40 percent of the undergraduate student body—which is about typical of national figures. Russell acknowledges that career-oriented fields, such as business, science, or computers, turn out students who are in much more demand. "But a liberal arts student who prepares for a corporate career is quite marketable." Potential employers that she has spoken with at conferences have expressed specific interest in liberal arts majors. "They have good thinking, research, and communications skills. They are also more flexible than business students, and the company can teach them business skills," she says.

Perhaps the key phrase in Russell's optimistic sentence is "prepares for a corporate career." It is fine to major in French because you love it. But Russell suggests that the French major also take elective courses in business and computers. He should find summer and part-time work in fields that he might have a career interest in. He should look into internships and volunteer work that would provide him with a chance to work directly with customers and clients and to observe how the business operates. She also likes co-op programs, in which a student alternates working on a job and going to school—a quarter on and a quarter off campus. Clearly, she doesn't mean the usual student part-time job in a pizza joint. What she is suggesting is that students get their feet wet in a kind of work they might like as a career, even if it means earning less money. It helps them make a decision, it looks good on their résumés, and it often provides the beginnings of a network of contacts in the field. Sometimes it even leads directly to a job.

"But students don't know this unless they come in here," she says. "Freshmen don't think about career plans at all. They just want their degrees. They take history because they love it. Then, in their senior year, they panic, but it's too late. They're afraid that nothing is out there and they don't want to graduate." Loyola is a small school, where students can count on personal support and guidance. The placement office reaches about 60 percent of its undergraduates.

But liberal arts students may be the last ones to come in. "These kids just don't believe in themselves," says Russell. "Stories in the media knock their self-confidence. We try to get their confidence up. Some of them bury their head in the sand and don't try. I think some of these kids can't take rejection. Maybe they were brought up with too much positive thinking. 'Prepare for rejection' is the best advice I can give them."

But avoiding rejection is the theme song of the generation. Expectations don't meet reality, so they avoid reality. And they do not risk failure. College has always been something of an escapist experience in America, but it used to be a luxury we could afford. It all worked. In a happier, earlier day, the most sheltered student emerged from his four-year cocoon, had some separation anxiety, made some adjustments, and went on to lead the life he expected to. He was willing to take some risks and explore a little, perhaps even move to another city. If he ended up with egg on his face, well, unless he had led a particularly charmed life, that had probably happened before. God knows, his parents and teachers—who worried about how tough it was out there—had warned him over and over about his many character flaws and bad habits (Who will hire a boy with such poor posture?), so a little rejection wouldn't be anything new. Besides, the cards were stacked in his favor. For almost thirty years, the economy was booming, and there weren't so many eager twenty-two-year-olds coming out of college. (The birthrate hit a trough in the thirties and early forties. And a considerably smaller percentage of the population went to college.) He could reasonably expect to be better off than his parents. He could even have a house on the hill that overlooks the old part of town where mom and dad live.

This generation is getting the reverse side of that fate. Today's college graduate leaves campus to find that the life-style he grew up with is not waiting at the corner for him. The economy has shrunk, his college class is large, and jobs are hard to get. If his parents' house were on the market, he wouldn't be able to afford it.

Sociologists call the predicament downward mobility. They mean simply that young adults will not have the income or the status that their parents had. They will almost certainly not enjoy the life-style. Alexa's mother's house on a hill sold for over $350,000. And even a young adult who could manage the monthly payments (probably in the neighborhood of four thousand dollars) would have difficulty coming up with the mortgage money. According to housing experts, a combination of factors—from the huge federal deficit to the bulge in the age distribution—will keep interest rates high and make housing loans hard to come by for the rest of this decade.

The situation has a depressing effect on even the most successful and directed members of the generation. Richard, the son of a successful lawyer and an *A* student at a top-tier university, expects to go to a top-tier law school. He assumes that his qualifications and connections will land him a very good job. But he wonders if he will ever be able to live the way his parents have. "What I worry about," he says, "is whether I will ever be able to own a house close enough to a city so I can practice law."

Those who have less of a toehold on the future can't even articulate what is worrying them. Bright and educated, they sense that they are not wanted or valued. No one seems impressed with them. Having grown up without failure, they don't know that they can fail and get up again. Subtly, unconsciously, they take themselves out of the running. They drift into low-status jobs without feeling the drop, as naturally as a river finding its course. One college senior said, "All this high-unemployment stuff scares everyone. I think it's crap. The whole problem is overblown. I never had a problem getting a job. I never carried a dish in my life, and I convinced this guy that I could be a waiter in a French restaurant. It's a matter of self-evaluation." In other words, what he had gotten from four years at a selective and demanding university was the ability to talk himself into a job as a waiter. Another senior, who searched long and hard for a job in journalism, took the test to be a county sheriff. "Actually, I've wanted to be in law enforcement since I was a kid. I just majored in journalism because I had to major in something," he rationalized gamely.

Even parents have learned to deny the problem and rationalize their disappointment. One mother—who has a Ph.D. and whose husband is a physician—explains her son's decision to go into construction work after college. "My children don't expect to live as beautifully as they have at home. They have other values. They grew up comfortably, but money wasn't important in our house."

Many of them work in offices and sales jobs, on the fuzzy border of college-status employment. Sometimes, like Alexa, they take low-status jobs in glamorous industries. Or they gild a basically boring job. Asked why Barnard graduates are seeking jobs in banking, career adviser Green says, "It doesn't matter what you major in for banking. It's retail sales, only you're selling money instead of ribbon. But it's dressy and clean."

"They move downscale and don't know it," notes reporter Moore. That may explain their puzzling optimism. In a group of surveys taken by Public Response Associates, a San Francisco based polling firm, 66 percent of the respondents between eighteen and thirty expected their personal economic situation to improve within the next year—compared to 50 percent of the total respondents. Similarly, more of the eighteen to thirty group than any other age group believed the country was headed in the right direction and that their own living conditions had improved within the past year. This is not a generation that protests or complains. This is a generation that avoids.

4

Going to College in an Age of Anxiety

Most college campuses look wonderful to those of us no longer enrolled. Big shade trees, brick walks, old buildings, some even covered with ivy. And huge new buildings that were never there in our day—labs and student union buildings with video games and indoor swimming pools and racquetball courts—impressive, modern structures with entrances at three levels. And of course, there are all of those healthy, attractive young people in Levi's and down jackets, walking casually but purposefully down those walks, backpacks bouncing lightly, almost weightless on their strong shoulders. There is some dawdling and some flirting, and if the weather's good, a little sexual byplay on the lawns or the benches, a frisbee or a football thrown in the quadrangle.

But mainly, there is a sense of well-being that is very comforting to the adults who pay for all of this, one way or another. Our children are growing in knowledge and in grace. How could they not with all of these buildings, these books, these laboratories, these other well-formed young people? We remember our own college days in the fifties or early sixties. Even with all of the rules and regulations—no visitors of the opposite sex in the dorm rooms; no visitors in the lounge after nine; week-day curfew at ten, weekends at midnight; no alcohol ever—it was a time of tremendous freedom and discovery. There was freedom from supervision, from routine, from the dreariness of wherever you grew up. (All homes and hometowns are boring.) There was discovery of the whole world of real culture. Music meant Bach and Vivaldi, not just the Top 40 or an aria from Carmen. There were books besides best sellers and the matched encyclopedias that sat untouched on our parents' shelves. There was food more elegant than roast beef and more exotic than lasagna. There were people who went to Europe as if it were a place at the lake and who could go to foreign films without reading the subtitles. And then there was the titillating game of acting familiar and cool about it all. Was the *Pastoral* the sixth or the seventh symphony? Is it all right to like Brahms? Was Courbet or Corot the sentimental one? It was a strain, sometimes, but that was a cheap price to pay for entrance to a higher plane of existence. Sometimes we faked it, but we learned and we grew. And when we left college, we had new values and a not-quite-gelled definition of ourselves. Whatever else we did at college, we had four safe years to do this.

We assume that this is the experience our children are having, and from the visitors' parking lot it looks reassuringly familiar.

In one way, it is. College is still the preferred initiation rite for the American middle class. In a national survey of almost two hundred thousand freshmen in 1982, 77.9 percent cited "getting a better job" as a very important reason for going to college; 69.8 percent cited making more money; 72.5 percent checked "learning more about things"; 54.6 percent wanted to "meet new and interesting people"; 33.1 percent were there because their parents wanted them to be; 33.8 percent wanted to "become a more cultured person"; 10.1 percent wanted to get away from home; 7.4 percent could not find a job; and 2.3 percent had nothing better to do. They could fill in the circle for as many reasons as they liked, and the total for all of the reasons added up to 473 percent. It may be that they didn't exactly know why they were there. As one young woman put it, "In my family, it was just assumed that you were going to college."

But the experience many students have at college is dramatically different from their parents'. Even if they wear Izod shirts and go to proms, their college years are often marked more by stress than by growth. Instead of being a safe place to grow up, college presents its own set of pressures above and beyond the existential pressure of growing up and entering what Carl Jung called "the monastery of the world." The struggle should build strength and resources, but there is something in its relentless nature that just derails and confuses, leaving the student with no lesson about reality except that life is mysteriously tough, continuity is impossible, and authorities are irrational. What used to be four years of room to grow is now more likely to be five and a half years of anxiety and aimlessness. The result, often, is a habit of not facing reality.

* * *

Almost any dorm or student lounge instantly provides the first clue that college life is different. Clue is a euphemism. Quadrophonic pop rock music blares out deafeningly over a powerful public address system, cheerfully and homogeneously assuming that everyone likes Lionel Richie and that no one wants to talk or think or read. A bulletin board announces "Activites," and it is not the last misspelled word. Punctuation is used at random. If it is early afternoon, there will be clusters of students gathered around the television set watching soap operas. They have arranged their schedules around it. At other times, they are watching sports or sitcoms. If there are books other than textbooks around, they are science fantasy or romance. This isn't a description of a party school. This is what it's like at selective schools, where students come from the top 10 percent of their high school class.

These students aren't slumming or putting on an act. They are genuinely intellectually underdeveloped, and one of the great sources of stress in American college life is that so many students are unequal to the task. Dormitory counselors report that freshmen most frequently come to them because of academic problems. "They're not well-prepared enough," said one junior who worked as a resident assistant on a freshman floor. "They don't know what to take or how to study." This is an old complaint at state universities and land grant institutions that are required by law or charter to admit anyone with a high school diploma. In those schools, the solution has always been simple: a massive attrition rate. Half the freshmen who go home for Thanksgiving never come back. But in the last decade, selective and even elite schools are getting poorly prepared students. They are not the bottom of the class in ability. They just don't know anything.

"Each generation of Americans has outstripped its parents in education, in literacy and in economic attainment," said a report by the National Commission on Excellence in Education. "For the first time in the history of our country, the educational skills of one generation will not surpass, will not equal, will not even approach, those of their parents."

It is easy to blame the high schools, and, in fact, most college students do. Apparently 54.5 percent of 1982's freshmen think that high school was too easy. Most parents think that high school is too easy. And the National Commission quoted above called American high school education "a tide of mediocrity," and likened our low educational standards to "an act of war" against the nation. Specifically, the commission blamed "a smorgasbord" of easy electives that have replaced traditional academic courses. A study of eighty-eight hundred high school transcripts, prepared for the commission, supported this contention. It found that over the years, a steady percentage of high school graduates go on to college. But the percentage who were in college preparatory tracks, rather than "general" tracks, had decreased by 12.4 between 1969 and 1981. The study also found that students in all tracks, even college preparatory, were spending less time on English, math, language, and other academic courses and more time on remedial and physical education and "personal service and development" courses, such as budgeting, band, chorus, and typing.

Clifford Adelman, the author of the study, told the *New York Times*, "Many high school students—and their parents—seem extraordinarily naïve concerning what it takes to prepare and compete in post-secondary education."

In 1984, a 4.0 average gain in Scholastic Aptitude Test scores made page-one headlines and even became an election issue for the Reagan administration. (Secretary of Education T. H. Bell held a news conference about the improved scores before the College Board even announced them, hoping perhaps that some voters would credit the administration for the rise.) But a 4.0 rise (3.0 in the math section and 1.0 in the verbal section) seems very modest when stacked against the 85.0 decline that occurred between 1963 and 1980.

As a result, remedial education is now a part of the curriculum at most universities. Twenty-two percent of entering freshmen say they will need remedial help in math, and 11 percent believe they will need it in English. Remedial courses now claim a big enough chunk of resources to have drawn ultimatums from some state legislatures: Get out of the tutoring business, they demand, or we will cut your funds. Lawmakers feel, not unreasonably, that scarce public money should not be spent to keep boneheads in college. The three *R*'s should be taught to children. But college officials have to live with the rueful knowledge that their students won't be able to read, write, or do sums unless they are taught on the premises. Even Harvard offers remedial education these days. And in a widely circulated "memo to secondary schools, students, and parents," Fred Hargadon, the dean of admissions at Stanford, wrote, "The Stanford faculty generally find their students to be exceptionally bright. But it is also the case that there are occasions on which they find them surprisingly lacking in one or another area of preparation. For example, it is not just a matter of observing that too few of them appear able to write well. Rather, upon closer inquiry, we have found that all too few appear to have been required to write much at all prior to entering college. And even for those who did do a good deal of writing in secondary school, too few report they were ever afforded the kind of sustained criticism which nurtures improvement.

"Much national attention has been given the particular problem just referred to. Less attention appears to have been given some of the other problems which have increasingly concerned our faculty. One set of these concerns relates to the content of secondary school courses in fields such as English, history, and the social sciences. Recognizing that our students are ones who for the most part achieved excellent records in high school, the faculty is all the more baffled by how little in the way of prior knowledge they can assume on the part of students whose records indicate they have in fact taken specific courses in a given field at the secondary school level."

Dr. Les Agnew is a courtly Scotsman and onetime medical doctor who gave up his practice because he liked the study of history better. He has spent most of the past thirty years as a student and "faculty-in-residence" at several prestigious campuses, including Yale, Harvard, and UCLA. What he really is is an erudite, sharp-tongued bearer of culture in a philistine land. Living in tiny dormitory quarters that double as a screening room for his collection of classic films and a lending library for his books and magazines, he is a campus spider, ensnaring students into an alien web of literature, film, and art. Only a few become part of his world, but he doesn't mind. "I'd rather light a candle than curse the darkness."

But the darkness fascinates and infuriates him. "They don't read," he sputters. "They don't even read newspapers except for sports and comics. They are abysmally ignorant of world figures. Mention Albert Schweitzer or Bertrand Russell, and they say, 'I didn't take the course.' The talk here is disappointing because they never talk about anything outside of their immediate ken. They have no common core of civilized knowledge to draw on. Their conversation is utterly devoid of intellectual curiosity or concern about social problems. They talk only of sports and television, with a little personal gossip. Their knowledge of popular television is astounding. They've seen every episode of these shows and even know the commercials by heart.

"They're the *Star Wars* generation. George Lucas understood them and fed them kids' stuff. They have the attention span of grasshoppers, and he met their emotional need for fantasy electronically. They want fast fantasy, just like fast food. Piping hot. They feel that learning must be fun. They don't understand the satisfaction in mastering a discipline. So they don't learn Spanish irregular verbs. They build a hacienda.

"They even refer to themselves as kids. The coaches refer to these huge Neanderthal hulks as kids. We would have killed anyone who called us kids when I was in medical school in Scotland. At twenty-two, I had the power to sign someone into an asylum. When do they assume responsibility?"

And here Agnew may have hit on something revealing. Students are not just victims of poor education. Their arrested intellectual development is a function of their reluctance to grow up. We put away childish things and imitated sophistication in college because we wanted to be grown-ups. These students live knee-deep in adolescent culture because they have no desire to be anything else. The youth mania of the sixties and the market power of the baby boom gave them hegemony, and they don't want to reach beyond the piping hot, fast fantasy of pop music, television, and sports. To do so would mean identifying with adults and assuming responsibility. Quadrophonic sound is so much nicer.

But even the most intellectually developed students might feel alienated by the crowded, impersonal nature of life on most campuses. During the years when the baby boomers were entering college, enrollment swelled geometrically. It is difficult for those of us who went through in quieter days to imagine the qualitative change that sheer quantity has wrought. In 1960, there were a little over 2.2 million young people enrolled in American colleges. In 1981, there were over 7.5 million. (There were not only more people of college age in 1981 but a higher percentage— 32.5 instead of 23.7—were enrolled in college.) Enrollment figures have begun to tail off as the baby boomers grow up, but not nearly as much as expected. High-tuition private schools have been most affected by the shrinking number of eighteen-year-olds. Public universities remain swollen with returning housewives and other older students who need more training; and of course, with eighteen-year-olds who can't afford the tuition at private schools.

Many of the nation's students are in "multiversities"—sprawling, large universities with complicated organizational structures. Nearly all of them are financially pinched, either by state budget cutbacks or mounting costs and shrinking revenues. Sometimes, the budget problems are as obvious as frayed collars and cuffs. The grass needs cutting, even the ivy needs to be trimmed. Inside the buildings, floors and bannisters show a film of dust; paint is chipped; stairs are worn into swaybacked crescents. But most feel the mean hand of economy in the curriculum. Where once there were five sections of a required course, there are now three. If the student doesn't have a good enough place on the registration line, he doesn't get in and he either juggles his schedule and takes something else or "runs for the class," i.e. he begs the professor to let him in even though the class is full. Similarly, if he chooses a popular major, he may find that it has been "capped," meaning that the department is accepting only a limited number of students and he has to compete *just to get in.*

Large universities are really small cities, with as many as fifty thousand students plus faculty and staff. The student is issued a number and that number is his identity for all of his days there. He begins to feel like a number, since no human being can be asked to wait on so many lines and fill out so many computerized forms. The University of Southern California, whose students were among the most complaisant and conservative during the anti-war days, faced a mini-revolt in 1982 over two-hour lines at clerical offices, seven-month waits to obtain a registrar's check on progress toward graduation, and too many courses taught by teaching assistants.

And many courses are given in large lecture halls that seat five hundred, with microphones and television monitors placed strategically to project the professor's face and voice to those in the rear. The professor has announced office hours, but most students would no sooner see him about a problem with the course than they would ask to speak to Dan Rather after the *CBS News*.

Some large universities—especially the intellectually distinguished ones like the University of California, Berkeley, and the University of Chicago—only suffer the presence of undergraduates. The real institutional focus is in the graduate and professional schools and the heavily funded research centers. Undergraduates are allowed in, often in large numbers, but no one takes much notice of them, and courses and requirements are not geared to the needs of eighteen-year-olds.

Given the impersonal and anonymous nature of the campuses, it is easy for a student to go into culture shock, especially if he has come from a smaller environment. James, a young man from a small town in Tennessee, describes his first year at the University of Tennessee at Knoxville. "I was shell-shocked. It was so big. I didn't know a soul. It was a traumatic transition, from knowing everybody to knowing nobody. I went to my counselor and he picked my courses. He didn't listen to me and I didn't understand him. I've pretty much blocked out my first year. For the first six or seven months, I think I just went to classes and then came back to my room and got high on drugs. It was very boring and very alienating."

Denise, who had attended a tiny convent school since kindergarten, became almost completely unstrung as a freshman at the University of Colorado. There were three hundred students—instead of eight or nine— in her classes and, by her standards, no privacy in the dorm or the bathrooms. She became so confused and depressed that she almost flunked out in her first semester. Instead, she went into counseling and private therapy and adjusted in the course of a long, painful first year.

But even students from large, urban high schools find it hard to settle in socially at large universities, and this appears to be one of the reasons that fraternities and sororities have been making a comeback after virtual extinction in the sixties. Dr. Carol Guardo, a University of Hartford psychologist who has written extensively on youth issues, believes that the upsurge shows a "desire for more controlled, personal interaction. It's a way of bringing order to a bewildering world." Revealingly, fraternities and sororities have always been more a part of campus life at large universities than at colleges. Those who don't join sometimes find themselves wandering from class to the dorm to the library waiting for college social life to start. Often it doesn't, and it isn't unusual to find sophomores and juniors rushing for sororities or fraternities—against all of their earlier and vocal objections—because they want a home base and a list of guaranteed friends.

They may also want a place to live. At many universities, dormitory rooms are hard to come by. Universities have different policies about who gets priority. At some, freshmen are at the top of the list; at others, upper classmen are rewarded; and some also factor in distance from home. In most cases, though, the dorm room is a dubious prize, a ten-by-twelve-foot oblong shared with another person from a different background, with a different life-style. Most newer dormitories were built on an emergency basis in the sixties and seventies to accommodate the baby boom onslaught. Since the most important considerations in their design were low cost and speed, builders turned out huge, high-rise boxes with thin walls and communal bathrooms. "The rooms and the architecture here create a lot of our problems," said Guy Sanders, an assistant dean at a UCLA residence hall. "There are only two similar living situations—prison and hospitals. You've got two people thrown together and the chances of explosion are great." Dorms are also noisy. Radios and slamming doors and loud conversation reverberate through the thin walls and ceilings. Privacy is almost nonexistent.

In a "guide" for freshmen, *Nutshell* magazine, a national publication for college students, warns about dorms:

University housing is based on the premise that 200 or 300 can live as cheaply as one—and in about the same space. It makes minimum use of minimum space in order to maximize sociocultural interaction. That means two showers per floor, walls you could read a newspaper through, stereo freaks to the left and right, a leaky waterbed above, a self-styled Louis Armstrong below, and fire drills at 4 A.M. in below-zero temperatures. . . . Each unit of university housing contains two orthopedically designed sacks of half-cooked Malt-o-Meal, linens, a pair of drapes from underneath the grease rack at Joe's Garage, and a desk that has a locked drawer with a key inside.

What many students do after a year or so in the dorms is take apartments in the student ghetto surrounding the campus. They pay high rents for quarters only marginally better than the dorms, but quieter. Often their parents pay their share of the rent, just as they paid the dormitory fees. It seems fair and reasonable at the time, but it sometimes has unexpected fall-out. Dorm fees end with graduation, but apartment life goes on. And a pattern that may not end with graduation has been established, wherein parents continue paying the rent.

Another and perhaps more serious cause of stress is money. College is increasingly expensive. At Harvard and Stanford, where tuition is close to eleven thousand dollars a year, the total cost—including room, board, and books—is about sixteen thousand dollars a year. At less costly private institutions, the annual total is still over ten thousand. And even at state universities, where tuition and fees for state residents typically range between one and two thousand a year, the total with room and board will come to almost six thousand. For most middle-class families—especially those with more than one child at college—these numbers present a staggering burden. Once, students took federal loans at low interest rates and paid them back after graduation. But in 1982 the Reagan administration proposed stringent eligibility requirements for federally guaranteed student loans and reduced student aid programs by one billion dollars.

The upshot is that more students are dependent on parental support and on part-time jobs. The percent of freshmen whose parents were contributing at least two thousand dollars a year to their college expenses increased in 1982 from 24 to 29 percent. Fifty-one percent of freshmen in that year said that financing college represented "some concern" to them, and 17 percent considered it a "major concern."

Many of them will hold jobs before long. About 40 percent of freshmen expect to hold a job to help pay their college expenses. For most students, a few hours a day stacking dishes in the cafeteria or working in the student store will suffice. But for a lot of others, "job" means real work and long hours off campus. At California State University, Northridge, a campus that serves twenty-eight thousand students in the comfortable suburbs of the San Fernando Valley, a 1981 report by the Counseling Center cited economic pressure as the leading cause of stress. "Students have to work many hours while attending CSUN," the report stated. "Long working hours interfere with their ability to study, which may result in poor grades. While this situation is not unlike that of previous generations of students facing economic realities, today's students face more uncertainty regarding their future."

The need to work long hours, according to the CSUN counselors, also led to social isolation and even poor health "as students face an increasingly fast pace of life." They have little time for activities that might be a social outlet or a growth experience. Many even have to plan their course schedules around their work hours.

And, in fact, it is not unusual for even serious students to be so preoccupied with the jobs they take to pay their way through college that school itself takes a backseat. Some especially cruel stories come from private institutions that have a "loss leader" policy about financial aid. They offer freshmen substantial scholarships and then, regardless of academic performance, cut them off after their first year, thinking that most will somehow or other come up with a way to pay the tuition rather than switch. Peggy, for instance, went to Boston University on a scholarship and got a 3.5 GPA. But her financial aid wasn't renewed after her freshmen year and, since she had two other sisters in college, there was no way her family could pick up the full tuition. So she got a series of part-time jobs, doing publicity for Boston theaters. She loved being around plays, and she cut classes to hang around the stage. "I loved the theater and the opportunity to experience the city," she reflects. "It was a much more educational experience than going to class," she notes, perhaps venting some bitterness at the school that lured her in and then cut her off. "I guess, with twenty-twenty hindsight, that I could have saved about thirty thousand dollars in tuition by dropping out and just working in the theater. But my parents really believed in that piece of paper. In their eyes, a diploma meant that you were a responsible member of society. I use it to mark the pizza listings in the Yellow Pages."

Kathy, a young Ohio woman, was even less lucky. She hung on at the University of Chicago after her financial aid was cut off by juggling as many as three part-time jobs. She was, at one time, a research assistant to a professor, a secretary in the philosophy department, and a cashier in a health food store. She found that she liked the last job best because it was off-campus and she got to deal with people. Finally, she realized that she just wasn't focused on school anymore and left in her fifth year without a degree. In retrospect, she thinks it would have been better to have transferred to a less intellectually demanding state university and been able to concentrate on school rather than working to pay for school. But at the time, she was just tired and depressed and wanted to be somewhere else.

Working at odd jobs and struggling to survive financially ought in theory to be growth experiences. But in reality, they present a detour. Both of these young women will appear in later pages of this book, and in their cases and many others it seems that survival has become a habit. Young people have become very resourceful at getting by, at putting out financial fires. What they are not so good at is finding direction for their lives. It may be that living hand-to-mouth became a pattern that they can't shake. Another possibility is that the gritty reality of coming up with the rent every month is itself an avoidance mechanism. As long as there is a wolf at the door, there is no time to think about who you are or what you want to do with your life. That's something you can do later, when the emergency is over. Meanwhile, you remain in a preadult limbo, doing whatever you have to in order to get by.

For looming over everything else is the great question of the future. No matter how well students manage to avoid the issue, it is coming and they know it. Some say that they think about it constantly, starting in their sophomore or junior years. "It just hangs over me like a cloud," said more than one student. Seniors develop a kind of gallows humor about it. "No need to say good-bye. We'll see each other all the time on the unemployment lines." They know that a college degree is no longer a guarantee of security. "Today's students face more uncertainty regarding their future," stated the CSUN counselors' report. "Counselors note less optimism about the value of a university degree in the current job market."

Even if they are in a hot field, students know that other hot fields have cooled off. Many of them are in debt, and many of them have given up the study of something they like for something that will win them a job. A lot of them have no idea what they want to do and that problem makes almost everything else a problem. One young woman, about to graduate, stared at the blank wall that her future seemed to be and collapsed into dependency on her boyfriend. He—not quite steady on his own feet—panicked and broke up with her. At one campus, the registrar discovered that he was harboring several hundred undergraduates who had completed at least fifty units over and above the requirements for graduation. "They stayed because they had nothing to do and no place to go," he said.

And indeed one of the most obvious changes in college life is that it lasts longer. It now takes the average student about five and a half years to get a bachelor's degree at an urban campus. All of the problems discussed here probably contribute to that state of affairs, but like most patterns, it takes on a life of its own. A few years ago, I interviewed a group of fraternity boys at UCLA. It was rush week and they were sitting out on the deck in front of the fraternity house watching girls go by and talking about life. They were bright, funny, a little raffish, and very engaging. After a while, I asked each of them to tell me about his own situation— his status at school, his major, and his plans for the future.

"I'm a philosophy major," said one. "I'm in my fourth year here, and I think I'm a sophomore."

"I'm in my fifth year. I'm a junior and an English major," said another.

"I'm in my third year. I have sophomore status, and I haven't declared a major yet."

Finally, I came to a bona fide senior—a history major. "What do you plan to do next year?" I asked.

He seemed startled by the question. "Be a senior again," he answered.

Despite the good humor of this group on a nice fall afternoon, college campuses have become communities with an underlying hum of stress. It doesn't show in the picturesque tableaux of young people in khakis riding bicycles through the streets, but it becomes almost palpable when you talk to them. It becomes even more evident when you talk to counselors and residence hall deans. Dr. Barbara McGowan, who heads the psychological counseling department at UCLA, says that her department's resources have been strained by a 10 percent increase in their caseload every year for the past few years. "We not only have more cases. We have more difficult cases," said McGowan, who is particularly concerned by the frequency with which students talk about, think about, and threaten suicide. "The actual number of suicides, thankfully, remains so low as to be negligible," says McGowan, who believes that the taboo about suicide talk no longer exists because "the culture is much more tolerant about violence in general."

Other counselors report similar increases in their caseload. At CSUN, the Counseling Center noted a 40 percent jump in one year. At the University of Maryland, between 11 and 18 percent of the student population will seek counseling in any given year, and 25 percent of all students have seen a counselor at some time in their years at college, according to Dr. Thomas Nagoon, director of the College and University Counseling Services Data Bank. And many counselors are having trouble simply keeping up with the new forms of illness produced by stress. Eating disorders— such as anorexia and bulimia—have become almost campus epidemics, the college woman's diseases, and some counseling departments now have therapy groups just for bulimics. (Bulimia is binge eating, followed by "compensation"—severe dieting, vomiting, or laxatives and diuretics.) One mother was warned to look for scars and chapping on the two first fingers. "They get it from putting them down their throats when they want to vomit." And at health centers gastrointestinal problems are as common as colds.

In fact, college stress has spawned a cottage industry: adjustment workshops for entering freshmen. A Summit, New Jersey, workshop was begun by a pediatric nurse-practitioner who noticed that her patients were either dropping out of college in their first year or coming home with stress-related illnesses. And on a more serious note, Dr. Samuel Klagsburn, a New York psychiatrist, recently opened a private psychiatric hospital called Four Winds exclusively for college students who have undergone emotional crises. Dr. Klagsburn told the New York Times that today's students are subject to stresses not experienced by previous generations. They have to deal with the information explosion, defining themselves, finding careers, and great uncertainty about the future.

Some students turn to nostalgia as a way to deal with stress. Why not go through college as your parents did, with sororities, fraternities, formals, and football weekends? It all seems traditional, innocent, part of another, safer time. Preppie clothes, bicycles, Thursday night mixers, Saturday night formals, pranks and raids, even curfews, give a comforting illusion of carefree, golden youth. But the students themselves know better. "It's all hypocrisy," observed one non-Greek. "They look so nice and have such a dignified facade. They go to formals and get flowers from their dates. They do charity lunches at fancy department stores. Then they go to parties and get completely bombed and throw up. Their songbooks are all dirty—about sex and drinking. It's like something out of Freud's Vienna." The golden youth facade papers over a lot of angst.

And indeed, fraternities and sororities are often the campus centers for bad behavior. Heavy drinking, fights, vandalism, and even rape at the Greek houses have become familiar items in college newspapers and sometimes make their way into the city papers. Students seem to accept the double vision of themselves. One woman, who was particularly proud of the graciousness of her sorority house, was asked if she minded its strict rules, which included a ban on alcohol. "If you want to drink, you just go over to the parking structure with a bottle," she explained, pointing to a concrete and steel-girdered building down the street.

"There's a lot of ugly behavior at fraternity houses," said one university vice-president. "Alcohol abuse is on the rise and it's become socially acceptable, even conservative." He went on to describe a recent fraternity party at which a young woman was—literally—bitten on the buttock and badly injured. "We've got a throwback to males linking up and taking coup, like warring Indians."

But while sororities and fraternities have made something of an art form of rowdy and dangerous behavior, they are hardly the owners of the franchise. Excessive drinking has become a serious problem among college students. A 1981 survey of two thousand college students vacationing in Daytona Beach, Florida, revealed that 29 percent drank alcoholic beverages at least three times a week, consuming six or more drinks on each occasion. That is serious drinking and a serious problem for college officials. Dartmouth College, which feels it has an undeserved reputation as a party school, began a campuswide effort in 1982 to raise the consciousness of undergraduates about alcohol abuse. The efforts include an Alcohol Concerns Committee, peer counseling on alcohol abuse, an outreach program, a professional alcohol counselor, and a campus chapter of Al-Anon.

At other schools, less famous for high living, residence hall deans say that alcohol accounts for 90 percent of discipline problems. "There's no party without alcohol," said one residence hall assistant. "And the goal is to get drunk. It's a big thing to brag, 'I was so wasted last night, I don't remember coming home.' Mostly, they drink beer and some hard liquor. They also get something called Ever-Clear, which is a big thing in the dorms. It's one-hundred-ninety proof grain alcohol, and it's not sold in the state. They bring it in from somewhere and they mix it with something sweet."

A male student dorm assistant found that a principal part of his job was carrying residents back to their rooms after they had passed out. One girl sat in a hot shower for hours. "I went out on my night off—it was about eight o'clock—and she was in the shower. I came back at midnight, and she was still there. I got a big robe and had these girls put it on her and carried her back to her room, still passed out. She could have drowned."

Another one of his young charges had a favorite drink—the Jellybean. "He puts three different kinds of alcohol in one glass. It's kind of a drinking game. They have a lot of drinking games here." He describes them. One is called "Quarters." "You bounce a quarter on the table. If it lands in a glass of beer, you make someone drink it." There is also the 101 club. To become a member, you have to drink a shot of beer every minute for 101 minutes. "They don't just drink on weekends. They arrange their schedules so they can start Thursday nights."

Judith Mack is director of counseling at UC Davis, where four alcohol-related driving deaths in two years have made alcohol abuse a major concern. Lately, Davis students have been complaining to counselors that there is so much drinking going on during the week that they can't study in the dorms. "The partying now starts on Wednesday," says Mack. "In one of our science departments, it has become a custom for students to drink at lunch." And her staff, she says, has seen an alarming increase in problem drinking. "A lot of kids are drinking to buy themselves some time off from the stress and confusion they feel. I'm not talking about college kids having a good time. I'm thinking of kids who drink alone and throw furniture in the pool or bust out walls. These are kids who often are brought here by their friends because their drinking has become such a problem."

In fairness, it should be said that drinking did not start in college. According to a 1981 study by the Research Triangle Institute, nearly one third of the nation's *high school* students are problem drinkers— meaning they were drunk at least six times in a year or experienced negative consequences of drinking with friends, family, school, the police, or while driving.

The drinking often leads to vandalism, to furniture in the pool and holes punched in walls. But even without alcohol, campus officials have noticed a disturbing rise in violent behavior. Pamela Grant, who has been a residence hall dean at Barnard, Ohio State, Buffalo State, and UCLA, says, "Once, students verbally harassed each other when they had disagreements. Now they will hit each other or have a fight. Sometimes, they throw furniture or break mirrors or destroy a couch because they are angry about something. One guy kicked in a window because a girl didn't show up at a floor party and he was disappointed. A girl who didn't like her roommate hung used tampons around the door like fringes."

But when students are called down to answer for destructive behavior, their response is often, "No big deal. We'll pay for all of it. Just send us the bill." The boy who kicked in the window said he was sorry and "It won't happen again." In other words, he didn't see it as anything to make a fuss over. The stress level has become so high that violence is acceptable.

Sometimes, the vandalism becomes arson. In the winter of 1983, minor fires broke out in dormitory after dormitory at the University of Massachusetts campus in Amherst. Alarm bells would clang in the middle of the night, and the building would be evacuated. There were at least forty fires, and though the physical damage was minimal, they came to dominate the thoughts of students whose sleep and work were interrupted.

It is hard to say whether bad behavior is more important as a symptom of stress or a cause. Marc Schuckit, a psychiatrist at the University of California, San Diego, conducted a study indicating that drinking was the *cause* of depression among many college men. It is probably both symptom and cause, a response to a problem that creates additional problems. But if college is, inadvertently, an education in the school of hard knocks for kids who have been given everything, it doesn't seem to be making them tougher or more realistic. Perhaps it is the beginning of a maturation process that will bear fruit years down the road. But in the immediate future, it seems that confusion and anxiety at college only make them confused and anxious. Instead of learning to cope, they learn disguises and diversions.

PART II

THE REALITY QUOTIENT

5
Super Students

At prep school, my classmates were the sons of national leaders. I just expected that at some point, I would have some voice, some influence. Right now, I'm a little confused about how to go about it. But I hate the specter of being powerless. —JOHN, TWENTY-FOUR, TWO YEARS AFTER GRADUATING FROM UC BERKELEY

I majored in art history because I took a great course in Dutch and Flemish painting when I was a freshman. It was nice to study. I had some vague ideas about working for a museum. I wasn't thinking hard about the future. Now I find that the only job you can get with an art history major is in an art gallery, and I really don't like galleries. I'd like to work for a nonprofit organization that does something useful—not just cultural. I think I'd like to write as part of my job, but I don't want to be a writer. —LISA, TWENTY-THREE, A YEAR AFTER GRADUATING FROM AMHERST COLLEGE

John and Lisa have never met. When I interview John, he is living at home and playing electric guitar with a rock band that has not yet had a booking. Lisa has a five-dollar-an-hour job with an agency that distributes free food to the needy. She does mainly office work, but the agency's funding is about to run out so it doesn't matter much how interesting it is.

Neither John nor Lisa will be heir to a fortune. Their parents are

57

middle-class professionals. Lisa's are both teachers in New York City. John's father is a psychiatrist in Los Angeles and his mother is an educational therapist. Their families lead comfortable lives, but there will be no fortune and no titles to leave behind. Yet both have a sense of themselves as special, as privileged people entitled to interesting lives.

The sense of entitlement comes with the territory. It pervades their generation. But while other young people just want money and the cars and homes and swimming pools that their parents have, John and Lisa have expectations that are deeper and subtler. They feel entitled to influence, even to power. They feel entitled to interesting, fulfilling work, without supervision or menial tasks. They feel that work should have *meaning*. Yet they don't seem to have any realistic notion of how to get those extraordinary privileges. They simply expect them.

The basis for their expectations is that they're very bright. They were the kids who learned to read instantly in kindergarten, the gifted kids, the straight *A* students in high school who went on to the top-ranked colleges. In an era in which every child was special, these kids were even more special. They went through school being told that they were wonderful. If they were asked to report to the office, they guessed it was for another award. No one ever spelled it out for them, but they assumed they were on a track that led automatically to leadership and achievement.

If their intellectual gifts had been in math, science, or technology, their expectations would have been squarely met. But this chapter is about those young people who are just free-lance intellectuals, mostly liberal arts majors, who expected that society would value them just as much as their teachers did.

A decade or two ago, it would have. And for that reason, many of us who are a generation or so older tend to be understanding about their predicament. We like them; they are bright and vulnerable and winning, and we see them as reminiscent of our own early years, especially if we too grew up bright, creative, and a little rebellious. We remember the confusion, the false starts, the naïve turns, the abrupt halts. We think that they will learn and grow, as we did. But this generation is different in three important ways.

The first is that the world valued us more when we were young and smart. There were grants and fellowships and academic careers. There were government agencies and nonprofit organizations doing interesting and idealistic things. There was journalism and publishing. There was law. And if none of that worked, there was always selling out to private industry. Bright young idealists got their hands in the dough of real life, professionalized their skills and tempered their ideals.

The second difference is in our history and the psychological makeup that resulted from it. We were raised insecure by parents who remembered depression and war. We expected life to be hard, and we were in awe of power, achievement, creativity. We understood that gratification wouldn't be instant and that amounting to something would take time and a bit of pain. We didn't feel entitled.

The third difference is that, for most of us, there wasn't the slightest chance that our parents would support us after college, unless we were going to medical school or something very much like it.

For today's young intellectuals the world is a less welcoming place. The jobs they get seldom meet their expectations or fully use their talents. It's a buyer's market, and employers aren't overly worried about compromising the ideals or self-esteem of young hires. At the same time, the young hires have very little ability to deal with disappointment and drudgery. Their history of entitlement interferes. A few hang in, but many find themselves cut off from the real world and isolated with their peers. They take jobs that go nowhere and turn to their parents for subsidies. And they live in their heads, making decisions out of thin air.

"I'm constantly tormented by the fact that I don't know what I want to do with my life," said a Berkeley junior with an A-minus average. Academically, she was good at everything. "I declared history as my major, but I feel I ought to do more with the sciences. I'm also interested in film-making lately. A lot of my friends are talking about film-making. I think that what I'd really like to do is write. I'm always observing things—like my family at dinner—and I know what's going on beneath the surface. I'm good with languages too. I think I'd like to be a foreign correspondent." I ask if she has worked for her campus newspaper. "Not yet. I'm thinking about it. I might look into it next semester."

She doesn't. Instead, she and her friends think about what, in a perfect world, they ought to do. Together, they wrap themselves in the cotton batting of their student idealism, a collective case of arrested development.

For when the eighties were indifferent to the promises of the sixties and seventies, they had even more reason than most of their peers to feel hurt and to develop defenses. They didn't get angry at any of the schools they had gone to for not telling them what the world would be like. They got angry at the world for not being like school, and they took permanent refuge in their identity as students. They are young people with a high Intelligence Quotient but a low reality quotient. They build their lives around holding on to that sense of specialness they had when they were still in school, and often this means avoiding reality and its challenges and the possibility of rejection that lurks around every new corner. It means clinging as much as possible to the student life-style and values instead of growing.

"These are my corporate clothes," says Jane apologetically. "I didn't have time to change into my Village clothes." Jane is twenty-three, wholesomely pretty, a little overweight, with a spill of long blond hair. She is wearing a print skirt and a blouse with ruffles that are not exactly out of a dress-for-success seminar. But if she had her way she would be in India cotton and faded jeans for lunch in Greenwich Village. The kind of clothes she wore at the University of Rochester. She has just come from a part-time secretarial job, which she explains as if it were an awkward secret. "The company makes these perfumes, like Oscar de la Renta, if you've ever heard of it." I explain that I am one of the nation's leading consumers. She is relieved. "I really like the business world, but my friends sneered when I took the job. They have certain values and there are things they consider selling out. One friend became a cop, and they were really appalled. They gave him a lot of grief." I know, without being told, what her friends' values are. What they value are the kinds of things they did as students, and that does not include making perfume or being a secretary or a cop.

So Jane is also a graduate student in psychology at New York University. "There's a nurse in one of my classes," she explains, trying to illustrate the unwritten rules she lives by. "She will come to class late rather than wear her uniform. Nursing is déclassé. People will wonder why she isn't a doctor. That's why I wouldn't think of being in an MSW program. I don't want to be typecast."

Jane went to the same experimental high school as Lisa, and for both young women, school provided an identity and a shelter. Lisa's parents divorced when she was fifteen and in the tenth grade. "I didn't really care that my mother was gone. I'd leave home at seven-thirty in the morning and not get home till five. I did my homework and went to sleep. I had very little time for anything but school."

"There were clear lines at our school. There were hippies and hitters," said Jane, who knew which she was. She acted in the repertory theater and dance groups. She spent a day a week doing art therapy with the learning disabled at a hospital. She worked in the English department office and the program office. Both young women had time to fall in love and to sample drugs and alcohol, but the center of their lives was school and its activities. Lisa describes in detail a high school history class in which students conducted a constitutional convention and did other special projects that went far beyond textbooks. And five years after graduation, she is still concerned that she learned math by procedure rather than logic.

College was even more intense, since they went to schools where there were no hitters. There were only other super students like themselves.

Jane made dean's list and developed a family of close friends, now scattered to the corners of the country. The memory of those friendships remains the most important force in her life. I ask Jane if she cares about making money or if she thinks that money will ever be important to her. She shrugs indifferently. She lives in a tiny apartment and her parents help with the rent. She also has college loans to pay off and graduate school tuition. "There's one thing I would like money for. I'd like to have air fare to visit my friends from college."

But an identity as super student lasts only so long. At some point, it becomes an outfit that is just wrong for the party. The super students find themselves at odds with the postgraduate world, and they handle the conflict by invoking the belief systems they constructed in school.

A persistent theme in their belief systems is a prejudice against technology. Modern-day Luddites, their rhetoric is filled with a naïve distrust of machines, and they are firmly convinced that anyone good with machines or numbers is boring, a nerd with pencils in his shirt pocket. It may be that they see the technocrats as clever younger siblings, competing more successfully for the world's attention. *Nutshell* magazine's satirical "Student Handbook" has special advice under the heading "If Your Roommate Is an Engineer." "All engineers tend to be smug about their employment prospects," author Kit Kiefer warns. "Remember: You'll be employed eventually. He'll be dull forever."

At Amherst, Lisa and her friends called the computer science students "hoseheads." She herself took some computer courses at college—in graphics for art. "My friends were very upset about it. They're very idealistic." After graduation, she spent a disastrous two months at a job as a programmer with a scholarly organization that used computers on some of its projects. She was, in her own view, unqualified for the job, and she had no one to talk to from nine to five. "I'd ask a question and they'd tell me to figure it out for myself. For two months, I watched the clock. I constantly had a stomachache. It was a horrible initiation into the world of work."

Kathy, a young woman whom we met in the last chapter, left the University of Chicago without a degree after five years. One of her three part-time jobs at college was with a business school professor who was doing computerized research. She was heading for New York, and, by happy chance, the professor was starting a firm that would do computerized research for Wall Street brokerage houses. He hired Kathy to look after the computers. Her skills were strictly seat of her pants, but she managed well as on-site operator, doing everything from simple programming to tearing up the floorboards to reconnecting loose wires. The firm prospered, and Kathy was soon earning twenty-five thousand dollars a year. The firm also moved to fancier headquarters and took on a more businesslike mien. A supervisor suggested to Kathy that she dress better than her usual jeans, sweatshirt, and Hush Puppies. "I'll think about it," she responded. A week later, she gave notice. The request to dress better, she felt, compromised her identity. She was also miffed that the company hadn't incorporated her design suggestions in the new office. "It sounds ridiculous" she explains, "but it wasn't really what I wanted to do. I didn't like the people or the values on Wall Street."

At the moment, she isn't certain what she does want to do. When I see her it is October, and since February she has been collecting unemployment and working on term papers for courses that she didn't complete at the University of Chicago. She is thinking of graduate school in history, but she doesn't want to commit herself to a Ph.D. program. She doesn't seem troubled by the fact that Ph.D.'s in history with degrees on the wall can't find jobs. She is also interested in New Age dance therapy, public interest lobbying, and public policy research. She would like to write—perhaps creative fiction or poetry or political journalism. "I wouldn't want to write unless it were something I believed in." She is twenty-five years old. Without passing judgment on her values, one can't help noticing that they interfere with her ability to make a commitment to anything. She can remain untested potential forever by invoking chapter and verse of her value system.

"The money isn't there for the things that I value and would like to do," she says. "One of my sisters is a musician and she makes fifteen thousand dollars a year teaching. Another is in oil company management and makes forty thousand. My third sister taught elementary school, but she got discouraged. She has kids and needed more money. She's now a computer programmer, and so is her husband. It seems to me there's a conflict between money and values."

It is sometimes hard to distinguish between values that are a defense against unpleasant reality and genuine naïveté. Donna, a senior at Barnard, plans to go to law school and then practice public interest law, dealing mainly with women's issues. When I point out that few lawyers can earn a living with such an exclusive clientele, her eyes glaze over. Somehow, she will be an exception to the rule. She is also considering a career in politics, but she doesn't plan to run for office. "I'd rather be the top staff person. Politicians are stupid, and I'd control their every move. Anyway, managing campaigns is more fun," she says. Somehow, she will earn a living as a lawyer doing only work that interests her. And somehow, she will attain power without risk or exposure, having constructed a world in which politicians are stupid and malleable.

Lisa also has an interest in politics as a possible career. When she was in college, she had an internship in the district office of a local congress-woman. She worked with constituents who had problems and liked it better than any job she has had. So she has sent out a bunch of résumés and letters to local elected officials. Had she asked the other employees in that congresswoman's office how they got their jobs, I am certain that not a single one could have honestly said that he got his start through a letter and résumé. What he did was work in a campaign. What is revealing is not that Lisa didn't know that things worked that way, but that—having spent some time among insiders—she didn't ask.

Another recurring theme among the former super students is the need to be different from their parents. This is usual for adolescents, but for intellectuals it persists into early adulthood. This is partly because adult-hood comes to them so slowly these days. But it is also because it is hard to be special or unique when your parents have already done it and when the odds of success are so much slimmer. For Kathy, carving out a new path was easy. For thirty-five years, her father hung by his fingernails to a white-collar job that barely supported his large family. Her mother raised six children and worked incredibly hard to make ends meet. Kathy saw it as "an oppressive way to live." Since they were trapped, she wants to be free. She sees her own confusion as "a junction I'm at. I think we have a lot of choices because we're not trapped into motherhood."

But for the children of the accomplished upper middle class, it is harder to find an unblazed trail. John, who longs to have influence, to change the world, sees his psychiatrist father sitting on presidential commissions that may reform drug use laws. He and his friends talk about the human potential movement and holistic health. "Sometimes," he confesses, "I'm sorry that I rebelled as much as I did. I should have just been more directed and gotten good grades in college and been in a position to have impact." He is thinking of applying to medical school and becom-ing a psychiatrist, like his father, but he feels ambivalent about going back to school to pick up his premed requirements. Also, he thinks that maybe he really belongs in the social sciences. Meanwhile he plays the guitar.

"Our parents were radical before we were. They got Ph.D.'s before we did. They got divorced before we did," says twenty-five-year-old Laura, whose father is a mathematician and whose mother is a psychotherapist. Laura left college after four and a half years, a few credits shy of a degree. "I left because I didn't want to finish my academic work and also because I had psychological difficulties about being a good girl at a paternalistic school, especially since my father is a professor." She seems to share many of her parents' interests and values but she does not want to be like her parents. "I think they're too isolated. All of their friends are other academics and therapists. They're interested in politics, but they find political power distasteful. I want the real thing. I want to make a more complex statement about what's out there"

Right now, Laura works in media, but she is on the verge of leaving her twenty-thousand-dollar-a-year job for a fellowship with the National Endowment for the Arts. "My father was shocked that I would leave a good job for a thirteen-week fellowship," she says, a little defiant. "But security just isn't worth the price. I'd rather have adventure than security. Class expectations are changing. It's just too hard to move up. We know we can't go much further than our parents. I know what they have, and I know what they had to do to get it. And I've asked myself, 'Do I want it?' And I suppose I don't."

Laura raises legitimate questions about ambition. Yet somehow, she is unconvincing. One senses that gifted young adults want what their parents have and more. They want personal gratification as part of the career bargain. They would like to achieve and have influence and recognition, but they are unwilling to take the risk. They talk a lot about freedom and adventure, which often turn out to be code words for not making a commitment. For as long as they haven't made a commitment, their illusions about life remain unchallenged. Caught between their sense of entitlement and their fear of failure, they live in a fantasy land of infinite choices.

Andrea is twenty-seven—almost twenty-eight—and she is a good example of her generation's reluctance to make commitments, their continued dependence on their parents, and most of all, their belief that an interesting, rewarding life should come easily.

Six years ago, Andrea graduated from Cornell, fluent in Russian. Right now she is unemployed and living with her parents in Westchester. She has just left a job as assignment editor at Cable News Network in Washington, and she is thinking about what she wants to do next. It is not television.

"I liked college," she says reflectively. "I liked the setting and the time structure. There was no separation between work and play. I liked learning and I was happy there." Instead of a conventional major, she was in a liberal arts mix called the "college scholar program." Basically, she took Russian studies and communications.

After graduation, she spent a year in Europe, traveling with her sister in France and England. She lived in London, sharing an apartment with friends, living on money saved from jobs, loans, and her parents. When that ran out, she cleaned houses and did other odd jobs that foreigners can get.

When she returned from her year abroad, her father, a network producer, helped her get a part-time job with the news department's election unit. The job ended shortly after the election, and was followed by another temporary job as fill-in at the reference library. "I hoped that by the end of the summer, I would really know what I wanted to do." Summer ended and she didn't know, so she went back to the election unit. During that time, she earned between $5 and $8 an hour. With overtime, it came to $250 a week. Her total earnings for the year were less than $4,000, but she managed because she was living at home part of the time. The rest of the time, she shared a westside apartment with another woman and had a low rent.

"I was always interviewing for jobs back then, and I was very flexible about what I wanted." She landed a job with a television news organization that provided video feeds to independent stations. "We bought, borrowed, and begged them," she explains. She began as a secretary to a friend of her father's but by the end of her first few months there, a half dozen or so employees had left with one of the directors, a founder of the brand new Cable News Network. The exodus left a huge vacuum, and Andrea rose quickly in the hierarchy, taking everyone's place in succession. It was chaotic and she worked evenings and Saturdays, but she learned to operate in television and to survive its constant, intense pressure.

Meanwhile, a long relationship was coming to an end, and New York was getting on her nerves. When she too was offered a job at CNN, she snapped it up and moved to company headquarters in Atlanta, just in time for the 1980 presidential election. She was an assignment editor, and the job made her last one seem as peaceful as a convent. "We were a community of transplants. We were very insular, and we worked hard I worked nights and right through the weekends. We never said goodbye to the job. It was exciting, but in the end, I was miserable. It just isn't normal to live that way. There's a narrowness that sets in. One man lived in a hotel across the street and never saw another thing in the city. We had no sense of anything except what was on the wires. All that mattered was hot news. Reality was a memory. Weather was a report." She spent nine months in Atlanta, and then CNN transferred her to their Washington office. It was a good career move. In Atlanta, she had been gathering news at a local level, and she had learned the inner machinery of the business—the satellite deliveries, the wheedling. She had also learned news judgment. "I knew what was a good story. But I didn't know whom to call or what to ask—the reporting process. And I learned that in Washington. I liked the city. It was familiar ground.

I had a daytime schedule and time for a life of my own. I took dance classes. The work was the same, but there was a smaller group of people, and it was a producers' shop, not an assignment-desk shop, as it was in Atlanta, where the assignment desk presented options and the producers picked among them—without making decisions or assuming responsibility. I liked that. I'd rather not make decisions unless I'm forced to. But that's not the way to behave at work.

"My news judgment is good, but we worried about the money we spent. The producers worried about coverage. I felt like an air-traffic controller and a bank manager at once. I was considered good at logistics. But that has nothing to do with news gathering. The role that I was playing needs someone who feeds on nervous anxiety. I'm nice, and an assignment editor has to be nasty or unemotional."

So when there was a lull between two chores—she had been tape supervisor/editor and was moving over to elections work—she took the summer off and went to Europe. "I learned during that summer that there was more to life than television. If I worked through the elections, I'd be thirty when I finished. I'm not so comfortable in my profession, not really committed. I got there on connections. I know elections work. It's compressed pressure. And I felt that my logistic/administrative role was growing, and I didn't like it.

"I feel I have to find what I really want to do. I was becoming a nasty person. I was treating people as roles. I wasn't being a friend but an editor. With a reporter, it was role to role, not person to person. I want to help. There must be a job where I can talk as a person."

Almost twenty-eight, she is now trying to decide what she wants to do when she grows up. She may go back to school in Russian studies or international studies and then work for the government or a journal. She is also interested in public health or health care, perhaps in an administrative capacity. She doesn't think she'd mind the responsibility. "They're slow-cooking decisions. That feeling of immediate pressure, as if thirty seconds on the air were life-threatening, won't be there. Those pressures are softer, subtler. For a while, I thought I couldn't work without an hourly deadline. I'd like to do something creative, but that's not the trend in television now. It's all very fast, and resources are limited. The future in TV is short takes. The networks aren't spending money on longer documentaries."

While she thinks, she is living at home. She likes home and she has nice memories of growing up. Her parents were flexible and gave her unconditional support, and she never gave them any trouble. The local high school—one of the best public schools in the country—offered an open-structured "school within a school" program, which she enjoyed.

And her parents are her principal role models. "My mother is a puppeteer and my father is in television. The examples rule out engineering.

"My mother was anxious for me to leave CNN for personal reasons. She thought the pressure wasn't doing me any good. But my father thought I was foolhardy to leave a good job. But he likes the idea of Russian studies. He sees me in the Moscow bureau of some news organization. And he thinks I'll go back to news after a rest."

Her personal life is also in flux. Before she went to Atlanta, she had been living with her college boyfriend, but "We outgrew each other, and it wasn't going anywhere." In Atlanta, there was no time for any social life. "It was easier in Washington, but everyone was so career-oriented. And the myth that there were so many more women screwed up expectations and resulted in just a lot of free and easy sex." Yet the problem is more than circumstance. "I wonder about permanence. It's not easy to integrate. It's hard to define yourself, your career, and meld it with personal needs. In five or ten years, I see myself working that way. Eventually, I'd like a family."

But meanwhile, "I have trouble with commitments. I tend to live in illusions. I'll have a boyfriend overseas and write or call long-distance. Reality doesn't work out as well.

"Besides, the job left me no time in the evenings. I was consumed by the job. It crushed my spirit. I was unhappy, less likable, less giving. Now, I'm confused, but I know I'm right not to have stayed. It's a great career for someone else.

"But I wonder, 'Who am I?' I'm basically normal, well adjusted, except for not knowing how I'm going to make a salary. I cried to a career counselor, 'It's a big world. What's my place in it?' I've traveled, and in other places, people don't emphasize work as much as we do. Here, your identity is your work. Maybe it was an impetuous decision not to go back to my job. But I think a job narrows your focus."

That last sentence tells us a lot. Commitment, of course, always narrows the focus because it requires that you choose one thing and give up something else. Perhaps a career in television is truly wrong for Andrea, but I can't help thinking that what she is really afraid of is commitment and adulthood. She might have parlayed her experience in a tough shop— and cable news is known in the industry as the toughest—into something pleasanter and more human. She might have learned to live with the commercial limitations of television. By not doing so, she remains tabula rasa, a child with the whole world still in front of her.

It is tempting to think that Andrea lingers in indecision because her parents provide a safety net. There was always Dad's money to tide her over, and Dad's connections to get her another job, and the house in

Larchmont when all else failed. There is some truth to this, but young people who in fact don't have a safety net act as if they do. The illusion of choice seems to be a cultural phenomenon of the generation.

Peggy is a good example. We met her in the last chapter as a college student working in Boston theaters to pay her tuition. She too grew up in Westchester, but in the far less glamorous reaches of Yonkers. Both of her parents had management jobs with large corporations. Peggy is the middle of three daughters. Right now, she is twenty-five and the only one not regularly employed.

In college, she did theater and arts reviews for the campus paper, and she also did a little free-lancing. She had hoped that her clips would win her a job with a magazine or the features section of a newspaper. But there were few jobs and lots of hopefuls that year, and the best she could get was an internship with a Knoxville, Tennessee, corporation that published a group of specialty magazines. A few months later, the company hired her as an editorial assistant, and she worked her way up through the ranks as staff writer, assistant editor, associate editor, and then editor of one of the magazines. Like others in this chapter, she has talent and she has spunk.

But a few months ago, her hard-won job began to go sour. A boss she liked left. In his place was someone who "doesn't like to share strategy decisions, and I had to implement his decisions." She didn't like that, and she found herself dwelling on other things she didn't like. "I hate office life. Quality just isn't important. The actual goals of the company are in MBO's [management by objectives] not human need. Maybe that's the way the world works, but I insist on remaining naïve." A while back, she drew up a proposal for a booklet for teenage mothers. It was turned down because teenage mothers aren't a good market. She did another proposal for a magazine for young adult consumers and that too was turned down. "I believe that we can do things that serve a need as well as make money. I worked and gave them my best and my best was never realized."

Meanwhile, she had developed another interest. During her years in Knoxville, she had begun cooking for her friends. She found she could improvise and do well. She made excellent soups and cheesecake. And she began toying with the idea of going into the food business. There wasn't, after all, any law that specifically prohibited college-educated women from Westchester County from working with their hands. A neighbor was a restaurant manager, and he approached her about opening a small restaurant that would serve interesting breakfasts and lunches in the downtown area. He would raise the financing and manage, and she would cook. They made plans and scouted sites. And she gave notice at the office. But somewhere between the dark and the daylight, he got an offer he couldn't refuse to manage a restaurant outside of Knoxville. Since she had absolutely no experience, there was no way that she could get financing on her own. "So I did a Butch and Sundance exit—jumping off the cliff when I couldn't swim. I left a good job with nothing lined up."

She survived the headlong jump because she had some savings and a three-month contract to do free-lance editing for the company. "I can manage," she says. "There'll be no new clothes and no movies for a while. I can sell my blood again if I have to." Like most of her peers, she has no health or dental insurance but counts on the rude health of being twenty-five. "I just made a radical left turn on instinct."

"It was back to words. I had to scramble." So she is doing some writing and editing. And she is also trying to market her chocolate cheesecake to local restaurants. (Her chocolate cheesecake is the best thing I have ever eaten. She would have to write *Gone with the Wind* to do anything as good at the typewriter.) "I'm going to be more flexible about life now that I haven't got firm plans. I won't resist change so much. I read somewhere that Dolly Parton has five-year plans for her career. I'm on a three-month plan. I have short-term goals. I drive a VW, and I'd like a Jag, but it's no big deal."

Asked how she envisions her future, she gets a faraway look in her eyes. "We visited an island off the coast of South Carolina this summer. It's called Pawleys Island. It has old beach houses and no neon signs. I'd like to live there and run a restaurant in the summer and write in the winter.

"I'm part Peter Pan. I don't want to grow up and face the nasty things." She reveals that her mother had a serious stroke three years before. "She is better now, but it was frightening. My mother was forty-six years old and she was immobile and needed a bedpan. Life is frightening and abrupt.

"I want to be there for my family, and I will. But I'm not looking forward to it. They supported me through a lot. They thought I was foolish to leave my job, but they listened to my point of view. They're good people. They raised three kids and none of us are screw-ups."

Does she see herself raising a family someday? "I'm just beginning to explore commitment. I don't know my depths as a writer or an editor. That's what this year is all about. But commitment to another person is more distant right now. I'm too young to say." She is twenty-five. Her mother was married at nineteen and had two children by the time she was twenty-two. "I see myself doing that—if I ever do it—when I'm in my thirties. Now, I have to learn to be single and self-reliant."

Like other young women, she has to do it without her mother as a role model. It is too late for her to define her life in terms of marriage and family.

"I guess the generations grew up differently. My mother never lived alone or talked to an accountant herself. I never went into labor. I suppose she was more mature at my age, but she didn't have as much choice."

6

Artists and Dreamers

An artist is a creature driven by demons. He don't know why they choose him and he's usually too busy to wonder why. He is completely amoral in that he will rob, beg, or steal from anybody to get the work done. . . . The writer's only responsibility is to his art. . . . The writer doesn't need economic freedom. All he needs is a pencil and some paper.
—WILLIAM FAULKNER IN AN INTERVIEW WITH THE *Paris Review*

I go to encounter for the millionth time the reality of experience and to forge in the smithy of my soul the uncreated conscience of the race.
—JAMES JOYCE, *Portrait of the Artist as a Young Man*

That was the old vision of the artist. He wanted nothing but the tools of his craft and the freedom to search his soul. His enemy was middle-class morality and middle-class comfort. His goal as an artist was to do something new and disturbing, to shock the bourgeoisie.

It is hard to say when that notion became an anachronism. But in the sixties, the middle class discovered art. Doctors and stockbrokers and their wives flocked to art classes and galleries and bought works. Elementary schoolchildren did expressionist painting, collages, murals, and sculpted with every imaginable material. They wrote haiku and made films. The useful arts and crafts projects, like ashtrays and paper flowers, had gone the way of desks nailed to the floor. Self-expression was the principal occupation of children in affluent American suburbs, and it seemed only natural to think of it as a life's work. (In poorer neighborhoods, parents were appalled to see their children bringing home all those paintings. "They do nothing but play," protested an angry *barrio* mother, worried that her children would never learn enough math and reading to become middle class.)

At about the same time, the artist discovered the middle class and all its new money. Andy Warhol showed artists that they also had to be businessmen. And like good businessmen, they needed contacts. "Jackson Pollock didn't hang out with Jackie Onassis and her friends," says Hunter Drohojowska, a Los Angeles art critic. "Andy Warhol started that. He was the first high-profile, media-oriented artist, and he became the role model for young artists today. He taught them to go to cocktail parties, to make the scene, to court critics and collectors and gallery owners. Art's become very chic, and artists work hand-in-hand with the bourgeoisie. There's no way to shock them anymore. The young artist goes to parties and gallery openings and shows with bankers and lawyers. He's part of the world. The starving artist mentality is gone."

Predictably, price tags for paintings rose. Young unknowns are now getting as much as $8,000 for their canvases, and artists under thirty with budding reputations are getting $20,000 and $30,000. Government and business became partners in the middle-class love affair with art. In 1970, the National Endowment for the Arts—which supports visual arts, performing arts, and literature—spent 15.7 million dollars. In 1981, the NEA disbursed 186.8 million, an increase of more than twelvefold. State support for the arts soared from 58 million in 1975 to 120 million in 1982. Private institutional support for art had an astonishing twentyfold increase—from 22 million in 1967 to 436 million in 1979. All that money created jobs. According to Department of Labor statistics, the number of people employed as artists, writers, or entertainers increased from 903,000 in 1972 to 1,388,000 in 1981.

Unfortunately the increased employment opportunities for artists didn't nearly keep pace with the rush of young adults who wanted careers in the arts. One whole percent of the population told the 1980 census taker that they were artists, which is almost twice the number that the Department of Labor said were employed as writers, artists, or entertainers. The affluent middle class and its elected government were supporting the arts, but not nearly as fast as its children were becoming artists. We may not have wanted this to happen, but the value message was unmistakable. It was hard to convince our children that careers in art were impractical while we were spending incalculable amounts of time and money on "culture."

"I got mixed signals from my mother," said Jenny, the young art student whom we met at the beginning of this book. "Officially, I was supposed to marry and have children. But my mother was a dilettante artist. She had talent, but no confidence. She painted; she took lessons with the local dance company. She played the piano for the Plantation Junior Women's Club. That was as far as she would go. But she wanted me to be a real artist."

And many of them are creative, productive artists. But many more seem to live on the margin of creativity.

Middle-class parents, having fought for affluence, could now indulge a part-time taste for something lovelier. But their children wanted to take it a step further. This was the generation that could afford to be impractical, to do what their parents timidly dreamed about: achieving in the arts, even becoming famous. And this is perhaps the group with the greatest burden of all. For not only do they have their own sense of destiny—and creative people often have grandiose delusions of greatness—but they have the impossible burden of fulfilling their parents' dreams while defying their wishes.

Careers in the arts are slow-growing by nature. Talent and the inner self have to develop and then mesh with opportunity. But again, this generation has added problems. First, there are so many of them because so many were special, identified as talented, and encouraged to pursue their talents. Like the super students, they were given a sense of destiny, but no one ever told them that achieving that destiny would require sacrifice and risk.

I first see Ellen through my office window. She is waiting for the traffic light across the street and I guess correctly that she is the young actress I am about to meet. She has the kind of friendly good looks that belong in dairy commercials: freckles, turned up nose, round cheeks, and hair that used to be called strawberry blond. She is carrying something on a hanger covered by a plastic bag.

It is an extra outfit. "I'm auditioning for a commercial after this," she explains a few minutes later. The commercial is not for milk, but for contact lenses. "I'm going to change in the ladies' room after lunch." It is a very hot summer day, and there is no doubt that whatever she is wearing now would be damp and wilted in a few hours. I give her extra credit for professionalism. She is twenty-eight, a serious actress with a degree from the prestigious New York University Professional Acting Program and a member of two Equity-waiver theater groups. But she is a practical woman and she supports herself doing voiceovers, commercials, and odd jobs.

I meet with Ellen a number of times, and I marvel at all the things she is involved with. She volunteers on a hotline for battered women. She has a job organizing a move for a rich couple. She is spending time with her sick grandfather. She is visiting her grandmother, who was in an accident. What I begin to notice is that she is not often involved with pursuing her acting career, and I wonder why.

"When I was little," she recalls, "my father used to tell me stories about Lilabelle the Lightbulb. She was the lightbulb in my bedroom, but in the stories, she was the prettiest, the brightest, the best. He used to ask me who I wanted to be like. Did I want to be John Muir? Did I want to be Eleonora Dusa? It was always someone great. From the time I was eight years old and on, my father was always telling me about great people to model myself after."

There are a lot of ways of being great. Ellen's father is a lawyer during working hours, but on his own time he pursues his passion for diaries. He writes diaries, he collects them, and he taught his children to keep diaries. He also shared with Ellen a devotion to old films and old songs. Her mother has a job in county government, but she is also a very good painter, and had a house full of artist friends. And when her parents divorced when Ellen was in her teens, her father promptly married a very good ceramic artist. They would all like to see Ellen do something more secure. But in Ellen's family, to be great means to do something in the arts.

"I always knew I wanted to be an actress," she says. It was a natural choice. Just living in her house was a work of art, an ongoing performance. Her family had a passion for recording everything—not only in diaries, but in tape recordings and photos on special occasions and anything that might be a milestone. Her sixteenth birthday party is fixed not only in her memory, but in photos and on tape. It was a costume party arranged by her mother. Everyone was in antique clothes except her father, who was no longer living at home. He arrived onstage late, in a red sport shirt and slacks, with a small check as her present. She remembers what he was wearing because she has the pictures. And she was so furious at him for slighting her that she ran off to her bedroom and taped her anger. "I want my parents to get a divorce," she told the recorder vengefully.

She went off to college determined to be an actress. She was eighteen, and it might be expected that a young woman with a sense of the dramatic would have dramatic relationships with men. Ellen's penchant was for what a therapist later called "wounded birds." One of her wounded birds made her decide to transfer from the University of California to New York University, where she soon had another boyfriend. "I went from one relationship to another in those years. I just couldn't be alone. I had this urge to be alone—a real longing—but I couldn't do it. I seemed to fall into instant passions." She offers some compelling psychological reasons for her dependency, reasons that go back to early childhood. But the behavior may be more interesting as a metaphor for her relationship to her talent. She longs to engage it, to be alone with it, but somehow she can't.

And stormy love affairs provide a constant diversion. A year after arriving in New York, she became involved with a troubled Vietnam veteran, an emotional casualty of the siege of Khe Sanh. He drank, had nightmares, and abused her, but she felt that he needed her constant attention. "I lost my friends and neglected my career. I felt I had to be with him all the time."

For many women, the old notion of living for and through a man remains an escape clause in every commitment they make with themselves.

She finally broke free and came home to California. She went into therapy, and her scars began to heal. She found assorted kinds of work to pay her bills—the commercials, the voiceovers, the occasional day on a television episode, and when all else failed, office work. But her acting career never quite took off. Months after that first meeting in the summer, we talk about it.

"I know I don't do the things I should do to get parts," she admits candidly. "I need new pictures. I need a new agent. I should go to more auditions. There's a whole list of things. But I just don't do them."

"Why?" I ask.

There is a long pause. "Because I've always felt I had to be famous," she explains, her well-pitched alto voice sliding out of register a little. "Since I was a kid, my fantasy was that I'd star in a Broadway play and I'd take the first row of seats and fly my family out to see me. Whatever I do is measured against that. So I always hesitate to take the next step because even if I'm very good, I might not be great. When I was in New York, I auditioned for the part of Liv Ullman's daughter in *I Remember Mama*, and I was absolutely convinced that I would get it. My family had always told me that I looked like her and had her sensibility. I was devastated when I didn't get the part."

Art student Jenny grew up in the South where her mother's bohemian ways were firmly fixed in a matrix of traditional values: church, family, position in the community. But like Ellen, Jenny feels she was set up. She is now twenty-nine, making a hefty salary as an installer for the telephone company, and taking film-making at the New School in New York. Her life is in order after several years of chaotic drifting, but her painting is on a back burner.

She spends a lot of time thinking about why she has had such a hard time. "By my expectations, I was a failure. My mother always told me that I was so talented, a genius. I thought she was just my mother and didn't know what she was saying. I wanted reality, but I didn't know where to find it. I felt I had to be special, in the top ranks to be acceptable. That makes it hard to be creative. To accept yourself. Since the second or third grade, I've had a fear of success, and I think it was a fear of finding out that I was just average. I believed that I was special and had to be to please others. In a way, I felt that something was robbed from me. I'd rather be average, without a destiny. Anything less than destiny is letting the side down. That's why I retreated into a job like this.

"But I didn't have any realistic options. My parents and teachers never gave me a realistic idea of where I stood, and it was hard to have a sense of myself apart from their expectations." Therapy helped. "The therapist guided me toward reality," she reflects.

Not all young would-be artists find a guide or even want one.

Twenty-six-year-old Nick would rather dream, and he has found the perfect place to do it. He is a part-time writer for a weekly alternative newspaper in a beach town in southern California. It is a sweet, messy, funky little town, dominated by the beach. I met him almost by accident. I was having lunch with his editor and another writer, and Nick passed, bronze, barefoot, and barrel-chested, in floral-print surf trunks. "There's one of our reporters," said the editor, who was trying to explain the ethos of the town to me. I grasped it instantly.

"I'm going to do some thinking," said Nick, heading for the beach.

"Good idea," said the editor. When Nick was out of earshot, the editor explained that he had just finished the reporting for a major story. "He's probably done much more research than the piece can possibly hold, and I'm glad he's going to let it all settle for a while." No one seemed to mind that he would be spending the afternoon at the beach.

I find Nick again at the newspaper office—a renovated loft over a movie theater—a few weeks later. His story has been a success, and he's pleased with himself. I suggest that we get a drink, and he explains that he doesn't drink anymore. Drinking became a problem for him and he had to give it up. But he leads me to a bar out of habit and orders coffee. The bartender and the waitress know him and they understand about the coffee.

"You know when I finished working on this piece I had an idea for a weekly alternative paper of my own. I talked to this journalism professor who's a friend of mine about helping me find backers. He keeps talking about getting me an internship at the *Times*. I don't know what I should do. I really want to lay the groundwork for this weekly of my own. I need a project besides writing and I need the freedom to do my own thing. But on the other hand, I keep asking myself, 'What's the use of freedom without money?' I mean, if I get offered six hundred a week at the *Times* I'll take it. A guy I know works for the *Times* here at the beach and he just does a couple of puffy pieces a week. I'm afraid I might end up like that—just comfortable."

Nick grew up a few miles from here in a suburb of sprawling homes that were more than just comfortable. The local public high school served the children of successful professionals and corporate executives, the kind of kids who wore topsiders to match their polo shirts as they worked their way toward top-tier colleges. Nick's foreign-born parents were self-made. His father is an engineer, and his mother owns a successful travel agency, and they moved there from a more modest area when he was a child.

"There were a lot of people with a lot of money in that community. One of my friends was a golfer on the pro tour. He had a Porsche and a lot of cash. We hung around a lot. Maybe that was part of it all. But I think I set it up so that I didn't have to go to school a lot. I was real smart in high school, and I could just not go."

The system didn't work as well in college. As a teenager, he had worked in his mother's travel business, so he decided to major in economics. He spent two years enrolled at UC San Diego and another year living nearby. "I just hung around. I started doing some writing. But I was losing interest in economics and I was taking drugs a lot. I just lost the momentum of go to school, go to law school. At twenty, it all seemed real boring. I liked writing music and playing with a rock band. But school without school was fun. I was still close with my friends there. It was nice."

Then, one summer Saturday, he drove up the coast closer to home and spent the day at the beach with a girl. He picked up a copy of the local weekly and noticed that there was a storywriting contest for readers. The deadline for entries was Sunday night.

"I slipped it in just in time. I remember I had a job at Sears then, stacking sheets. They called me at work to tell me that I won."

He began writing regularly for the paper and he was instantly adopted by older staffers. There always seemed to be someone around who wanted to take him out for a drink or over to a good party. "There was a lot of madness," he remembers. "I went to bars, got drunk. Sometimes I worked for fourteen hours straight to get a story done. I had romantic notions about things. I thought it was a badge of honor to do crazy things. And this town is great for that kind of stuff. I met all kinds of people who liked fun. I guess that's why I've stayed here all these years. There are a lot of people I enjoy here."

One of them was Tim, the paper's cartoonist. "He was really fun. We pushed each other a lot."

A few months ago, they pushed each other too far. They left a party together at three in the morning, and Nick plowed into another car, wrecking both cars and throwing Tim through the windshield. He was jailed for drunk driving, and his publisher had to bail him out. And since he wasn't insured, his legal and financial problems have consumed him since. "Now, I'm working for my lawyer and the lady in the other car."

I ask why he didn't have insurance. "I don't know," he shrugs. "I just didn't think about stuff like that. I thought about money for rent and food and gas. I just never thought about insurance.

"My girlfriend is just the opposite. She's organized. She teaches fitness for a big corporation. She's got lots of lists and long-range goals. I like instant gratification. Get the story now.

"If I didn't have all these legal problems now, I'd start moving up. Being out here is like being an expert on some obscure African tribe. It's just out of the way. Nobody knows it's here. And I don't really think of myself as a newspaper reporter. I'm more a writer. I'd like to do a cover story for *California* or a national magazine. I'm also working on a screenplay with my brother-in-law."

When it's time to go, I ask if he knows a better way back to town than the major north-south boulevard, which I know will be jammed with rush hour traffic. He has never heard of the boulevard. "I just know my way around here. I know these streets."

I am stunned enough to gossip with his editor, a perceptive and experienced newspaperman who has taken refuge here for reasons of his own. "You have to see the copy that Nick turns in," he offers by way of explanation. "It has to be completely rewritten. It's full of tortured facts and bureaucratic garbage. It's painful for him to write, and what he turns in is never the story that he talked about. He has very little professionalism, but he wants to be a writer. He has a first-rate mind. What he lacks is killer instinct. It requires a commitment to extract the story from a maze of facts, and he just can't make it.

"Nick doesn't get it together because he doesn't need to. He makes a little money. His girlfriend has a salary. His parents help out. There's an absence of struggle there. He adapts. You don't really choose this kind of life-style. It's just arrived at."

Psychoanalyst Rollo May writes in *The Courage to Create* of a patient who never took his work beyond the idea stage. "A talented professional, this man had rich and varied creative potentialities, but he always stopped just short of actualizing them. He would suddenly get the idea for an excellent story, would work it out in his mind to a full outline which could have then been written up without much further ado, and would relish and enjoy the ecstasy of the experience. Then he would stop there, writing down nothing at all. It was as though the experience of *seeing himself as one who was able to write, as being just about to write,* had within it what he was really seeking and brought its own reward. Hence he never actually created."

May calls this "escapist creativity." "There is no real encounter, no engagement with reality. That isn't what the young man is after; he wants to be passively accepted and admired by his mother. In cases of this kind it is accurate to speak of *regression* in the negative sense."

Escapist creativity may now be something of a social malaise, the neurosis of a generation brought up to be creative. In a looser, less Freudian sense, today's young artists see their talent as a great attention getter. It allows them to be admired, dependent children forever. And that of course feeds itself. If you assume responsibility for your talent and produce, you run the risk of not being as good as your potential. The trick then is to remain potential.

So disorganization and irresponsibility become a way of life for some. It is, after all, part of the artists' life-style, and it even reinforces their image. Sometimes, like Nick, they keep their lives in such a state of confusion that work is impossible. Others live on the border of creativity. They hang out a shingle and make the scene. But real work is yet to come, and no definite date has been set for its commencement.

Eric is a nice, big, dark-haired, rumpled boy of twenty-four. He is very bright. "I was the best student in my junior high school," he tells me, "and I have trophies in general excellence to prove it." His junior high school was a cozy enough place in a lower-middle-class suburb outside of Boston. Eric grew up there, the youngest of five children, and his father operated a dry-cleaning shop. "Everybody knew me and my family there. It was a real neighborhood." He was plucked out of that bowl of warm oatmeal when he won a scholarship to an elite prep school in the city. It was a progressive, socially conscious school. "During the energy crisis, they turned the heat off and we all froze. We wore our coats and gloves and you could see your breath condensing in front of you." But it was there, Eric feels, that he became an educated person.

It was also where he learned about the choices that his parents didn't have. He is also a good example of the power of peer culture. Almost instantly, Eric took on the class prerogatives and privileges of the wealthy kids he went to school with. "I think I'm incapable of holding a nine-to-five job," he explains. "The school reinforced those values. They taught us to be happy. To grow. A career doesn't matter."

So at Brandeis, Eric spent three years majoring in theoretical math. "I didn't want to be practical. It would be contrary to my nature." After three years, he decided that he would be at best a mediocre mathematician, but he could be a star as a painter. Somehow, he convinced Brandeis to allow him to switch majors in his senior year. He graduated on time, *magna cum laude*. "I don't know how I did it. I had no paintings. Just a thesis. And raw talent." He is also a wonderful talker.

But all the hustle and raw talent in the world couldn't provide him with any sense of direction after graduation. It was one thing to razzle-dazzle college officials, and quite another to make it as a painter in the real world. So he went home and spent three months watching television—soap operas, game shows, old movies, sitcom reruns—whatever was on. "What else could I do?" he asks, remembering Dustin Hoffman in *The Graduate*. "I can't swim, and Jews don't camp."

In the fall, he found a job as a customer serviceman with a mutual fund company. "That means I sat on the phone and took abuse for eight hours a day. It was okay. I didn't care. The customers called up and yelled at me about their million dollar accounts while I was making a hundred and fifty a week." He had moved out of his parents' house and was living in Boston with a girlfriend. He was also getting very good at his job, and he set a company record for handling five hundred complaints in a day. Then he knew it was time to move on.

"Somebody in that office said that you could only get so close to someone and then you had to fuck him or kill him. It's sad but true. I knew that I had to get out of that job or embrace it. And I only took it to get out of the house." So one day, dressed in his paint-smeared clothes, he arrived at the office, picked up his paycheck, cashed it, and never returned.

It seemed like a dramatic, over-the-cliff ending, but Eric was not about to become a starving artist. He already had another job lined up, as a computer operator. "Painters used to work as carpenters," he muses. "Now they do computer work." His job was ideal. "It consisted of twenty minutes of work in each eight-hour day. I sat in front of a digital system and made a phone call when it was down. I got twelve thousand a year for that." He worked a shift from four P.M. until midnight, slept till eight A.M., and then got up and painted. His girlfriend left him because "she wanted to marry and be taken care of, and she didn't see a painter filling that role. I was glad that she was gone because I could paint during the day."

The job lasted ten months. He left because an art professor convinced him that a painter ought to live in New York. It was where the scene was. He now has another pay-the-rent job, as an office boy for a design firm. "I do what I'm told," is his vague description of the job. He takes home $150 a week, and he shares a loft with another painter, a woman who is his friend, not his lover. "I've always lived with girls. I've never roomed with a guy. Girls are easier. They're less competitive." The loft costs each of them three hundred dollars a month, and he manages to paint two nights a week. The rest of the time, he enjoys New York. "We're meeting a lot of people in New York. We go to galleries and openings. I really like it. And the contacts are important."

I ask if he's made any progress toward showing or selling his work. "Gimme a break," he pleads disarmingly. "I'm just a kid. I'm not ready for that yet." He thinks about it for a minute. "Actually, there is someone. I'm a good squash player, and I play with this guy who's a curator. This guy thinks that I should do some squash paintings. He offered to help me sell them to rich people who love squash." Nothing has come of the offer yet. Eric has never mentioned it again because he considers the man too important to bother.

He has fantasies about marrying one of the designers in his office. "She makes a thousand dollars a week, and she's cute." They haven't gone out yet. He expects that at some point he will accept his parents' offer of financial support. Basically, it is the way young artists get started. They paint, get into a show, sell a canvas, and try to get reviewed. It is a long, hard progress for serious artists. It is not only hard work, but it means taking risks, doing what Tom Wolfe called "hanging your ass out over the edge."

"I'd be happy to be left alone in a corner to paint," Eric says. But he works in an office all day, and he goes out to openings at night. He is preoccupied by *weltschmerz*. "The world may be coming to an end, and I worry about what red to use. I think in small terms, and horrible images keep me awake. I think of babies with swollen bellies. My mind races all over the place. I need television and two beers to sleep." It may be that he needs to paint, to commit those images to canvas; but for now, he is delaying that moment of truth. "I have only forty more years to live, and I don't want to spend one minute of it unhappy." But making art, of course, is uncomfortable, often painful. So it stays in the background, his identity and his raison d'être. "Art gives life meaning. I couldn't give it up." But it is not yet his occupation.

7
Santa Cruz as a State of Mind

There is something about the angle or the color of the sun here on the northern curve of Monterey Bay that makes even the seediness of Pacific Avenue mall lovely. It pours down through the magnolia leaves, superimposing a pattern of dappled light and shadow on the strict geometry of the brick walk. It is a nice, mellow sun that makes yellow swatches on the bare legs of a girl in a drooping India cotton skirt dancing in a doorway to a beat of her own and on the dirty blankets of the young transients sleeping on the planter ledges. It shines on the outdoor patio restaurants, where tourists are having chicken salads and white wine, and on the family-owned department store that shows mannequins in knee-length skirts and stock-tied blouses, and on the health food store and the Woolworth's that sells pads of linen-finish stationery with purple flowers and beanies with propellers mounted on top.

It must be the quality of the light here, or magic, that keeps Santa Cruz from feeling like a depression-era seaside town invaded by hippies who have come to hide out from the eighties. A blend of small-town conservatism, arts and crafts bohemia, and counterculture battiness, it seems as if the clocks here stopped before the Arab oil embargo in 1974.

Rather good jazz comes from the patio of the old courthouse—now a restaurant, a bar, and a bunch of halfhearted tourist shops. It almost drowns out the group from the Lighthouse Christian Fellowship singing hymns across the street; but there are no hard feelings. A man with a front tooth missing smiles and hands passersby a little booklet entitled *How to Have a Happy and Meaningful Life.*

Farther down, toward the end of the mall, a street musician in kilts plays bagpipes. A bulletin board behind him is thatched with layers of messages about rides to be shared, massage therapists, postural realignment, Nicaragua, hatha yoga, lesbian health care. Two men hawk a newspaper about repression in Iran.

There have been some particularly grisly murders in Santa Cruz; the police have been accused of brutalizing the "transient element" at the request of local merchants; and the city council is divided between a no-growth left and pro-growth right. (At the moment, the left has four votes out of seven.) But mostly, coexistence is a way of life here. Other American cities have street performers, but Santa Cruz is the only one where the street performers have organized into a guild and written a manifesto. Its points—such as, each performer may remain at a location for no more than one hour if others are waiting—are largely ignored, but it is posted in the window of the sporting goods store.

On a nice summer day, the tourists cruise the street, drop a few coins in the performers' hats, look at the mostly disappointing merchandise in the shop windows, and then try to find a place to eat lunch. There are lots of restaurants on the mall: Chinese, Mexican, Indian, German, casual French and fancy French, general salad and crepes, vegetarian. But wherever you eat it will seem as if the place just opened and it's the waiter's first day on the job. He will be out of the special, bring the wrong order, and then disappear when you want to pay the check.

The chances are that the waiter, or waitperson, used to be a student at UC Santa Cruz or maybe somewhere else. He may even have advanced degrees, so he doesn't mind not being a good waiter. On the other hand, he doesn't mind being a waiter either. Ambition is not an ingredient in the brew of life here. Good drugs, the right coffee beans, the presence or absence of a breeze are far more important.

"There's no shame at all in a college graduate being a waiter here," says Lee Quarnstrom, a newspaperman who has lived in Santa Cruz off and on for the past fifteen years. "There is absolutely no peer pressure to succeed. The role models for success here are cocaine dealers. They drive Mercedes, but no one envies them. They have to work too hard." He warns me not to make appointments in Santa Cruz. "People don't understand them. Appointments are a big-city notion. I think I am the only owner of a telephone answering machine in the county. When locals call and get the machine, they hang up in wonder. 'You mean they've got machines that answer phones?'"

Quarnstrom tells of a young woman who worked for his wife. She was twenty-one, the daughter of accomplished parents, and she herself was a rather good graphic artist. Her car was totaled in an accident. When she collected the insurance, she went out and bought drugs and partied her way through the money. Weeks later, when it was gone, it dawned on her that she had no car and no way of getting to work. She shrugged, and without regrets bought a bicycle and got another job closer to home. That it paid less and had less of a future didn't matter much. It was just work.

"The big division in Santa Cruz," says Quarnstrom, "is a class split—those who work versus those who don't. A few years ago, the city commissioned a study on the 'undesirable transient element' or UTE's as they began to call themselves. They liked the name. One guy ran for city council as a UTE. He won, but then he left town because he decided he was gay and didn't want to live with his wife anymore. The UTE's have a real fear of employed people. They're afraid that if there are too many employed people, the balance of power will change, and they won't be able to get their benefits."

Santa Cruz is the capital of the sixties. It has counterparts in dozens of mountain, beach, and country towns all over the country and in bits and pieces of virtually every city in America. They are living proof that no matter what the media say, the sixties—or more accurately, an eighties adaptation of the memory of the sixties—are still an option. The option, though, is the shell of the sixties, the style without the substance. There are no real issues, no real rebellion, and certainly no activity that would have any bearing on anything outside of Santa Cruz. Sometimes the lack of reality frays the nerves.

It isn't anyone's fault. Young people often just need to rebel, to be different. In any generation, there will be a given number of young people who don't know what they do want, but they know that they don't want to be like their parents or do what society tells them to. In other times there were clear and praiseworthy ways of being different. They involved a struggle with reality, perhaps with real authorities, and they sometimes led to real results or real consequences. And that led to growth. But rebellion in the eighties is more like a fun-house stairway that goes nowhere.

In a 1981 *Esquire* article, author and Santa Cruz resident Page Stegner wrote angrily of the increasingly bizarre and antisocial behavior in the town he had come to in the 1960's "because it was still possible to entertain the illusion of living with, and off, the land." Fifteen years later, there were not only grotesque murders in Santa Cruz, but there were meth freaks in the street and unsolicited offers of drugs in the men's room and deadbeats urinating in the parking lot. "Something ominous was slithering into the garden," Stegner wrote.

"These chickens, unlike their distant cousins from the bohemian, beatnik, and hippie eras, have no credo, no goals, no ideology. They want nothing more immediate than the gratification of various cravings, and they don't care in the least who picks up the tab.

". . . Few of the people (or that element of the street people who have increasingly taken over the center of town) bear any relationship to the youth movements of the sixties. They are, on the contrary, the ring around the tub, a residue of human marginalia, a drug culture spin-off that exists not only on what it can bilk out of a liberal democratic society but on the tolerance that society has developed for aberrant behavior, even when it is clearly deranged."

Stegner's views caused a little bit of a stir in Santa Cruz, which is not a town that rushes to judgment. Culture-proud Santa Cruz bookstores reserve a section for "local authors," but none of them had copies of *American Places*, the book from which Stegner's *Esquire* piece was adapted. Two years later, the weekly Santa Cruz *Express* ran a rejoinder by another local author. Page Smith, a historian and a founder of the University of California, Santa Cruz, offered the theory that his city was the reincarnation of the American small town. He wrote of sitting with friends and watching an anti-nuclear demonstration. "All the rich and varied cultural life of Santa Cruz passed before us—the African dancers, the mimes, the poets, the singers, the politicians, the talented and the only modestly talented and the not-so-talented—all bathed in the pellucid and enchanting sunlight of late summer. Jack Zajac looked around and said, 'Just a typical Sunday afternoon in a typical American small town!'

"In any event I love Santa Cruz's general looniness as well as its earnestness in good causes and not-so-good causes. Perhaps because no picturesque idler has peed on my shoes or stolen my wallet I wouldn't want to be anywhere else. Sometimes I have a fantasy: I reinvented the small town; it turned out to be Santa Cruz."

But whether Santa Cruz, and towns like it, represents the new barbarism or an enlightened version of the small town, it continues to be a mecca for disaffected young people. They come here daily and nightly, from all parts of the country, riding the Green Tortoise, a weekly bus from Los Angeles with a twenty-dollar fare, or a Greyhound bus, or hitchhiking, or driving aging Volkswagens or even the Toyotas and Datsuns their parents gave them as high school graduation presents. Waifs come here because they heard it was pretty and the weather was good and the drugs were plentiful. But it is also the kind of place that educated, middle-class young people come to when they would rather be waiters.

Brian is a handsome, even-featured boy with dark curly hair and beard, blue-green eyes, and a gentle voice. He is a waiter at the Cooper House, the restaurant in the old courthouse-turned tourist attraction. That is his bicycle chained to the low iron railing around the patio. When his shift is over, he will unlock it and ride over to the Caffe Pergolessi, a little coffeehouse behind the Santa Cruz Bookshop that shares courtyard tables with a Chinese restaurant and a pastry shop. On most days, Brian will have a caffe con latte from the counter at the Pergolessi and maybe a chocolate croissant from the pastry shop, and sit at a table in the courtyard in the mustard-colored afternoon sun. He is trim from running and biking, but no one in Santa Cruz worries about calories much.

He has been around long enough so that a steady stream of girls wave to him and stop to chat. They are flirtatious, but it will do no good just now. Brian is in love with one of his co-workers, a sturdy, suntanned girl named Judy. The affair isn't going well and that is part of the reason he seems depressed. The rest is more complicated and has to do with being thirty and a fugitive from the life he was supposed to lead.

Brian grew up in Westchester County and in Connecticut, one of five sons in a successful, professionally ambitious Irish family. His father is president of a high technology company, his mother is a mother. One of his brothers is an accountant, one is a lawyer. The other two are still in college, majoring in business.

Brian was a psychology major at the University of Connecticut. He settled on psychology after first trying anthropology, sociology, and English. Practically speaking, it didn't matter what he majored in. After graduation, he went to work for his father's company, as an electronics buyer. At first, he liked it. He liked the challenge and he liked the money. He had taken out loans to go to school, and he was glad to have a steady income now. He had an interesting loft apartment in New York and a nice car. He went out to dinner a lot and he went to great bars, like the Ritz in the Village. But as time went on, he found that he just wasn't happy. He was part of the great status quo, and in some vague way he had wanted to change the world. "I wanted to make a difference," is all he can say to explain it. He participated in some demonstrations, he started a solar company of his own, and he had some love affairs.

"The love affairs stifled me," he says. "They either held me down or they made me move on." One of them was a long-distance relationship with a very career-oriented law student who lived in Washington, D.C. He was traveling back and forth on weekends and finding it all frustrating. "New York was dirty and getting me down. It was like beating my head against a wall." He found himself observing everyone he knew and concluding that they weren't happy. He didn't think of it as a projection of his own depression. It was fact, the way things were.

"My parents aren't happy people. They have a beautiful home and material things. But my father is a very unhealthy man. He has cataracts; he's overweight. He can't express his feelings, to us or to others. He has that quiet Irish pride. My mother is very hardworking. I don't know if she's happy. She doesn't complain.

"But I looked at my friends and they were all into drugs or alcohol—some form of escape. I did all sorts of drugs myself. I used cocaine, LSD. It had some good effects. It made me look inside myself. I think I used drugs because I was bored. I wanted stimulation and challenge. I was searching for something. Spirituality. Something was missing."

Then he met a woman who had been living on Maui. She was in New York on a visit, and she suggested that Maui would suit him also. "People are more spiritual there. The life-style is simpler, more accepting." She couldn't be happy in New York either, she admitted. So Brian left his father's business and the loft apartment and the Ritz bar and went off to Maui. He lived there with the young woman who convinced him to make the move, but they were roommates, not lovers. Maui was beautiful and accepting and spiritual. He developed an interest in the "healing arts" there. But it was hard to make a living on an island whose only legal industries are sugar cane, pineapples, and tourism. He worked as a waiter, and even that was unsteady.

Then someone approached him about a business venture—growing magic mushrooms. They raised a crop and Brian flew it back to the mainland. He made almost twelve thousand dollars and decided that would be it for his career in the drug business. "It was too much risk," he concluded sensibly. Later on, he told his parents about the deal. "They weren't too pleased," is his understated account of their reaction. "But I explained what the mushrooms did and how they affected people, how they opened minds, and they were less upset. I didn't do mushrooms much myself," he adds.

After two years, he decided that he had exhausted what Maui could offer. Thanks to the magic mushrooms, he had a stake, and what he wanted to do was study the healing arts—polarity therapy (massage based on Eastern theories of body energy), massage, herbology, acupuncture, and nutrition. He saw a magazine ad for the Hartwood College of the Healing Arts in Santa Cruz. "I decided to go for it."

He spent a year at Hartwood College. At the end of the year, he earned a certificate as practitioner of the healing arts, and decided to stay in Santa Cruz, a sympathetic place where he had a lot of friends. Armed with his degree, he hung out a shingle and did a few massages. But he soon discovered that a large percentage of the population of Santa Cruz were also massage therapists and hardly anyone had the money for massages. His mushroom money had run out and in desperation he took a sales job in high-tech San Jose. It lasted for nine months. "I hated it. I hated sales. I didn't like commuting. I don't like cities. It was the same routine I was escaping from."

Being a waiter though is all right. His days start with a four-mile run between the beach and the San Lorenzo River. Then he goes back to the wood-frame house he shares with a friend, showers, and bikes the few miles to Pacific Avenue. He has coffee and croissants at the Pergolessi, reads the papers, and then works the lunch shift at the Cooper House. On his days off, he goes to the beach or rides horses in the country. If he isn't working a dinner shift, he visits Judy at her house in the mountains after work.

"The summer is hectic because of the tourists," he says with little complaint. Sometimes he goes two weeks without a day off. But in the winter, there's little work, so he tries to save money. "I cut wood then or do whatever."

He reads a lot all year long, mostly fiction or personal therapy. Leo Buscaglia is a favorite. He read *Love Is Letting Go of Fear* and gave it to his lover. He has had no therapy except what he has provided for himself.

It is not a bad life, this biking from beach to mountains to coffeehouse. It is certainly more appealing than congested freeways and sales quotas. Brian has been here for three years, discovering these pathways and little pleasures. He would probably like it more if he didn't have a broken heart most of the time. Despite his appeal, he has trouble with women. Maybe they don't like the wounded look in his eyes.

"I love to be in love, but I also hate it," he explains. "The problem is my expectations. I want feelings returned. Maybe I want a soul mate. But all my relationships end in friendship. There's always a crisis. One of us wants more. Lately, I've been involved in triangles. The women I've cared for have been involved with other men. Everyone ends up getting hurt."

He is in that kind of situation with Judy right now. They met three months ago at the restaurant where they both work. Brian fell unreservedly in love. "But Judy is in a state of confusion right now. She tells me she loves me, but she also loves this chiropractor in Los Angeles. She left L.A. because the relationship wasn't going well, but then he came back into her life. He started calling, and next week, she's going down to L.A. to see him. She wants to see if the relationship can be saved." He relates all this flatly, factually, but the pain in his eyes is unmistakable.

"If I could do anything I wanted with my life, I'd like to work with mentally retarded and handicapped kids. I'd like to have a farm, a big house for them, and run it with Judy. I don't know how I'd get it started.

Things like that aren't funded anymore. I think I'd like to go to UC Santa Cruz and study handicapped education.

"I feel a lot of confusion right now. A lot of people I know are in a similar situation. They don't know where their lives are going. They can't decide where the world is going or if it's all worth the investment."

Even from across the street, Judy projects strength. Tan, slender, her wavy brown hair is combed back into a neat, thick braid that hangs almost to the small of her back. Wearing a thin tank top and short skirt under her dark green restaurant apron, she balances trays of food and mugs of beer effortlessly, the muscles in her forearms and back rippling with her movements. Even her face, bare of makeup, is strong, with prominent jaw and cheekbones and brown eyes that look right at you. She is clearly her own person, if she could only figure out who she is and where she fits.

She is twenty-one and struggling with it. "It seems as if adolescence goes on forever now," she says matter-of-factly, as if she were giving directions to the men's room. "Kids don't discover themselves in time to make the right choices. They start at something they think they'll like and then they learn the external forces." By "external forces" she means things like money and degrees and market demand. "The eighties are tough," she adds.

When Judy was born, things weren't so tough but they were confusing. Her parents separated when she was two and divorced when she was four. She, her older sister, and her middle brother and sister, who were twins, were shuffled back and forth between the two households. At the time, both households were in the Virginia suburbs of Washington. Her mother was a chemist and her father worked for the CIA. He is still with the CIA, but she doesn't know exactly what he does. "He's an economist, and he was in the START talks. I think he speaks five languages." He is a shadowy figure in her life. "I see him every two or three years. I probably won't see him for another year or so. Last year, he sent me five hundred dollars out of the blue. That's the way he is. He never asks me if I'm happy. He asks if I have money for insurance."

Her operative father is Simon, whom her mother married when Judy was seven. Simon was a violinist with the Metropolitan Opera, so the family moved to New York and then settled in a house in New Jersey. And her mother had a change of careers as well as heart. She left science for art, becoming a singer in the chorus at the Met. Despite these changes, her daughter describes her as "English—very straight and very conservative. A real hardass."

Judy never was straight or conservative. By the time she was in eighth grade, she heartily hated public school. "There's no way I'll go back," she announced to her family. She did manage to survive the ninth grade, and in the course of the year, she heard about a private alternative school in the area. It was almost a free school, without structure or requirements. Her parents were firmly opposed to any such place, so she went on her own to see the principal. Marv, as she calls him, was impressed with her gumption, and agreed to give her a partial scholarship. She convinced her mother to pay half of the two-thousand-dollar annual tuition, and she would get a job and come up with the rest.

It was a remarkable negotiation for a fourteen-year-old. She cleaned houses to earn her share of the tuition and she had enough left over to keep herself supplied with drugs. "I learned about making money then. Other kids don't do so well on their own. They're not so together. I learned to be resourceful."

Her parents admired that but they were less happy about what she was doing in school. "There were no term papers, no memorizing. We'd read a book and talk about it. There was no structure. We talked with professionals in different fields. We did what we wanted to. If I was tired, I didn't go to class. Why sit there and space out?" What she liked most were the apprenticeships. "We could pick a field and work in it. I taught senior citizens painting and drawing. The old ladies loved me. I did it for a year. Then I worked with retarded and emotionally disturbed kids the second year. And then I stopped going to school altogether. I just worked with the kids from January on. I graduated anyway. I arranged to get credits for the work with the kids."

Her parents, who had a more traditional notion of education, were appalled. But they were busy people, and she was the youngest of four. Battle-weary, they had surrendered and let her go to a school that they didn't approve of. But they did what parents often do when defeated by a strong, rebellious child: They criticized.

"They attacked my choice of school," says Judy bitterly. "They made me think that I wasn't intelligent, that I couldn't do things. They said I couldn't write a letter or a term paper. They were constantly calling me stupid because I came home from school without books. They felt that I was undereducated."

But school wasn't the only source of friction between Judy and her mother. "She had really had it with kids and being a mother by then" is Judy's explanation. "I wore old jeans and didn't shave my legs. They also didn't like my politics. I went to some protests. I used to stay out really late, and she didn't like that. She told me not to eat the food in the refrigerator. We were fighting constantly." She was also using drugs a good deal. Her housecleaning money provided her with cocaine three nights a week, and she also liked marijuana. "I was stoned the whole ninth grade."

"I think it was because she was having menopause and facing the empty nest," Judy says of her mother. "I learned at the open school that adults were people. We called our teachers by their first name. We partied with them. We had an interaction class that was very therapeutic. We learned that they go through stuff too. My mother was a real person, and she had problems—with money and paying the bills and so on."

She also, of course, had real problems with her daughter. When Judy was eighteen and finished with high school, she decided that she had had enough of home. She moved in with her brother who lived in the next town, and cleaned houses until she had enough money to go to Europe with a girlfriend.

After two months of traveling, she came home and took a psychology course as a nonmatriculated student at a nearby state college. "At first I got an F, then a B, then I got all A's." She teamed up with her sister and went back to housecleaning, earning more money than she wants anyone to know about. Her parents admired her initiative and hard work. "The key is trust," she explains. "We were fast and honest. I liked it. I love hard, physical work. I like waiting on tables. You do a different act for different people, and you learn to interact."

By the next summer, she was ready for another adventure. She and her brother packed up and took off across country in a little red Colt. In August, they arrived in California, and Judy headed up to the San Francisco Bay area, where she had some friends. She taught at a private kindergarten during the day and waited on tables at night. When she wasn't working, she lived in a rickety old building known as the Pink Palace. "It used to be a whorehouse, and it was full of drunks and sleazy characters. I felt very insecure. I was separated from my family and my friends. I got really depressed."

Then, in January, her high school boyfriend came to California, and together they moved to Los Angeles and looked for work. She waited on tables and cleaned houses. He was a guitarist and had a harder time. In May, he had a chance to do an album back East, and left. Judy stayed and met Ted, the chiropractor. He was twenty-eight and still in school. "We had a hot and cold relationship," she tells. "He's a sweet, beautiful man, but he's uncommitted. It ended because he said we had no future. That was February. In April, I came to Santa Cruz.

"There was nothing to keep me in Los Angeles. Hollywood and Beverly Hills were ugh. I was there a total of ten times. Everyone seemed depressed. Maybe that's because I was depressed. George kept me going while I was there, and without him, there was no point in staying."

She chose Santa Cruz because seven years earlier, when she was in the ninth grade, she saw a picture of UC Santa Cruz in a college handbook. It was her dream of a place to go to school. She quickly found another waitress job in time for the tourist season and a cabin back in the mountains where she could garden. She also met Brian.

"He's a beautiful man too. Very different from Ted. Ted really takes care of his temple. He works out and he's a vegetarian. Brian does too, but not as much. But I'm not in love with Brian. I'm in love with Ted. There was a lot of misunderstanding in that relationship. He didn't really want me to leave L.A. He just wasn't ready for a commitment. He wasn't ready to marry me. Anyway, he called and he came up here July fourth, and I wanted to keep the connection. So I'm going down to L.A. to see if the relationship can be continued. He sees me as a perfect mate, but he doesn't feel it. I'm in Brian's position with him and Ted's position with Brian. I don't know what I'll do but whatever I do will tear me apart. The relationship with Brian has been completely honest. I told him at the beginning, 'Don't fall in love with me.' We were just casual lovers."

After a week together in Los Angeles, Ted comes back to Santa Cruz with Judy. "It seems to be working out. We're happy, but Brian is depressed," she sums up. I begin to understand that she talks about complicated relationships and feelings in such a businesslike way because they are in fact her business. They are her principal products, like coffee beans or hemp.

And, sadly, finding someone who will love her may have to be her life's work for a while. Her three parents—talented, high-achieving, well educated—seem to have rejected her, each for different reasons. They are busy and preoccupied with the rich possibilities of their own lives. She is trying valiantly to find some ground that is her own, that makes her special, *but not them.* At the same time, she is drawn to self-absorbed, elusive, rejecting men, men like her shadowy father. Caught up in this complicated emotional agenda, reality is pushed to a back burner. For all her uniqueness, Judy is very much a child of her times.

Working the tables at the Cooper House, Brian seems more subdued than ever, even with customers and passing girls. He is ready for the inevitable. "Judy saw a psychic who told her that Ted would be her life mate."

Only a psychic could predict the future for someone like Judy. What will happen to a young woman so rich in survival skills and so utterly bereft of everything else that a rich background might have offered? It is hard to see her just as Ted's or anyone else's wife. Perceptive, strong, resourceful, hardworking, erratically worldly, she is also seriously undereducated. She turns to psychics for advice about whom to marry. She talks about a healthy life and "caring for your temple," yet she smokes constantly. And she addresses her future with the choplogic fantasy that her generation applies to that subject.

"What I'd like to do is live in a small town and start a home for the functionally retarded. They're so neglected, and there's so much you can do for them. They can be brought into society. They can farm. They can have schooling and apprenticeships. I'd like it to be in California, Washington, or Oregon. Mostly, I'd like California; it's less rainy. And it's fairly liberal and open here."

I raise the subject of funding. "The cost of keeping a kid there would be close to five thousand dollars a year. It would take federal and state funding, private funds where possible." It is news to her that funding for social programs has been dramatically reduced. It doesn't affect her dream. "I'd like to have ten or twenty acres, a large house, thirty kids and five in staff. The staff could live in at home or come there—four days on, three days off, with one person overnight all the time.

"I don't want it to be near a city. I want it to be in the mountains or at the beach. A beautiful environment is very important to me. I want the school to be in a healthy place, with animals and fertile soil for flowers and gardening. I've loved gardening since the second grade."

She knows that running a school requires credentials. "The only way for me to get anyplace doing what I'd like to do is to get a doctorate." What she has is a ragtag collection of courses from community colleges in each of the cities she has lived in. She will get some more in the fall at a community college near here. And some day, maybe in a year or two, she will get to UC Santa Cruz, her dream school, if only she can come up with the money. It is a bit late in the game to go to her parents. "My real father was supposed to pay for college, but I refuse to ask him. It's like getting blood from a stone. He's a real hardass."

Yet she and Brian present us with other puzzles, less easily solved. Why are these attractive, healthy children of the American dream so preoccupied with healing and the handicapped? Towns like Santa Cruz are cluttered with dusty little clinics and health food stores and odd therapies, as if we all lived in constant pain. The town has an undertone of convalescence. "Even the environment in Santa Cruz is calming and soothing. The mountains and the ocean have that effect," says Brian. One gets the sense that in some way their idealism, their longing for transcendence makes them unfit for the times, and they have taken refuge here like wounded deer. They want something different from their parents' world of education, success, even cultural achievement, but they don't know what it is. The outside world offers no clues or maps. They would like to change the world, to make it better, but there don't seem to be ways to do it. There's just massage, acupuncture, vegetarianism, and unhappy love affairs. That seems to be all that's available to rebels in the eighties.

Santa Cruz—and other counterculture choices—may seem like an avoidance of the pressure to compete and fit in, but it is a sweet escapism, and sometimes it has a point. The young publisher of an alternative weekly in another seaside town explained his career choice with brutal honesty: "I started the paper because I couldn't get a job with one of the dailies." On the other hand, he says that he is glad that he failed. "Reporters who were cream of the class are writing drivel. I like what I'm doing." But sophisticated, ambitious parents who have given their children every opportunity to make it in the real world are mystified when they go off and live on a farm in Oregon or make health food in Vermont or build reconstructions of ancient boats in Maine.

Carolyn Lewis, associate dean of the Columbia Graduate School of Journalism, wrote in a 1982 Newsweek column ("My Turn") of her own sons, who were living in small rural places. "In this society, where material riches and a certain notoriety are considered admirable achievement, it takes some courage to say no thanks, not for me.

"Plainly, what my sons want and need is something different—something smaller, simpler, and more manageable. They march to a different drummer, searching for an ethic that recognizes limits, that scorns overbearing competition and what it does to human relations, and that says simply and gently, enough is enough."

Lewis draws an idyllic picture of her sons' lives. "They till the earth around their modest houses to grow vegetables, trees, and flowers. They are entertained by shared festivities with neighbors, wives, and children. They have records for music, books for learning, and each lives close enough to the sea to enjoy the esthetic pleasures of blue vistas and open sky."

It is exactly the life that young people like Judy dream about. "My basic goal—when I'm in my forties or fifties—is to have fifty or a hundred acres between the beach and the mountains. I'd build a house, a garden, a small community of people. We'd be self-sufficient, not dependent on society." Yet even she understands that this is hard to do. "Society is going in the wrong direction. The jobs are all in the cities." Her logic is her own, but at least she perceives the fact.

The realization that the idyllic life has its own dues comes slowly. A very bad but commercial painter in Santa Cruz has it all worked out. "Twice a year, I load my paintings in the car, drive to Los Angeles, and sell them to clients. Then I buy myself lunch at the Beverly Hills

Hotel and head back here as fast as I can." He has his dues down to a minimum: He is a bad but commercial painter, and he spends two days a year in Los Angeles. Render unto Caesar what is Caesar's.

For others, the choices are harder. What they would have to give up is exactly what brought them here: the promise of a lovely, unstructured, uncommitted life, without appointments or telephone answering machines or the pressure to succeed.

Barbara sits on a low stool in front of a pottery wheel at the Center Street Clayworks, surrounded by blocks of clay and works in various stages of completion—bare clay, thrown pots that have been painted but not glazed, glazed pots that have not yet been fired. It is a cool room with a film of clay dust over everything. The partition that separates her work space from another potter's is lined with shelves displaying finished pots for sale. A lot of the pieces are done in celadon, a blue-gray or gray-green glaze that she is working with lately. It is very good work, distinctive, well executed, playful, and modestly priced.

She is a stocky young woman, with a friendly, sensible face, and short, blond hair that looks like it has been cut with nothing in mind except keeping it out of her eyes. She wears shorts and a T-shirt and rubber zoris. She seems to like what she is doing, and it is hard to believe that she came to it more or less by accident.

Barbara is from a nice suburb of Chicago, where she spent a happy and uneventful childhood. Her father is an engineer and he has been at the same job since she and her brother and sister were little. "He's typical of his generation," she says. "He did all the right things. He was calm. He took care of us. My mother was more emotional and more verbal." Barbara too did all the right things at first. She was a good student who got A's and B's in high school. But she found it boring. "I was never excited or interested. I just followed the form."

There was no question about going to college, but she had no idea what she wanted to learn or do once she got there. She chose Antioch, an experimental college, because it had a work-study program and it was nontraditional, unlike her high school. In the summer after her sophomore year, she was looking for an interesting work-study opportunity. She scanned the lists provided by the college and noticed that there was a summer room-and-board apprenticeship with a potter in Los Angeles. Barbara had a friend in Los Angeles. "I did it because it sounded like fun. I didn't know anything about pottery. At the time, I was depressed. I had to pick a major. I had no direction or sense of what I was doing, and that bothered me. Going to school was expensive, and my parents were paying the bills. They couldn't figure out what I was doing. I'd always been very responsible."

It was a hard summer. She was unsure of herself; she had little money and few friends and only a bicycle for transportation in a city that ran by car. "It was a period of indecision," she remembers. " 'Who am I? What am I doing?' I kept asking myself."

But the potter she was apprenticing with was a motherly woman who worked out of a garage studio behind her tree-shaded, Spanish-style house. Barbara liked working with clay, and the house and the studio and the older woman offered security. Summer turned to fall, and she decided not to go back to school. "It made so little sense. It was too much money, and I wasn't doing anything there. Helen [the potter] liked me and I wanted to stay. So I dropped out of school."

She promised her parents that she would finish college eventually, but needed some time off. Her older sister had dropped out and then gone back, so they had a precedent. "I guess they were worrying and wondering," Barbara says, "but they were glad that I had a reason and something to do."

The summer apprenticeship stretched into a year. "I learned a lot from Helen that year, not so much about ceramics because I was just starting. I learned that you could make a life around clay. She was middle-aged and she was married and raised kids and was working as an artist and potter. I guess you could say she was a role model."

After a year, it was time to go back to school. "I needed a degree, for my family and for myself. I had a friend at UC Santa Cruz. They had a pottery major and it wasn't expensive to go there. I was there for two years, and I feel I should frame my high school and college diplomas and put them up behind my wheel."

When she graduated, she set up shop in Santa Cruz. That was eight years ago. She is thirty-one now, and she assesses the life she has made for herself. She has never held a conventional job. "I've had part-time jobs but never a nine-to-five job where I had to wear nylons. If I had to, I'd think of a trade, where I could work with my hands.

"When I was younger, I never thought of being a potter or anything else. I lead my life as an organic process. I'm not goal-oriented. I do things till they don't feel right and then I do something that feels better. It's like the progress in learning clay. The next step always came along when I needed it. I went back to school in ceramics because I couldn't think of getting a B.A. in anything else. I was never dedicated or committed in high school, but I worked real hard at this, so I knew it was right for me."

It is not a bad life. "My days have no routine. I take off when I want to. But I go to the studio most days. It makes me feel connected and secure." In the evenings, she plays on a softball league or goes to the movies or the theater or a concert. There is always culture in Santa Cruz. And on holidays, they have huge potluck dinners. "A lot of us here are transplants, and most of my friends are in crafts." She lives a few minutes away from the studio in a house she shares with friends. She likes to travel, and she takes off a lot sometimes just to hike or spend the day in San Francisco, sometimes for a longer trip. "I've been gone about three months this year." It is unthreatening and pleasant and communal, almost a student's life, but without finals or grades.

She nets between seven and nine thousand dollars a year. "I feel I have enough if I can take care of my obligations and travel. I pretty much do what I want to do. I'm exceptionally lucky. I have a backup system. My parents will help out if I'm in a jam. I don't turn to them a lot, but I got a loan from them that became a gift."

Another gift from her parents was a health insurance policy. "I started to worry about what would happen to me if I got sick. So did my mother. It was wise of her, since she'd feel she had to take care of things if something happened to me."

Yet even with her parents there as a safety net, she has begun to feel that she is growing older and her life-style isn't keeping pace. Her expenses are low since she shares her house with three others—a man, a woman, and a seventeen-year-old girl, all involved in crafts. She likes them, but she is starting to feel that she needs some privacy. She would like a house and a studio of her own. "I'd like more control. I'd prefer to live alone, but I'm social and I want to stay close to town, not be out in the boonies, which is all I could afford." Her studio is also a complicated, shared arrangement, and she has grown tired of it. "It takes time and psychic energy."

What she needs is more money, and she knows that her work is good enough to make it. She also knows that she can't make it in Santa Cruz. "My style doesn't sell well here. I'm too playful and New Wavish. I'm not obviously craftsy, which people here like. I need a more educated market, like Los Angeles or San Francisco.

"I've tried to market in galleries around the country, and I'm in a few." But getting into new markets takes sustained effort, and it's easier to live for today, which is usually so pleasant. "I know that I don't do that extra. I don't do all I could. I can always get by, so I don't do it. Commitment—to work, to friends, to life—is one of my problems. I don't want to be a workaholic, but it's a matter of self-esteem, of pushing yourself."

She seldom thinks of the future. "It seems so grim. It's hard to think of saving money when I wonder if I'll survive that long. There may be a holocaust or, more likely, life will just become so wretched, with the cold war and the proliferation of weapons. I'm not hopeful about the prospects of government sanity. And there are so many chemicals polluting the system and nuclear power plants being dismantled and hazardous waste dumps. It isn't just surviving, but will we survive in a manner that we like.

"Economics also make this a real uncertain time to grow up. Once you could grow up thinking you could plan. You could be wrong and get wiped out, but at least you thought things were predictable. I couldn't begin to plan. I just can't foresee the future." Perhaps it is an excuse for inaction, but she is the first interviewee to mention concern about the world beyond her own life. She is not politically involved—just worried.

Unlike her mother or Helen, the older potter who was once her role model, she doesn't see herself marrying or having children. "I like independence and have a fear of giving it up." It is a choice that other generations didn't have, but freedom presents its own dilemmas. So she takes things as they come, without plans or goals. She reads a lot, mostly novels.

"For a while," she says, "I was on a Japan kick, especially medieval Japan. I liked the visuals in the samurai movies. But even more, I liked something about the society. It was rigid and structured. Living within a structure is so different from me. The roles, the honor. Sometimes a character would have to do what everyone knew was the wrong thing because he had to follow the form, even if it was disastrous. Everything was simple and beautiful, down to the details."

8

Renaissance Women

There are fifteen people—eleven women and four men—sitting around the long conference table in this air-conditioned, windowless room. Each one has a pile of mimeographed material and a place card with her (or his) first name on it. This is their fourth meeting, and the cards seem unnecessary. They all know each other. There is, in fact, a friendly bond among these people that seems incongruous in a conference room piled with papers.

This is a career change workshop at a major urban university. It is a service provided by the career and placement department, free to alumnae and for a fee to the public. What these fifteen people have in common is that they have been out of school for years, they have carved out careers for themselves, and now they want to do something entirely different. There are, predictably, a divorcée or two and a housewife or two. But there are also a teacher, a government bureaucrat, a breathtakingly beautiful French woman who wants to trade an adventurous career for a lucrative one, an art administrator, a designer, an actor, a translator, a speech therapist, and a social worker.

"I always had a fear of assertiveness because if I asserted myself I could be rejected," says one of the women. The leaders have asked for reactions to last week's session on assertiveness training. It starts slowly, with statements like these that seem to go nowhere.

"I thought I was nonassertive," says one of the recent divorcées. "So

I took another class on assertiveness training and decided that I wasn't so bad. Most of those people were much worse than I was."

"It convinced me that I have to make those phone calls," says a dark, curly-haired woman named Melanie. "The worst can't happen all the time. Sometimes I get interviews out of the calls. I'm learning to take risks."

The discussion is desultory. The beautiful French woman says that assertiveness training helped her tell a friend she couldn't listen to her troubles right away. Then, a young woman across the table interrupts. She has found something in the pile of mimeographed material that irritates her. "Hey, hang on a second," she says, holding up the offending sheet. It is a list of the "developmental tasks" of adults in their twenties. "This is from some other world," she protests, exasperated. "According to this, a person in her late twenties should be establishing a permanent relationship with a mate, a home, and a life's work. I'm nowhere near that. Neither is anybody else I know in their late twenties." Everyone seems to agree with her. Those may have been realistic goals once upon a time, but now, in the eighties, they are clearly impossible. The review of assertiveness training is dropped. A new topic has emerged: time.

"Time is on my mind a lot," says Melanie. "And I think it's on a lot of people's minds. I'm going to be twenty-eight in a few weeks, and my high school class's ten-year reunion is in the fall. It's a good time to start reevaluating. Some of the people who will be at that reunion will have found these years very successful. They have a career, a marriage, a house. My ten years haven't been so successful. I've quit my job and I'm still waiting for the house and the relationship."

"The twenty-year reunion is better," says a woman in her late thirties, a former speech therapist. "You're more honest with each other. And you tend to just appreciate each other because you're all in the same boat. Or rather, we all missed the same boat. No woman went and got an M.B.A. back in the sixties. Back then, you went into the humanities and the arts and helping other people. Those things just don't cut it in the eighties. They don't matter. Just look around this room. You don't see any scientists or engineers or dentists here trying to change careers. I guess what I'm trying to say is that right now, I wish I had something in my back pocket that isn't there."

And suddenly the session comes alive. It is the underlying theme of why they are here. They chose wrong for the eighties. And time is working against them. They are twenty-eight and thirty, and life still hasn't happened for them yet. Educated, articulate, well dressed, they are still searching for the job, the career, the direction that will make their status real instead of a hollow entitlement.

"I have too many choices," says Melanie. "I'm waiting for my niche to find me."

"I'm angry at myself," says another woman. "I got hooked. I keep wondering, why did I waste myself?"

"There's just no market for the renaissance woman in the eighties," says Melanie, summing up succinctly. Everyone laughs. It is the quote of the day.

The unmarketable renaissance woman in Melanie's quip is a young adult in the eighties whose values and life choices were formed in the sixties, when she was growing up. She was taught to be helpful and humanistic, to be concerned with people and feelings, rather than things or money, to live for others.

She is, in short, a figure out of the past, acting out a script for life that combines sixties idealism and outdated notions of a woman's role. And what she wants to do is move into the present.

The present is about making money and it has very little to do with serving others. According to the 1982 American Freshman Survey, fewer students than ever were interested in becoming teachers. In 1966, 21.7 percent of entering freshmen planned to teach. In 1982, only 4.7 percent saw their future in a classroom, and these, it seemed, were the bottom of the academic barrel. Similarly, potential social workers dropped from 2.9 percent in 1966 to 1.1 percent in 1982. The dramatic increases were in business, engineering, and computer work.

"In the last five or six years, we've seen a dramatic shift to the private sector," says Robert Ehrmann, director of the career development unit at UCLA. "It's up forty-five percent. It's both student preference and the reality of the labor market. There's little interest in government jobs or nonprofit agency jobs."

"Consistent with the trends in career choices, the attitudes and values of the 1982 freshmen showed a greater degree of materialism and less altruism and social concern than those of any previous entering class," said Alexander W. Astin, director of the study. "Being well off financially" was considered an important goal by 68.9 percent of the class—compared to 43.5 percent in 1967. And 69.8 percent—compared to 49.9 percent in 1971—said that "to be able to make more money" was a very important reason for attending college. Meanwhile, goals such as "helping others in difficulty," "participating in programs to clean up the environment," "helping to promote racial understanding," and "developing a meaningful philosophy of life" continued to decline.

"This continuing pattern of increasing materialism and declining altruism and idealism may in part be a by-product of the women's movement, since the women have shown much larger changes in career interests and values than have the men," said Astin. "Nevertheless, since men's values and plans have also changed in similar directions, this would appear to be a general societal phenomenon."

It is an easy shift for freshmen who were never caught up in the old mode. Career advisers say that women students are gradually moving into all fields, and psychological counselors say that women often seek help over conflict between career plans and relationships. And more and more, they are deciding the conflict in favor of careers. "Realism has set in," says Dr. Barbara McGowan, counseling director at UCLA. "Women know their career is for twenty-five or thirty years."

But for women a few years out of college, their feet firmly planted in careers and values they chose perhaps ten years earlier, it is a painful transition. They are the ones caught between two eras and two sets of assumptions. They were raised to care for others and to be cared for. Both promises are being broken. They look around and find that the traditional helping professions—teaching, social work, nursing—aren't valued or rewarded. They also find that no one is taking care of them. The husbands leave or the boyfriends don't want to get married or the dates don't want to become boyfriends.

So they come to workshops like this one to shed their old expectations and to brace themselves for change. It is slow and difficult work. For a radical change in values can be as painful for a young woman as a divorce. It means separation—from a way of thinking and an image of herself that she still loves. It means risk and insecurity. It means wanting reality so badly that she is willing to trade in her fantasies to get it.

At the time of that workshop, Melanie had been unemployed for two months. She was a clinical social worker, with a master's degree, and in her last job, she was a counselor at a rape treatment center in one of the city's best hospitals. "It was the Cadillac of social work jobs," she says.

"Going into social work was natural for me," she says. "I decided to be a social worker in high school, but as far back as the fourth grade, I knew I'd be a psychologist or a social worker. Everyone thought so. I was the helper in my family, the adult child. I was a Girl Scout for ten years, and I was active in the community center. In high school, I was a radical and a feminist."

So she went to Berkeley, as everyone thought she would. "I was involved in peer counseling and prisoners' rights and various protests." She spent the year after graduation in Washington, working for what was then the Department of Health, Education, and Welfare, and then went to graduate school and got her M.S.W.—as everyone thought she would.

Her first job was counseling gang kids at a drug prevention center;

and her next job—with a substantial raise in salary—was with the rape clinic she just left. By most standards, it was an enviable job. She was single and making twenty-two thousand dollars a year. The hospital was in a nice area, and it was close to the garden apartment she shared with her best friend. And surely she had reason to feel that she was making the world a better place every day.

Except that she hated her job. "I got burned out listening to those really horrible stories. I felt, 'I've nailed myself to the cross. I'm taking on everyone's suffering.' I had reached a point where I couldn't cope with my own feelings. I wanted to lash out at the poor rape victims for telling me those terrible things and expecting me to help them." Social worker burnout, of course, is an old story. Social workers used to deal with it by changing jobs within the field. When they got tired of rape victims and gang members, they went to adoption agencies or family counseling or even administration. But Melanie wanted more change than that. She began to think that a lot of the assumptions she had been making about her life weren't working.

"My family is traditional. My father is a pharmacist, my mother is a secretary. They didn't think a career was so important for a woman. The fantasy I grew up with is: 'I'll be taken care of.' But that's all breaking down. I don't see anybody taking care of me. But the fantasy that I would be taken care of allowed me to remain in human services longer. It was just a job, not a career.

"But after three years as a social worker, I realized that I had unacknowledged values. I wanted to make money. I wanted to be in an environment without pathology. And I wanted to meet men. I had always rejected these values because of my radical politics.

"When I was burned out, I felt stuck. Security is better than the unknown. That's why people stay in jobs that beat them up. My feeling was, 'I'm trying to keep things the same, but I want change. I don't know what I have to do.' For instance, I wanted to meet men, but when I was working, I met only women, naturally. But I refused to admit that I minded. I held on to my sixties values. Now I feel that those values have kept me stuck.

"But I have no pact with the gods. I can change. It's such a relief. Whew. I actually said that. I don't have to do that anymore. Now, two months later, I realize that I need more for me. Back then, that thought was taboo. To me, the metaphor for not wanting to help others was masturbation. Sex without giving. Selfishness was the cardinal sin in my family. My mother's family was very giving. And I swallowed it all.

"Now I'm doing the self-exploration I should have done when I was younger. I need reality. The more reality I take in, the more I can use it. The more I defend against it, the more I stay stuck. It's very easy to criticize other people. This person just thinks about her career. This one just has children. I'm looking at the world now in a way that isn't critical but functional. Everything serves a function. We don't know good and bad values. There are no clear-cut values."

She is a metaphor for our times, but that is not much of a living. "What I would like to do is carve out a niche for myself in the corporate world as an expert in personnel and social problems, such as absenteeism. I'm exploring that but I'm finding it a little disappointing. A lot of companies have drug and alcohol programs for their employees, and they are interested in me for that—as a counselor. But that's social work all over in a corporate setting. I want something different. The problem is finding some company that will take a chance on me, since I have no corporate experience."

She has no savings, so for immediate income she works for a friend who organizes trade shows, and she sees a few private clients. She likes the trade-show work. "It's interesting to be in an environment where people talk about things instead of problems." But it's temporary work and when it ends, the money starts to run out. Her monthly rent is $650, and she is still repaying college loans. "I'm on a tight budget," she says. Even when she was working, her take-home pay—between $1,200 and $1,300 a month—didn't leave very much over. "I don't buy drugs. But in the past three years, I've gone to Europe and I've bought a new car. I like clothes and I have expensive taste." At the moment, she is wearing a red linen blazer and gun metal gray linen slacks. They are expensively tailored and they are this year's.

Two months stretch into five. There are helpful leads and letters and résumés and phone calls and interviews, but no jobs. She begins to panic and wonder if she hadn't underestimated security. And then she finds a mentor. It turns out to be an old friend who has confronted her own unacknowledged values and made the difficult journey from sixties woman—helpful, supportive, dedicated to the welfare of others—to eighties woman—independent, materially successful, and enjoying it all so much that she has a lot left to give.

Erica was her roommate at Berkeley. When she separated from her husband two years later, Melanie was in social-work school studying divorce, and Erica became her first case. They shared an apartment for a while, and Melanie helped her make it through the night. Now it is Erica's turn to help Melanie.

Erica is a knockout. She is slender, on the tall side, and has a mass of honey-colored hair and a Botticelli face made over by *Vogue*. She is the small-town princess, the high school cheerleader, the family pet. Her mother was operations manager at a bank, and her father, "the kind of truck driver who played golf. I never knew we weren't wealthy. I always had everything I wanted. I guess you could say they indulged me.

"The plan for me was always that I would marry someone wealthy. My mother is extremely intelligent and capable. She was really the strong partner, but she did it diplomatically. The clear message in my family was that Dad was the head of the household, and mother seldom challenged him."

So Erica went through school ready to carry out the program. She was pretty, and she paid attention to it. She dressed well, and she took care of her hair and her skin and did her nails. She was a cheerleader, and a "good girl student." The fly in the smooth ointment was that she was very smart. Teachers kept advising her to take honors classes, but she begged off. They always seemed to conflict with cheerleading practice, and besides, she didn't relate to "eggheads." In her senior year, she took honors English because a teacher virtually forced her into it. Her term paper, on Jane Austen, was the best in the class, and the only one read aloud. Suddenly, she was interested in academics and even had an egghead boyfriend. "He changed my values. He convinced me that getting A's was what life was about."

She went to a local community college and was named "Woman of Distinction" when she graduated two years later. It was a substantial honor, replete with a banquet. "I got to invite all the significant people in my life—my honors English teacher, my boyfriend's mother." The following year, she went off to Berkeley. She majored in English, planned to become a high school English teacher, and was still in love with her high school boyfriend, who was at another campus less than two hours away.

"We got married ten days after I graduated, on the hottest day of the year." She took a fifth year to get her teaching certificate and then they both applied for jobs close to their hometown.

Erica, who had been a star as a student teacher, was quickly placed in one of the most affluent school districts in the state. Her new husband was less of a star, and he spent the year as a substitute teacher and a janitor. It didn't matter, they told each other, but in the course of the year, they were quietly going their separate ways. "He is one of the most intellectual people I know," she says of him now. "But something is missing. He couldn't even hustle himself a teaching job."

Erica, on the other hand, is a succeeder. When she does things, she does them well. She was a strong, committed teacher, and at the end of the year she spent seventy-two hours without sleep grading final essays, because good English teachers gave essays, not short-answer tests. On the day she went to turn in her grades, she found a memo in her faculty letter box. It was an announcement of the new salary schedule for teachers. Bleary-eyed, she glanced at it, and then she studied it, but no matter how she looked at it, the bottom line was the same: If she taught for fifteen years and got a Ph.D. in English, she would earn twenty-six thousand dollars a year.

"I just said to myself, 'I'm worth more than that,' and I decided I was quitting. I cried when I went to tell my chairman but my mind was made up. I cut myself off. I thought, 'Hello, private sector, good-bye public sector.' "

The salary memo wasn't the only reason, but it was the last one she needed. The country was in the middle of a taxpayers' revolt, and only days earlier, California voters had passed Proposition 13, a constitutional amendment that radically cut property taxes—the revenue base that supported the schools. And a story had gotten around the teachers' lounge that a mother—in this school district of sprawling estate homes—had casually announced at a meeting that she saw no reason why she should pay a teacher more than a maid.

Erica had no intention of being anyone's underpaid servant, not even the public's. That summer, she got a sales job at Gucci, and she started a course in the fashion industry. The course turned out to be expensive and useless, and she dropped it, but in the fall, she landed a spot in a management training program for a high-priced department store chain. And one day she came home from her new job and her husband told her that he just didn't want to be married anymore.

"It took forty-five minutes to end the marriage. Both of us packed some things and went home to our parents. Looking back, I realize that he felt threatened by me, but he made it a question of values. In his view, I was shallow and materialistic.

"My parents formed an absolutely solid wall of support behind me. My mother's advice was, 'Get on with your life.' "

So she did. She moved in with Melanie for a while and was "frenetically single." On the job, however, she was just single-minded, moving up the ladder at a record pace. "I was promoted every four months." She became manager of the sweater department at one of the larger branches and increased sales by 287 percent over the previous season. "I did it by being a real retail bitch," she says with characteristic directness. "Anyway, I was paid the same salary as a manager who had dropped in sales." Her reward was a chance to manage the chain's new Las Vegas store. It was a flattering offer, but she assessed it with the same instant dollars and cents realism that she brought to everything else. "I would be responsible for an operation that took in twenty-seven million dollars in annual revenues and employed over two hundred fifty people. My salary would have been twenty-one thousand dollars a year."

She had a second reason for saying no. There was a new man in her life, a competing manager who was just as ambitious as she was. "The competition turned to admiration and respect. And then we fell in love." Together, they realized the limits of their prospects in retail management and they left for something hotter—computer sales.

Erica knew absolutely nothing about computers, but she went for an interview. "I sat forward in my chair and I got the job." She was supposed to spend two weeks in the office learning the products, but she realized that she was "on draw"—meaning that her salary was paid against future commissions. "While I'm sitting here reading this stuff, I'm going in the hole," she thought. After three days, she told her employers that she wanted to make cold calls. She told herself that she couldn't have lunch until she made at least one sales pitch.

"The customers asked questions. Sometimes I figured out what I needed to know. Sometimes I said I'd get back to them. But it worked out. I did well." That is an understatement. In her first six months, she earned twenty-six thousand dollars in commissions, which must be a record for a beginner.

At any rate, she was number one sales representative in the area that year. Understandably, a "headhunter" (a recruiter who finds and places corporate employees for a fee) called her, trying to raid her for another company. They talked, and before long, he had recruited her to become a headhunter herself. "I took the job against all advice. Everyone said that recruiters were sleazy, fast-buck, con artists.

"But I like sales. I was a good teacher, and I liked the human interface. I thought I'd rather sell people than things. It seemed right for me. After three days, I knew that everything people said about the industry was true. These people did the most unethical things. I was in a state of moral indignation. They were the scum of the earth." She held on for three months, long enough for a crash course in the recruiting business. Then she took another big risk. She went out on her own.

"A wealthy businessman I had sold a computer to had become a friend of mine. He had offered to back me if I wanted to go into business myself, and I decided to take him up on it. He was always looking for business ventures, and he had a lot of confidence in me." It is easy to read things into such an arrangement, but in Erica's case, the man was making a business investment.

But Erica's confidence in herself wasn't so high, and she took a partner— another recruiter with years of experience—for security. With her backer's money, they took three thousand feet of expensive office space and hired a staff. Her partner loved it, but as the months went by, she noticed that they were nearly out of money. He was spending freely and not producing. "He hadn't brought in a single dollar. So I sat down and assessed the situation and created a business plan. I announced that the business was over. I told him that our financial condition was untenable and the backer wanted his money. And I moved what was left of the business, which consisted of a secretary and a recruiter and five telephone lines, to my house. As soon as I made the decision, things started to work out. The momentum picked up."

But there was another complication. She had not only started her own business that year, but she had married her boyfriend, who was now doing well in a sales operation of his own. Soon after opening her doors, she discovered that she was pregnant. She was eight and a half months pregnant when she fired her partner and moved the business into her house. "I was tired a lot of the time, and I was filled with self-hate because I couldn't get it all done. It was a horrible time."

But she got it all done. She had the baby—a healthy boy—and when she came out of the delivery room, she picked up the phone and completed a job placement that had been hanging fire. "The candidate was irritated because I hadn't returned his calls while I was in labor. We had dealt with each other over the phone, and he didn't know that I was pregnant. 'I'm sorry,' I said, 'but Mother Nature interfered.' "

Seven weeks later, she moved back into a real office. The business proceeded to gross over a hundred thousand dollars in its first year, with a net of thirty-five thousand for her. She was twenty-nine years old. "I can't wait to turn thirty," she said. "It will give me more clout." Ten months later, she hired a new recruiter—Melanie.

The real office is in one of the mirrored towers of a high-rise office complex. There is a reception area with cobalt blue plush carpeting, blond wood cube tables, and beige tweed modular furniture. Two receptionists greet visitors with courteous efficiency and handle the switchboard. All of this corporate grandeur isn't theirs. This is a practical arrangement called an "executive suite," in which a dozen or so professionals have private offices off a main corridor, but share the reception area, secretarial services, copiers, and other office machines.

Erica and Melanie are dressed for success in silk shirts and impeccably severe skirt suits. That is their concession to the banks and data processing companies who are their clients. But it is all the concession they make. The rest is themselves. The hair and makeup are playful and contemporary; the eyelids are violet, the lips pink. Erica's office is unabashedly feminine, with a rose and ecru floral print couch covered with pillows, a small teak desk, a vivid Georgia O'Keefe print.

Melanie, who has her own office down the hall, has been with her for five months. They have been difficult months, but she is getting a toehold. After months of plowing and sowing and making mistakes, she is finally beginning to reap. In the past few weeks, she has made four placements, each bringing in a fee of several thousand dollars.

"In the first three months, everything that could possibly go wrong went wrong." They were the kinds of things that would upset a young woman who was used to being helpful. For instance, the manager of a company where they had candidates (a candidate is a job seeker in head-hunter parlance) intercepted a call and told her in no uncertain terms that she was persona non grata. Melanie was furious and upset, and it was Erica who taught her how to handle it. "When things like that happened, she would say, 'Don't get mad. Get ahead. Act in your own interest.' This was a different approach to life for me. I've always been involved in feelings and principles.

"I've also learned about taking care of myself from Erica. She is very caring and very conscientious, but no matter how busy and crazy everything gets, she still gets her hair and her nails done. I like the message in that. It says, 'I count too. I'm worth taking care of.' "

Interestingly enough, there is now a man in Melanie's life, a sound engineer whom she met a year and a half ago. "We went out for a few months and then I got scared. I had problems with intimacy, and I broke it off." Then, last fall, when she started working with Erica, they had dinner and this time, magically, the relationship took.

"He's different from the other men Melanie's been with," Erica volunteers. "He's not a judgmental, intellectual snob. He's warm, funny, and unpretentious." It is a change in taste similar to her own. As students, their heroes were intellectuals. Now, they are free to pick men who are nice to be with. They want company, not an identity, from the men in their lives. They would do their own achieving. Melanie's sea change is also another example of something that love songs try to hide from us. Good relationships are for the strong. And love does not save the weak.

"It has to do with taking risks," says Melanie. "I've had the courage to take a risk with my career, and that gave me the courage to take another risk. I feel differently about myself. I'm no longer asking, 'Who's going to give it to me?' I'm going to get it for myself.

"I think I bring a lot to the business from my social-work background," says Melanie. "I have good listening skills, and I communicate to people that their lives are important. I understand that a job change is a crisis, and I know how to work with people in crisis. It's especially hard for salespeople because they tend to be cocky and they need help to admit that they're in trouble."

The two women often meet job candidates together, as a team. Melanie draws them out and restores their soul; Erica supplies the adrenaline, the persuasive force that closes the deal. "We're very seductive together," says Melanie frankly. "We make people feel that they're safe with us." She is right. As a pair, they exude buoyancy, competence. They know how to take care of people because they did it before, in previous lives. And now, they are also taking care of themselves.

They have begun to think about a partnership and an expansion of the firm. "Our goal," says Erica, "isn't to build a two-hundred recruiter firm. What we want is quality. Our analogy isn't Sears, but Giorgio's. I want us to be nationally respected and recognized as an elite firm because of the unwavering quality of our service."

They have done so much together, why shouldn't they be rich and famous also?

There is an obvious down side to this upbeat story. Their success is society's failure. If we don't care about or reward teachers and social workers, the ones who are strong enough and smart enough—in other words, the good ones—will do something else. Erica and Melanie are a modern morality play with the values reversed. Mammon wins, and the God who preaches selflessness and charity loses. Yet these are sensitive, caring, intelligent women. What has happened is that they have begun to see the old values as exploitive. When they were growing up, serving humanity made you a heroine. In the eighties, it makes you a sucker.

It is a fact that has not gone unnoticed, and young women are quietly leaving real and secure jobs in human services and setting off after uncertain new careers in business and technology. Like Melanie, they want more money, glamour, and social opportunities than classrooms and hospitals offer. They don't want to save the world anymore. They want carpeted offices decorated with modern furniture and attractive men. They want to dress well and have expense-account lunches and business trips with drinks on the plane. Without too many regrets, they are saying good-bye to the dreariness of public sector/nonprofit work, with its hopeless problems, institutional green walls, and sturdy pine desks made by prisoners.

Denise is thirty. She is very pretty, tiny, blue-eyed, with a warm, eager-to-please way about her. She is also high-strung, and it shows through her poise, like the blue of veins through translucent skin. If a customer in the computer shop where she now works doesn't come back, she is quick to conclude, "I must have turned him off." Not that he got a better deal somewhere else or that he wasn't ready to buy. When a sick friend calls, she becomes nervous and upset. "I feel so helpless," she says afterward. "I wish I could do something, but he has shingles and that just has to run its course." She knows because she used to be a nurse.

Denise was never a flower child. She never protested anything or tried to change anything. She grew up in Denver, the oldest of three daughters in a wealthy, conservative family. Her parents traveled a lot, and she went to a convent boarding school from kindergarten to the end of high school. Her ideal of a life of service came from the nuns who taught her and the parents who left her. "The nuns always seemed so happy and so orderly. I wanted to be like them. I think I also had an emotional need to be helpful. I thought that if I were good enough, my parents would stay home with me." Like so many women, she learned that caring for others was the way to be cared for.

She graduated from a large public university and then went on for a master's degree in nursing, a career her parents didn't approve of. "They believed that a woman should marry first and have children, and then go back to have a career. They also considered nursing too subservient." But Denise liked science, and she saw in nursing an opportunity to help.

For a few years, she worked in a large, prestigious hospital, where she became friendly with a group of doctors who were starting a new clinic. They asked her to be its general administrator. It was a better paying, less wearing job than hospital nursing, and she accepted. One of her responsibilities on her new job was to set up a computerized billing system, at the time a new notion in doctor's offices. She got in touch with a software company that specialized in programs for medical offices and learned about the systems. They fascinated her, and the owner of the company saw her as a valuable resource in developing his programs. A year later, when he decided to open a retail computer shop in the high-rent part of town, he asked Denise to join his sales staff.

"I had burned out dealing with people's problems, with the sick and the dying and the constant cycle of depression in medicine," she says. Like Melanie, she wanted to make money, meet new men, and deal with things instead of pathology. And she has gotten exactly that. Her specialty in the store is selling computer systems for medical offices— the kind that she bought and helped develop. Word has gotten around town that she is the person a doctor ought to see when he is ready to computerize. They are expensive systems, running about $30,000 each, and she works on commission. She earned $17,000 a year as a nurse and $46,000 as clinic administrator. This year, she made $150,000 selling computers. She has gone out with a number of men whom she sold systems to—doctors and lawyers and businessmen—and she loves what she does. "I think I'm good at it because I like helping people."

Vicki, twenty-seven, and Nancy, thirty-one, are both graduate students in the master's program in computer information science at Ohio State. Vicki was an elementary-school teacher until a year and a half ago. Nancy used to be a medical technician. Both of them are back in school, earning small stipends as teaching assistants instead of real salaries at jobs they were already trained for. They are sensible midwestern women, without grandiose notions of life. They have just seen the handwriting on the wall. As a teacher and a medical technician, they were social servants, underpaid, unthanked, and buried in menial work. As computer specialists, they will be sought after and rewarded.

"I was disillusioned with teaching," says Vicki. "I didn't enjoy it anymore. I was in a public school in the country, and the kids were very nice. But teaching isn't working with kids anymore. It's mounds of paperwork and the principal's demands, which have nothing to do with the kids. 'Don't make waves' was the attitude. I felt stagnant. I felt that I was getting no recognition, and that it would be the same for the next fifteen years. I wasn't making as much money as I will in computer work, but money was a secondary consideration."

She had taken exploratory courses in accounting and computers during the period when teaching was losing its luster, and decided that she liked computers. She will have a master's in computer information science in two months, and is unruffled at the prospect of looking for a job. The jobs are looking for her. Recruiters were up and down the department corridors today, offering starting salaries of thirty thousand, and boasting about the perks the company provides, like health spas, swimming pools, ski clubs, and scenic locations. "I think I'd like to stay here in Columbus because my husband likes his job here. But he says he'd move if I were offered something wonderful somewhere else. It's not that big of a deal. I really have a lot of choice."

Jill doesn't have a husband to help her through school. She lives in a tiny apartment with two cats, and at age thirty-one, she is living on a teaching assistantship, her savings, and some help from her parents. It isn't easy, having real life on hold. She would like, someday, to have a family and own a home. But for now, she is "letting things happen. You never find what you go out and look for."

An A student in college, with a major in biochemistry, she had worked as a laboratory technician, specializing in blood work, for six years after graduation. It wasn't exactly that she didn't like her work, though working night shifts in a hospital isn't every young woman's vision of life. Other things about her profession started to bother her: the high attrition rate, the low pay, the lack of recognition or credit. "We had a poor image within the medical profession. People would ask, 'What do technicians do?' Doctors talked down to us. It was a real ego struggle. I liked the job, but I couldn't see myself doing it in twenty years."

So she did what people in doubt often do. She got a master's degree. Ohio State offered her a teaching assistantship in clinical pathology and blood banking, and she completed the degree two years ago. She took a course in computers because she was interested in their potential application to blood-bank work. It was fun, and she took another, and she started having doubts about what she would do with a master's in blood banking. A friend asked her, "What do you want to be doing five years from now?"

"I knew I didn't want to be in blood banking. So I jumped right into the deep end of computer science." It took her three quarters just to complete the prerequisites for the master's program, but she expects to finish at the end of the next quarter, "unless I hit a brick wall in my thesis."

Like the other women, she is combining her old career and her new one. She plans to specialize in biomedical systems and hospital information. "I don't need training in medical information," she says with an undertone of relief that at least on that score, she is ahead of the game after the years of playing catch-up.

But she knows that it will all be worth it. While her contemporaries worry about finding a job, she thinks about the ideal location. "I'm much less conservative than most computer people. I like purple and red Norma Kamali clothes and tights in bright primary colors. I think I'll fit in better in Los Angeles. I'd like to work on the East Coast or the West Coast or maybe Colorado. I can be selective now."

At last. Like the other women in this chapter, she is almost a decade out of college. Change takes time.

9
Heroes

Real people are so full of surprises that you wonder why there are so many boring novels and movies. Perhaps it is because fiction has to be plausible and subtle, while real life can do whatever it pleases. It can take bizarre plot turns and teach preachy lessons. It doesn't have to be credible or fashionable.

One of the unfashionable messages that comes from real people is about courage, what athletes and politicians call "hanging tough." We don't like to talk about hanging tough anymore, perhaps because it makes us nervous. We were hoping that life would be easy and risk-free, and there wouldn't be anything to hang tough about. We have already achieved a Brave New World belief that when things go wrong, there has been an error, and there should be some therapy, some soma-like drug, some relaxation technique that will correct it.

It took a writer as extraordinary as Tom Wolfe to make us care about heroes in *The Right Stuff*, and even at that, the movie lost money, and the real-life hero, John Glenn, was an early casualty in the 1984 Democratic primary, a disappointment who never drew crowds or captured our imagination. Granted, he lacked sparkle as a candidate, but so did the winner. Even test pilot Chuck Yeager, the ultimate American hero, the gumchewing loner who defies death as part of his government job, has the safe appeal of fantasy rather than reality. Like Superman or Captain Marvel, he travels faster than the speed of sound. Like the Lone Ranger, he thunders out of the West.

In real life, we would rather admire people who are not quite so unsettling and challenging. Perhaps, on a deeper level, we reject what they stand for: the need to take risks and to have courage in our own more ordinary lives. Heroes are nice for Westerns and other genres that we don't have to believe. In reality, we prefer people who take care of themselves in a prudent, sensible way that doesn't put any of us to the test. A Los Angeles doctor who saved a man from a burning car was honored by the city and the county, but his colleagues in the hospital cafeteria politely questioned his wisdom. "Wasn't that a bit risky? You're a surgeon. What if you had burned your hands?" they asked resentfully.

The idea that life ought to be easy is especially popular among today's young adults. "My parents had not wanted life to be difficult for me," Jill Robinson wrote in *Dr. Rocksinger and the Age of Longing*. "In fact, they expected it would be easy. That perhaps was their only mistake, and such a forgivable one. And I believed in that expectation, that it would be easy. And if life has any universal characteristic, it is not ease." As a group, they had the richest, most attentive parents in the world, and life's wrinkles were always smoothed away. They were brought up in pretty suburbs, places without litter or crime or raised voices. Their parents may have divorced, but they didn't fight or talk about money in front of them. They were always positive about their children's achievements. The kid who never moved the bat off his shoulders had "a good eye" because he never swung at a bad pitch. The child who could never remember the right answers had "a lively imagination." Whatever they did, they were interesting, creative, special children. If they had a problem, it was quickly labeled—"dyslexia," "poor memory retention," "low concentration"—all things specialists could take care of.

The lucky ones, sometimes, were those who had problems. They learned early that life could be tough and sometimes they had to be too. This chapter is about the heroes of the eighties. They didn't test new planes or get shot into space. They are just kids who had a hard time growing up and by some alchemy of the spirit, turned it into strength. It is not a prescription for raising children, but it has a message about the value of working hard and risking failure.

When we first meet, Barney is working as a waiter. Not an ordinary waiter to be sure, but a singing waiter at a popular, zany restaurant where people go for birthdays and graduations and drunken Friday nights. Still, he is a waiter, and he is twenty-eight years old, and sometimes the customer is a guy he went to high school with. "He's a doctor and he's ordering me around."

Barney is short, with curly hair and a small beard and eyes that seem to take in everything, while he is apparently doing something else. He is open, engaging, and so full of energy that he is sometimes hard to follow. He comes from the kind of family that we have been talking about: affluent, cultured, devoted parents who offered their children everything. If he had an interest in something, it was nurtured with lessons. If he had a problem, he was given help. His father is a successful businessman, "the only honest businessman I've ever met," says Barney. His mother is a reading specialist at a university. It is hard to believe that he ever had problems.

But, in fact, he had two problems. The first was that he comes from the kind of home we've been talking about, a home that breeds high expectations and infinite choices. He could be a doctor, a lawyer, an artist, or a musician. He could go into his father's business and be an artist and a musician in his spare time.

The second problem was that he was a very poor student, and that turned out to be his greatest source of strength. It taught him that it wasn't easy to be special. "I was the kind of kid who always got notes home from the teacher because I wasn't living up to my potential. I never did well in school," says Barney. "I was always in the lowest reading and math group." He says all this by way of introduction, as if it were something he has to establish and get out of the way. It's in the category of "I've served time," or "I've been married before." He wasn't a bad kid or a rebel. Parents like his know about rebels from their friends. They come with the territory. But Barney was a genuinely good kid. He was the youngest of three, and they tended to be lenient with him. "I was never punished for doing anything bad, but then again, I never did anything bad."

He was just an undeniably inept student, and his anxious parents provided him with a series of private tutors who became fixtures of his childhood. His favorite was Jack. "He looked like Frank Sinatra and he was very popular," says Barney, as if he were talking about a young uncle who lived with the family.

But helping Barney keep up with a roomful of college-bound, middle-class kids who were born reading and doing long division was a thankless job. Barney was creative and nonlinear, and school was relentlessly linear. "I just blocked school out. I hated it. I liked nursery school, but my kindergarten teacher scared me, and from then on I always felt bad about school. It was bad for my ego because I didn't do well, and I think it had a major effect on me."

Luckily, there were other, more positive strands in his life. His artistic mother painted and shared a studio with other artists. So at ten, Barney was sent to Saturday art classes, and one of his favorite childhood memories is of the smell of clay in a cool studio. A woman named Dorothy ran the studio, and he learned pottery, sculpture, and painting. "Mostly," he says, "it was a place to play. My parents weren't interested in Little League or competitive sports. They would rather that we read or did creative things. I never owned a coloring book."

Art was fun, but back in the mid-sixties, a boy in need of status wanted to be a Beatle. So Barney also took guitar lessons. "It didn't come to me naturally, at first," he says, but not very much did. At one point, his teacher suggested that he quit music. But Barney was used to discouragement, and he stayed with it, learning by himself and from his friends. "It was a nice escape from life." For the next sixteen years, music was a major part of his life. He played in one band or another, and became a good enough musician to be offered a job with the New Christie Minstrels. (He turned it down because he thought their music was too commercial.) And he might well have been a musician if other things hadn't happened.

Meanwhile, Barney went through school as an artist and a musician, but never a student in the academic sense. In the ninth grade, he was held back a semester and took ceramics, flute, and typing to make up for missing credits. For once, he tasted success. "I got all A's and I felt okay."

During this time, his family moved up from a comfortable neighborhood to a very wealthy one. On his first day in his new junior high, a girl asked if was wearing English Leather. Puzzled, Barney responded that he had no idea where his moccasins came from. The girl laughed at this unbelievable naïveté. It would turn out to be one of his most valuable qualities. It enabled him to do the obvious, while other people looked for excuses.

He got through high school in a popular, sixties-style program called "School without Walls." "You could write a song for a term paper," he remembers cheerfully. His problems by then were social. "I had lousy feelings about myself all through school. My girlfriends' parents always disapproved of me. I guess I didn't seem to have prospects. They thought my drawings were cute, but I didn't do well in school, so I wouldn't amount to much."

He went on to college because in his family, it was the thing to do. "My folks embraced me when I told them I decided to go to college." He chose a rural campus, fondly known as "Granola State" because of its hippie student body. But still, it was a college and they gave real diplomas. It had a good art department, and if he could draw and have some time for his music, it wouldn't be too bad.

As it turned out, he loved it. He played in a band, and he worked for a guitar maker, and most of all he drew. One day, he drew for eight hours straight without realizing how much time had gone by. "This is what I do," he thought with a kind of white joy that most people never know. It was one of those flashes of insight that he was prone to. Wisely, he listened to them.

His parents did not mind his spending collegé this way. In their view, education was for development, not to get a job. When he wanted a job, there was always one waiting in Dad's business. But after four years of this idyllic life, he wasn't ready for much else, and he did what a lot of other interesting young college graduates did then. He drifted. He went to Europe for three months, and when he returned he crawled back into the comfortable womb of the college town he had left behind. For six months, he worked for the guitar maker again. "Our band broke up when I left for Europe and some of the others got married. Disco was big then, and we were disillusioned. I played a little, at clubs here and there. But basically, I was dormant. It was the first time since I was nine or ten that I didn't have a band."

So he went to work for his father in the leather parts business. "He kept telling me that someday the business would be mine. It scared the hell out of me. My life, from now on, was selling shoe leather." He did it for two years, hating almost every day.

He drew in the evenings, and he sent his drawings to an agent, who suggested that he go back to art school. Barney thought she might be right. "I didn't actually go back to art school, but I took a course. I picked the course by accident, but the teacher turned out to be a famous writer and illustrator of children's books. I couldn't do any of her assignments right, but I started a book of my own." It turned out to be an enchanting book about children's fears in the night called *It Must Have Been the Wind*. The drawings are large and primitive, with a childlike charm and simplicity that isn't childish. After his teacher saw the early drawings, she told him to stop doing the assignments and finish the book.

"She had no doubts about my talent, and that was an incredible boost." It was all that he needed. While she was working on selling *It Must Have Been the Wind*, he turned out another book, a collection of visual puns called *Utter Nonsense*. When it was finished, he tucked the manuscript under his arm and headed for New York. "I knew that if I wanted something, I had to go after it," he explains simply. "When I was playing in bands, I used to see all these big record companies from the freeway. There were these big buildings, and they were making all these records, and one day it just hit me that they were inside and no one was going to come out and get me because I'm so creative."

So when he got to New York, he hit the streets, as if he were selling leather parts. At McGraw-Hill, he asked the security guard in the lobby, "What floor do I go to to sell a book?"

"You don't," the guard answered. That wasn't the way books were sold. You got an agent and the agent submitted a proposal.

"Well, if this were the way to sell a book, what floor would I go to?"

Finally, the guard succumbed and directed him to a floor, where a receptionist put him through the same drill. But Barney persisted and showed her the manuscript. Maybe because she liked it and maybe because it was the course of least resistance, she brought it back to an editor— who promptly bought it.

"Barney is really naïve," said a friend of his. "He doesn't understand the way things are done in this world, so he goes ahead and does the wrong thing and it works."

The books bolstered his sagging ego, but they didn't pay his rent. For a while, he played the guitar in a honky-tonk, and then he got the job as a singing waiter. He worked nights, and at first, it was great. The other waiters were also aspiring musicians, and after work they all went out and drank till the bars closed. Then they went to a deli for breakfast and crawled home to sleep all day. Barney did this with them for a few weeks, and then he had another of his naïve insights. "If I go on this way, I'm going to be a waiter when I'm forty."

So he established a regimen. Unable to choose between art and music, he linked up with another band and, on the nights when he wasn't working, he rehearsed with them from midnight till five in the morning. Then he would go home and sleep, get up at seven-thirty to call his agent in New York about art work, nap till nine, and then draw till five. He was working on another book and on individual drawings for galleries.

As it happened his career choice was made for him. To make some extra money, he drew cartoon characters on chefs' aprons and peddled them to kitchenware stores. One of his characters was a chef with a moustache, and a manufacturer saw one and loved it. He had Barney design a whole line of hats, aprons, and kitchen linens and arranged for licensing to a ceramics company for mugs, spoon rests, trivets, and other items. Barney got a little money up front and a royalties arrangement, but meanwhile he was still waiting on tables and trying to get through the summer. "It's time to be serious," his father said. "You're twenty-eight, and you're too old for fantasies. If the aprons don't sell, you'll feel let down. What you need is a real job." And he offered to stake him to some more schooling in something practical.

In the fall, the manufacturer flew him to New York for an industry show. They did it up in style, with an airport limo and a luxury hotel suite, but what really impressed Barney was that when he walked into the showroom, the salespeople gave him a standing ovation. He had the hot item that year. Within three days, there were orders for a quarter of a million dollars' worth of merchandise. In the weeks before Christmas, the little chef with the moustache was in department store displays all over the country, and in three-quarter-page ads in the newspapers. Barney didn't have to be a waiter anymore.

The chefs line has since mushroomed into more products and even a book. He has still another book out and an album cover. His drawings in galleries have tripled in price. "My parents finally stopped telling me to go back to school," he says triumphantly. In fact, his father, who is retiring, will spend some of his new free time managing Barney's complicated business affairs. Best of all, he ran into one of his high school girlfriends and her mother—one of the mothers who thought he was a nice boy but not for her daughter. "I always knew you'd be successful," gushed the girl's mother, with absolute sincerity.

Barney's problem, relatively speaking, was a sweet one. What he had to overcome was an embarrassment of riches and minor inadequacy. What makes his story unusual is that so many young adults with his kind of background don't know the meaning of overcome because they have always been carefully insulated from any kind of unpleasantness. Parents believed religiously in a psychological doctrine that held that childhood trauma led inexorably to adult maladjustment. For perfect parents, anything might turn out to be a trauma, so they shielded their children from everything. Ironically, a number of recent studies show that children are more resilient than fragile. Even abandoned children found scavenging in garbage cans showed no psychological problems years after being adopted. The prestigious New York Longitudinal Study showed that among its subjects who had serious problems in childhood or adolescence, the majority—thirty-five out of fifty-three—were completely recovered by early adulthood. It is a nice statistic, but there are the eighteen who didn't recover. So I am not suggesting that children be subjected to trauma or abuse or that educational handicaps lead to success. What I am saying is that our children have more capacity for survival than we think and that the struggle is often character forming.

Julie is sitting in the student lounge at Barnard, drinking coffee and studying. She is alone at a table in the ebb of a gray New York afternoon, going through the pages of a heavy textbook, underlining with a yellow highlighter, and making notes in a spiral pad. She does this in a poised, calm way, without urgency, as if she is comfortably ahead on all her assignments. She is a very pretty blonde, nicely dressed in camel's hair skirt and tailored blouse. On the third finger of the hand holding the coffee cup is a large diamond ring with a matching band. If I had to guess, I would say she is a suburban debutante, from Scarsdale or Greenwich, and she transferred to Barnard after she married because her husband works on Wall Street.

She is in fact from Connecticut; she is a transfer student and her husband is a Wall Street lawyer. After that come the surprises. Her last school was the University of Hawaii, which conjures a totally different set of images than Barnard on a chilly afternoon: white on fuchsia prints, Plexiglas surfboards, hibiscus and plumeria, barefoot students, sand in the textbooks; a warm, vivid hedonism; a school for swimmers and surfers, not serious students. Barnard transfers come from Wellesley or Brandeis or Connecticut College for Women.

"And before that," she says in the same pleasant voice, "I lived in Florida and Louisiana and some other places in the South." She wasn't a student in these other places. "I was a waitress. I was a salesgirl. I worked in factories."

This poised young woman, it turns out, was never a suburban deb. She was a teenage runaway who left home when she was fifteen. "I have one high school credit, in band," she says with a shrug.

Home was in a nice, middle-class community in Connecticut. Her father was an engineer, and she was the younger and luckier of two daughters. It was her older sister whom her mother abused. "My mother was mentally ill and my father just stood by and watched. Materially, they gave me everything, but they never merited my respect."

In this troubled constellation, Julie was the classic teenage rebel, resenting her parents and defying them in every way she could. She used a variety of drugs, "everything except heroin," and she kept running away from a home that profered no security or role models, just oppressive rules. She wanted nothing except her independence, and when she took off for Florida one day, they just gave up.

For the next two years, she drifted around the South, working at odd jobs, and moving on to cities because she had a friend or a boyfriend there. After two years of wandering, she came back to Connecticut, but didn't return home. She worked as a waitress and became friendly with some sophisticated professional men who were her steady customers. They played backgammon together, which she did well, and when she needed a new place to live, they rented her a room in their house. She had left waitressing and taken a factory job, and suddenly, she was frightened that this was to be her lot in life. Her new housemates, realizing how bright she was, encouraged her to develop her intellectual ability. She began taking courses at a nearby state college and got good enough grades to matriculate and become a real student.

She had a friend at a school in New Orleans, so she applied there and was accepted. She roomed with the friend, and one weekend, the friend had a date with a Harvard Law student. He had a friend along, another Harvard Law student, and it was only natural that Julie was paired with him. True to script, they fell in love, and six weeks later, she moved to Cambridge. They lived together and she got a job, putting aside school until he finished law school. Nine months later, they were married.

Her new husband was born and raised in Hawaii—the son of a Honolulu missionary family—and his plan was to go home to practice law. They crossed the continent and the Pacific, and Julie enrolled at the University of Hawaii. Like a lot of women accustomed to independence, she discovered that it wasn't easy to build a marriage on the "whither thou goest" principle. Honolulu had lovely weather, but her husband was busy working and studying for the bar exam. She had no car and no furniture. Her missionary-bred mother-in-law didn't care for this interloper of a daughter-in-law who used makeup and committed other vaguely cited sins. Her father-in-law drank. She felt out of place, and she began to think that the marriage was a mistake.

Then they saw a marriage counselor. "It was the best thing that we could have done," she reflects. "I learned to deal with my mother-in-law's competitive feelings toward me and mine toward her. And my husband and I learned to relate to each other better." It was the only therapy she had, but it was enough to convince her that she needed to be her own person again. (There is marvelous irony in the fact that as a teenager she managed perfectly well on her own in strange cities, without help from anyone. What she needed therapy for was dealing with a husband and in-laws. But that is another subject for another time.)

She was doing well in school and the education she had never cared about when she was a teenager took on increasing importance. Her husband had a top-tier education, and she saw the status, the mobility it gave him. She wanted it too. "I began wondering about the value of a degree from the University of Hawaii. On the mainland, it would be a joke. I wanted the kind of education that he had." So they made a deal. They would go back to the mainland until she completed her degree. He contacted the Wall Street law firm where he had worked summers during law school, and she applied to Barnard, a school not known for accepting high school dropouts.

"They were puzzled by my background. I'm not their normal type, but I guess they decided, 'Why not?' I was a borderline decision for them, and they didn't take me right away."

This is her second year there and her self-possession and sense of direction are impressive, even for Barnard, which is populated by purposeful women. "I felt freaked out at first. But I just dug in and I got good grades." She is now a senior and a full-time graduate student, working simultaneously on a B.A. and an M.A. in public administration. She will get the B.A. in June, and the M.A. the following year. When she finishes, they will move back to Hawaii because "that's the deal we made." She plans to work as a government analyst for a few years and then move to the private sector. "I'd like to be pregnant by the summer after I finish graduate school."

College social life, though, is something she missed. "I'm twenty-four instead of twenty-one, and I don't live on campus or even near campus. I have a few friends my age—other women who have taken time off." They are often surprised by her story, and she has mixed feelings about that. "I sometimes feel smug because I've done so many things they haven't. On the other hand, I can't talk about my trips to Europe. So mostly, I don't talk about my background.

"In a way, I'd like to erase the years from fifteen to seventeen, but I'm not sure. I wouldn't change a thing. I'm very lucky to have my husband and my friends. They've been critical."

Her relationship with her parents is better now. "They're very proud of me, and they love my husband. But they're very traditional, and they didn't like my displacing him so I could get the kind of education I wanted. I felt that he was so well-qualified that he could accommodate me without setting himself back very much. Their view is that it's his career that matters." She says this with a shrug, as if she were reporting the views of a particularly backward sector of a community she had been asked to analyze for a paper. There is no rancor in her voice. She separated from her parents a long time ago.

Lisa and Joshua live together in a small, modern apartment on the West Side of Manhattan. They are both in their early twenties. We talk, on a fall Saturday afternoon, amid a pile of unsorted laundry. He is a second-year medical student, and she has a temporary job with a nonprofit agency that distributes food to the poor. We met Lisa in an earlier chapter, as a super student trying to find her niche in the postgraduate world. Part of her story belonged there. The rest was saved for this chapter on heroes. The fact that she belongs in both chapters is part of the contrariness of real life.

Both she and Joshua have every right to be casualties of sixties childhoods, hopelessly unable to adjust to the harsh demands of the eighties. Yet they turned out with enough strength and clarity to get them through a great deal more.

They were babies when the sixties began. Lisa's father was a high school teacher in New York City; Joshua's was a physicist in California.

Their mothers were mothers, not career women who had taken six weeks for maternity leave, and in the last generation of women to use cloth diapers. Both families changed with the era.

When Joshua was two, his mother and father took him to London for a year. When they came back to California, his parents divorced, and he and his mother moved in with another family. The other family consisted of a mother and five children, and Joshua thought it was just great. He shared a room with a boy four years older, and he went to public school in a nice suburb, and his mother went to work for a travel agent. There were so many divorced families in the neighborhood that it wasn't until years later that he discovered that it wasn't usual to live without fathers. He was invited on a birthday outing for a friend who had a normal family—a mother, a father, a sister, and a station wagon— and somehow it all clicked. His household was the one that was different. He was a scientific child, and he took it as simply an interesting fact, an example of inductive reasoning. When he was eight—five years later— his mother got a job with a television station, and they moved to San Francisco, breaking up the communal ménage of women and children. They moved around a lot, living mostly in North Beach, and his interesting mother had a wide range of friends. "Most of them were sort of arty. They used drugs and had pot parties. I would hide. I was afraid to leave my room. I stayed there with my guitar. All those weird people scared me. I remember that one artist who was into drugs jumped out from behind a tree and scared me. It all made a big impression on me. During the time I was applying to medical schools, I thought a lot about my need for stability.

"My mother was a major influence on me. She wasn't crazy or childish. She was stable and wanted independence for both of us. We had a rule: If you weren't home by six, you had to call. It didn't matter where we were or what we were doing. I slept and ate at friends' houses. I fooled around all over the city. I really had a lot of freedom while my mother was at work. I also worried if she was late. It was a good model—freedom and responsibility." He and his mother were sort of "co-parents" to each other. "It wasn't emotional—just pragmatic. I did the grocery shopping, but I never felt I had to support her emotionally. She often said, 'You don't have to be my mother. I'm grown up.'" He was ten years old at the time.

For a while, he went to a sternly disciplined military academy, which he hated, and then to a "free" school, where he did lucite sculpture and protested the war in Vietnam. Meanwhile, his father had remarried and was spending a year with his new family in a mountain area where they were going to build a cabin. Joshua joined them there, and they lived in tents for the summer and had to build fast enough to have a roof up before the snow fell. During this year, he went to a small-town public school where he was called "Joshurina" because of his long hair. He also taught math instead of taking it because he was so far ahead of his country classmates.

He returned to his mother at the end of the year and learned that she too was about to marry again. And there was to be another dramatic change in his life. His new stepfather was an old family friend, also a physicist, who lived in Boston. He was also extremely wealthy, heir to a vast family fortune. Joshua took the change in stride. It was just change and that, he had learned, was one of life's constants. His new family divided its time between a modest apartment in Cambridge and a country house in what his mother called "the family compound."

Joshua chose his own high school, a small, academically demanding private day school, liberal enough to offer scholarships to half of its students. Joshua's mother worried that it would be too academic for him, and his math teacher told him that his "California tendencies" made him too undisciplined. At the end of the first year, he was a star pupil in math—and in science and English. He learned to work on computers, he sang in the special chorus, and he was on his way to being a state squash champion. He also tutored the scholarship students who hadn't grown up with his advantages.

It is hard to explain why being buffeted by change produced the best young man in the world instead of a hopelessly confused neurotic. It is clear that his mother—despite all of her own changes—was indeed a strong and solid parent. His own cheerful explanation is this: "I took from all of them. I learned flexibility and tolerance. I'm open-minded, and I respect other people's lives."

It may also be that he never quite needed to be a child. He had done that in another life and he arrived in this one ready to be an adult. "Somehow, I was never on the slope of the hill of adolescence," he reflects. He developed relationships with girls—each one serious and monogamous. "I always dated girls with an eye toward finding the perfect one for a long-term relationship." Asked what he looks for in women, he explains that he values intelligence most. "I want an equal, a full-time companion. I'm not just interested in women who are pretty or in having sex just to have it." He didn't do any drugs and he didn't get drunk because he'd had enough of his mother's friends and felt that it was important to have control. In fact, he decided that it was his role to drive everyone else home from the party. "I was happy with that role. I purposely didn't drink because I wanted to perform that job. I worried about everyone." At one point, his mother worried that he was too good. She instructed a friend to take him out and get him drunk. The friend did and Joshua spent a few hours under the influence of something other than his own formidable intelligence.

He also felt that it was his job to make people happy. "Sometimes I forget to have a good time myself. I play host all the time, even in other people's houses," he confesses.

In the age of narcissism-is-beautiful, it is necessary to emphasize that this is a true story.

Lisa grew up in a sturdy brick house in a safe, treelined neighborhood in Queens. When she and her brother were babies, her mother had few concerns besides the well-being of her family.

Her father was a high school history teacher, and he loved his work, in a bemused, dispassionate way. He was constantly grading papers and relating funny anecdotes about his students. The house was furnished mainly in books. They lined the walls and spilled from the coffee tables and sat in little piles near every chair. They all read constantly, and maybe that's why no one noticed that mom was changing.

The devoted mother and homebody of the early sixties had developed outside interests—in civil rights, in the peace movement, and in other causes. It was only natural that she drift into the women's movement too; it had a special message for someone buried in the role of wife and mother, and she found herself envious of women who seemed so free when she was so tied down.

One year, they had a "Feminist Thanksgiving." They had turkey, sweet potatoes, cranberry sauce, cornbread stuffing, and pie for dessert, and her mother's new friends as guests. The feminist guests were so hostile to men and children that Lisa and her father finally felt driven out of the house. "We went to a movie and came back after they were gone. It was us against them," she remembers.

"My father was the strong alternative. My mother sort of disappeared." A few months later, her mother left the family.

"At the time," Lisa recalls, "I didn't care that my mother left. I liked my father better anyway. I was closer to him. He was more reliable; he was there for us. He was the parent to turn to, and he could help with schoolwork." Helping with schoolwork was critical because that was what Lisa did during those years. An excellent student, she immersed herself in school.

She got along well with her father, a cool and kind man, who was cerebral, funny, and very devoted to Lisa. His coolness both irritated her and suited her perfectly. "I once told him I was going to sleep over at this guy's house. He didn't bat an eye. He had such control. He never said anything or interfered. I lost my virginity that weekend, and I'm glad he didn't stop me."

Lisa herself had boyfriends throughout high school, and once in a while, she got high on marijuana or hash. But mostly, she studied, and she did well enough to get into Amherst. She met Joshua at the end of her freshman year. He was handsome, and he was good in literature and science and an even better tennis player than she was.

The relationship was still new and not quite rooted when they parted for the summer. She had a job in New York, and he went home to Boston. She was a little tired that summer and her glands were suspiciously swollen. She was certain that her symptoms were the stubborn remains of the mononucleosis she had had earlier in the year, but to satisfy her worried parents, she had a biopsy. The diagnosis was Hodgkin's disease—cancer of the lymph system.

She called Joshua from a pay phone at the hospital. Eighteen and still immortal, her main concern was what would happen to her new love. Stunned, he sounded evasive on the phone, and she burst into tears. She could live with the threat of death, but not with losing him. The next day, he flew in and spent the summer with her family while she recovered from a splenectomy and began chemotherapy and radiation. For the next year and a half, he was with her every weekend while her treatment continued. It was interrupted by bouts of hepatitis and shingles, because the therapy lowered her immune system. She was constantly throwing up. She lost her hair and had to wear a wig. She was tired. But handsome, high-powered Joshua—the super athlete and super student, with money and energy to burn—was always there. So were her parents and their new partners, a modern foursome.

That was four years ago, and Lisa has been clear of cancer and has every reason to expect to remain so. While Lisa was in treatment at Sloan-Kettering, she saw a psychologist to help her deal with her illness. The psychologist is now in private practice, and Lisa is seeing her to help her deal with her past. "The divorce had a bigger effect than I thought. I think it finally caught up with me."

During the two years of her illness, she reached for her own kind of strength. She lived with cancer just as she had lived with her parents' divorce. "I focused on other things—an exam, my friends. I never questioned that I'd get better." Curiously, the breakup of her family forced her to develop that discipline. Once again, she was shifting her concentration from a painful situation she had no control over to intellectual activity and other relationships. It is far healthier than self-absorption and depression.

Her illness had another result for Joshua. He had majored in English and physics at Amherst and was searching for a career that would combine his humanistic and scientific interests. He did internships and work-study programs with public agencies that dealt with the environment and energy.

But he sat through endless hearings and met people who wrote reports and he wasn't inspired. When Lisa had cancer, he found his role models. He decided to go into medicine. It was science, and it helped people.

So he applied to the best medical schools, which was appropriate since he had an outstanding record. The next part tells us as much about ourselves and our distrust of heroes as it does about Joshua. Applicants were asked to include essays explaining why they wanted to be doctors. Joshua told the truth in his. He wanted to be a doctor because doctors saved Lisa. A family friend who was a doctor and who knew the medical school admissions process shook his head. It was the wrong thing to say. But Joshua persisted and sent it in. It was, after all, the truth.

Harvard turned him down, despite what he modestly calls "a good, strong application." Columbia's Physicians and Surgeons put him on the waiting list. Tufts accepted him. He let his decision hang till the end of the summer, when he called the dean of admissions at Columbia. The dean knew exactly who he was and suggested that he come over for a talk. The talk lasted for three hours, long enough for the dean to be certain that Joshua was not a wild-eyed radical, and he was admitted instantly. Wanting to save lives, after all, is a rather emotional reason for going into medicine. It's heroic, and it puts a strain on the rest of us.

The family friend who read his essay knew that and is still guilt-ridden that Joshua didn't get into Harvard. "I should have insisted that you not write that essay," he said recently. Joshua, for his part, would not have done it differently.

PART III

DEPENDENCIES

10

Cutting the Cord

Ideally, the separation between parents and their young adult children ought to be a rite of passage. An old-fashioned wedding is a good example. The bride walks down the aisle on her father's arm. In front of the altar, her father steps back and she walks forward. When the ceremony is over, she walks back down the aisle with the groom. A few minutes ago, she was a girl in the care of her father. Now she is a married woman, a grown-up. The boy with her is magically a man ready to assume the responsibility of a family. Those of us who cry at weddings usually do it at this point, perhaps because we know it won't be that easy.

Graduations are also good metaphors, though they tend to be sunbaked and overlong. There are a lot of speeches because this is the elders' last chance to give advice. At the end, in a movement as simultaneous as rehearsal can make it, several hundred black-robed graduates flip the tassel on the mortarboard from one side to the other. It's done. The student is a graduate, ready to go forth into the adult world, perhaps the next day.

Once, these rites of passage had real meaning. Parents watched them with an assortment of emotions, mainly relief and satisfaction. Their job was to raise the child, launch him into independent, responsible adulthood, experience the empty nest syndrome, and then wait for grandchildren and the repetition of the whole process. In middle-class America, the process was supposed to begin when the child was about eighteen and going off to college, and culminate when he was twenty-two and graduating. Anyway, that's the way parents remember it. You went off to school, learned to do your own laundry, made new attachments, graduated and then got married, went into the service, started your first job, or, if you were very promising, continued on in graduate school. You didn't live at home, except in exceptional or temporary circumstances, and even those were suspect. A twenty-two-year-old in his parents' home, except as a visitor, was an embarrassment.

But in recent years, there has been a blurring of the lines between adulthood and adolescence. The ceremonies don't happen on schedule, and even when they do, they are not followed by a dramatic passage to another phase of life. The twenty-two-year-old, and even the thirty-year-old, continues living in his parents' home or in some other, more subtle way remains a child, financially and emotionally dependent. The parents, who thought that by now they would be retired from the active-parent role, and could have their income and home to themselves, find that they have taken on a much longer job than they bargained for. The kids are still very much their responsibility, often in some way that seems to be no one's fault.

"My daughter did very well in college and then spent two years in France because she had a boyfriend there," explains the mother of a twenty-four-year-old. "Now she's back and she hasn't got a job or any real plans, so she's living with us." The mother is sitting at a lunch counter, riffling through a packet of forms. "She's thinking about law school, so I've been picking up applications for her, and I thought while I was out, I might as well get information about this course that prepares them for the LSAT's." She is a little embarrassed by what she is saying. "Nancy doesn't have a car so I end up doing these things for her. Otherwise, I have to lend her my car, and I need it for work," she adds.

The grown-up kids who come back home to live have been an almost obligatory newspaper feature story of the eighties. "A New Generation Finds It Hard to Leave the Nest," said a *New York Times* headline. " 'Refilled Nest Syndrome' Reflects Economy," said a similar story in the Los Angeles *Times*. Both stories go on to describe the adjustment problems of households in which grown children have moved back. "It's like being caught in midair above a hurdle," a twenty-two-year-old graduate of Hamilton College told the L.A. *Times*. And a twenty-seven-year-old woman said plaintively to the *New York Times:* "My mother knows I'm not trying to be a leech; she knows it's only temporary."

The media and demographers blame the situation on a poor job market, high housing costs, and unrealistic expectations. And they are not wrong. In 1984, the Census Bureau reported a sharp drop in the number of young Americans who started new households the previous year, though the pool of young adults who might be expected to do so had not gotten smaller. According to the Bureau's report, the change "seems more likely to be a response to economic conditions that may have discouraged the formation of new households, particularly among young adults." It cited high interest rates on home mortgages and went on to observe that "more adult sons and daughters appear to be living with their parents and many young adults are postponing marriage as they pursue educational and career goals."

All of this brings to mind the image of an economic victim, an employable, well-intentioned young person reluctantly living with mom and dad while he papers the city with résumés or waits for a promotion. Some are like that. There are also some young adults who have deeply neurotic relationships with their parents, and they would find a reason to remain dependent even in a boom economy. But most of the young people that I interviewed who were dependent on their parents were afloat somewhere between emotional and economic dependency, a fuzzy, indeterminate gray rather than black or white. How does one classify Nancy, who manages on her own in a foreign country for two years and then collapses in her mother's lap, without plans or marketable skills? Or super student Andrea, in Chapter 5, who uses home and her father's connections whenever she is stuck? Or Jenny, the artist in the first chapter who took refuge in her father's office when she couldn't learn to operate the bank's change machines? Or Alexa in Chapter 3, who has a low-paying newspaper job but prefers her mother's spacious, modern hillside house to the "cracker box in a bad neighborhood" that she could afford?

It seems almost impossible to untangle the real and practical problems from the emotional ones. Perhaps it is best to look at it as a social problem that arises from their history. These were the special children of perfect parents, and they've had very little practice in dealing with failure or rejection. But fate has taken these bright, charming middle-class aristocrats and dumped them into a rude, tightfisted world. They tried independence; it didn't work, and that sapped their confidence and sent them home crying. They are like Romanovs driving taxis in Paris and trying not to go mad. If the czar were still in power, they would be fine. But the czar was gone, and the eighties are very different from the sixties. (Perhaps it would be more accurate to say that the eighties are different from what we believed the world was like in the sixties. We deluded ourselves a lot back then.) So they are not so fine.

And they are not home or dependent by accident of circumstances. As the Joan Baez song goes, "Whoever treasures freedom, like the swallow, would learn to fly." A young woman who wanted to manage her own life would arrange somehow to get her own law school applications. And a twenty-four-year-old who wanted to be an adult rather than a child would see a small apartment with a futon bed and butcher-block table as a step forward from her mother's elegant house, perhaps toward the day when she has her own. Alexa sees it as a frightening plummet. For these young people have taken a look at the grown-up world and found it scary.

"We aren't children, but we are unwilling to become adults. We are vexed by maturity," wrote a young man named Jeff Nelligan in a provocative 1982 op-ed piece in the Los Angeles *Times*. "We grow older, and our experience broadens, yet we avoid, sometimes reject, steps that would make us accept the life-style responsibilities of adulthood. . . .

"My peers are not lazy, but brought up as we were in playpens ringed by safety nets, we don't have much fear of failing. We are living in a compassionate age, the first in which parents, however exasperated, seem to take pride in not 'pushing' their kids out of the family home. And it is a fortunate age—no wars or other national calamity that in the past created an automatic transition to adulthood.

"We're lucky, I guess."

Nelligan himself graduated from college, held a job for seven months, and then quit to ricochet around the country in pursuit of a girl. At the time he wrote the article, he was back home with no car, no money, no job, and no girl. He was hanging around with his old friends and having confrontational talks with his parents about borrowing the car and mowing the lawn, as if he were a true teenager rather than a teenager in his mid-twenties.

Jacqueline is a slender brunet with creamy skin and luminous, tilted eyes. Like her mother, she has a personal style that is both refined and interesting. Physically, there isn't a strong resemblance, but they are obviously mother and daughter.

"Our family was different," says Jacqueline, who is always called Jacqueline, never Jackie. "It always surprised me when I visited my friends, the way they had dinner whenever they felt like or passed the platters around, family style. In our house, dinner was always *served;* and on Saturday nights, there were flowers and candles and classical music. There was sort of an unwritten rule: You couldn't just gripe or talk about personal things at the table. My father always steered the conversation to something more educational—the decline and fall of whatever. Dad wasn't cold. He was always there in a pinch. But he was cool—detached. If we had a problem, we talked to Mom."

And Mom was always there—sympathetic, intelligent, ready to listen and solve problems or even to avert them before they happened. She was the mother who found the best ballet classes and music teachers and art courses for her gifted children. She drove her daughters to these activities and picked them up on time. If they had a difficult school project, she would find an unusual bookstore only a few towns away where she would buy the materials—sometimes old books or rare prints. She planned their parties and scouted the stores for clothes they would like. "Jacqueline likes avant-garde things. Deirdre is more romantic and traditional," she would say.

What she did for Jacqueline was present her with an image of life that wasn't going to work. She herself had left college to marry and had worked at desultory jobs while her husband got started in his business. Once the children came along, they were her job. For her, being an interesting, cultured, elegant person was enough of an addition to that. For her daughter, it was anachronistic. There were few jobs in culture, and women were now expected to hold their own financially. Jacqueline had learned about a way of life from her mother. What she needed to know was how her father paid for it.

In college, Jacqueline majored in theater arts, perhaps because it was a way to stay center stage. She didn't work at an outside job while she was in school because drama students were supposed to help with shows from four to eleven every evening. Besides, her parents could afford to support her. "I had a great time in college," she admits with a self-conscious shrug. "I got okay grades, and I took whatever I wanted to— French lit, Italian cinema. I didn't know what I wanted to do. I sort of wanted to act. But whenever I thought about the future, it was like looking at a brick wall. I just took for granted that my parents would be there."

By her senior year, she was more than a little panicky and began depending on her boyfriend as well. They had been going together since high school and had talked about getting married. If she married, the life script that had been written for her would work. All the pieces would fall into place. But today's young men—certainly, the sophisticated, interesting "new men" that Jacqueline would meet—aren't programmed to support a woman. Her boyfriend had no clear notion of his own future, and he was certainly not ready to take on hers. "He suddenly didn't want to see me or return my phone calls. He felt I was smothering him."

They broke up, and she graduated feeling depressed and aimless. Officially, she wanted to be an actress, and convinced her parents to stake her. She took an apartment with two other girls, and her parents paid her share of the rent. She drove a car that had been a graduation present from her parents, and they paid for the insurance, gas, and repairs. In fact, they paid most of her bills. "I had part-time jobs so I could buy my own clothes," she says.

She did a lot of hanging around, the principal activity of the generation. In the course of it, she met Tom, a lanky, charming saxophone player who wanted to be a professional musician in much the same way that she wanted to be an actress. "We were both without any drive or ambition. And we made it okay for each other to be that way. We'd go to the zoo in the afternoon during the week. He was living on some student-loan money and doing a little music. I would go to about one audition a week, but I wasn't really trying. I never even got an agent," she recalls.

But eventually her parents understood that they were supporting her dependency rather than her acting career. "My father caught on and started to scale down the amount of money he gave me." They were basically healthy people, without any neurotic need to keep her tied to them. They had simply made the mistake of raising her for another era. When they saw reality, they began to act on it.

During that time, Jacqueline would call her parents often—sometimes late at night—because she was upset or depressed or her car needed tires or a bill was past due. "I just didn't want to be on my own. It was so much torment. I didn't know what I wanted to do. I just had no direction," she recalls.

For their part, her parents found themselves with a twenty-two-year-old daughter, ostensibly on her own, who needed constant emotional and financial support. Yet they had no control over her and no leverage. She would ignore their advice and when she stumbled and fell, there would be a tearful call, a desperate S.O.S.

Jacqueline turned twenty-three in early January of the following year. The new year and the birthday together made it a time of reckoning. She decided that a change was due, and she started seeing a therapist. Her parents paid for the treatment, but it may well have been the best money they spent on her in those years, for Jacqueline credits the therapy for what happened next. "I told my parents that I was going to get a full-time job and support myself."

It was a year when jobs were hard to get, and she had a frightening false start on a job that didn't work out. "I got fired after a month, and it really wasn't my fault. There was a personality conflict, and I was out on my ear. But I couldn't go back to getting handouts from my parents." Job situations are complicated. In this case, Jacqueline was hired by an employer who knew that she was a beginner and paid her accordingly. But he expected her to perform like an accomplished veteran and became enraged when she didn't. Jacqueline could have seized on this as a perfect excuse to crawl home again and ask for her parents' help. The world is unfair and unmanageable and there are no decent jobs. But she had grown beyond that.

She spent a few anxious weeks looking, and then fell gratefully into a job as a receptionist for a film company. "It was a nowhere job, but it was a paycheck, and I held on for eight months. I took pride in being the greatest receptionist in the world."

Even that goal had limited appeal, but it was a start, a toe in the water. For one thing, she learned that she was good on the phone, as actors often are. For another, she had a chance to pore over the want ads of the media trade magazines that came across her desk. She learned that advertising salespeople made good money, and when she came across an ad that specified "eager and willing" instead of "five years' experience," she responded immediately. She got the job, and her first year has been a clear success. She is good at selling ads, she likes her boss, and she likes making money on her own.

By coincidence, or because of her example, her boyfriend started to grow up at the same time. He decided to take his music career seriously, and he began to practice and to "hustle for gigs." Now he has regular recording-studio work and club dates. Even Jacqueline's parents, who once considered him an attractive lounge lizard, are now impressed. After a dinner together, her father confided to her mother, "Actually, I think I like him better than I like her. He's good company."

But the young boyfriend still has things to learn about fitting in with the family. "A couple of weeks ago, we were sitting in my kitchen eating canned soup," Jacqueline tells. "We had been jogging and we were both in sweats. Suddenly he said, 'Don't you think we ought to get married?' I said, 'No!' He looked stunned. Finally, I explained that I just didn't want to be asked in that way. Well, tonight, we're going to dinner somewhere special. He won't say where or what this is about. He just told me to get dressed up." She pauses. "Of course, I know what it's about." She is finding a way to be her mother's daughter, to be her own person, and to live in the 1980's. It isn't easy.

What brought Jacqueline out of dependency was that hers was obvious and painful. Barry is a twenty-four-year-old student, and he and his parents found a socially acceptable way to disguise the fact that he was remaining a child. They all liked it that way and saw no pressing reason for him to grow up. They, too, provided their child with an enviable life-style and very little information about how to earn it on his own. He was, after all, a special child, and he didn't need to take on the kind of burdens his father had. And his father also provided him with a role model that wouldn't work: the strong, selfless, eternal provider.

When Barry was a little boy, they lived in a famous community of mansionlike homes fronted by expanses of lawn and year-round garden color. His family's home was spacious and modern and distinguished even in this neighborhood because it was designed by a famous architect. Barry was the youngest of four and the only boy, engaging, polite, and a star athlete. It was all perfect, until he was seventeen and the last of his older sisters married. His parents decided the house was too big (and too valuable) for just the three of them, sold it, and moved to a condominium in a slightly more modest part of town. Barry was allowed to finish his senior year of high school in the old neighborhood, but the move was the great blow of his life. "I've had better days," he reflects six years later. "I still drive by The House and think of it as mine. I want to have it back someday. I think of all of this time as an extended vacation."

In short, he thinks of his life as a temporary interruption of the perfect childhood. He went off to college where he did enough to get by. The rest of the time, he pursued sports, women, and chances to gamble. "I like to play poker, bet on football games with a bookie. My parents disapproved of that. My dad is very puritanical." After graduation, he moved back to his parents' condo and for a year worked unenthusiastically in the file room at a law firm. "I had a rebellious attitude toward them," he explains. "Working for a big law firm is an indoctrination process, and it's hard to be nonconforming." His employers perhaps thought he was just a file clerk and gave him things to file. It was the kind of humiliation that kept occurring since he had moved out of The House.

The following year, he started law school himself. It is a "country club" law school, but his grades hover around D. "Maybe $D+$," he says optimistically. "I suppose I could get better grades, but I just don't want to tax myself that much. I don't really see myself as a lawyer, and I don't know if I'm going to stay in law school. My father wants me to, and maybe I should. I think I'd rather go into some business, but even in business, it's nice to be able to say you have a law degree. And also, if you're a lawyer yourself, other lawyers can't take advantage of you."

Those are unconvincing reasons to plow through three years of law school. The real reason, of course, is that it gives Dad a reason to support him. "They pay for my tuition, my gas, my car insurance. Whatever I need when I run short," he says with a deprecatory shrug. "I guess I'm one of those spoiled rich kids."

"But I love the relationship with my parents. I wouldn't trade it for anything. Families should be tight. Everywhere you look, the family is eroding. My parents are European, and European families are more close-knit. My parents are also a lot older than most parents of people my age, and that makes a difference. I mean, they could be my grandparents. They provide stability and security. They're always there behind me. And they support whatever I do."

It is a curious kind of support and curious closeness. "In a way, I feel guilty toward my parents. I mean, we never spend any time together. Our life-styles are radically different. They're very staid and quiet. I'm hardly ever home, but the phone is always ringing for me, and they have to take messages. I leave for school around seven forty-five in the morning. I get home around four and usually sleep for a while. I eat dinner at seven, and then I go out again. I study at the library or I go somewhere. I like to stay out late, and they think it's unhealthy and wrong. I go to events and concerts, and I go away weekends. They think it doesn't make sense to run around like that. The funny thing is, they're right ninety-nine percent of the time. For instance, they told me not to go away last weekend. And you know what happened? It rained the whole time.

"Still, I feel guilty about not being home more. I think I move around a lot because I only enjoyed being home in the old house. Next year, though, I'm going to have my own apartment. It's part of my deal with my parents."

His parents' part of the deal, of course, is paying the rent. "My dad is the single most unselfish person I've ever met. He has always thought of the family first. When he buys a new car, he thinks what we would like, not what he likes. But that's what makes him feel good.

"I don't think he feels I'm abusing the relationship. I'm not depriving them of anything. And my dad loves me more than himself. I know that. I guess I'll be the same way with my kids and with my wife. My parents have been married for forty-one years. That's the kind of marriage I'd like to have."

But he has a long way to go before he will be his father, the unselfish provider. Right now, he is still a kid who wants the most expensive new toys and then cries when they don't work right. "The women I like are the gorgeous model types. I love going out with them, but I never have a good time. I just spend a lot of money. The cute ones are spoiled, and it's better not to do stuff for them. They're very materialistic and they just take advantage."

Twenty-two-year-old Jack is a punk singer and songwriter. He is tall and very thin, and he wears a striped, long-sleeved shirt, flapping open at the cuffs. His glistening dark hair is spiked around the crown and swept back on the sides, a trick accomplished by a sweet-smelling gel. His skin is pale, still scarred by acne, and his lower lids are rimmed in teal-blue eyeliner.

He is diffident in talking about himself, but articulate and voluble about music: "Ninety-five percent of pop music is just product, like dog food, and ninety percent of what's called New Wave is trash. New Wave itself is a reaction against the sixties bands, which teenagers view as hopelessly establishment. It was supposed to be radical, but it had become cynical, artless show biz. The punk movement was created to give rock 'n' roll back to the teenagers, to take it away from the musical technocrats who had come out of the sixties bands.

"Back in 1977, when I got into music, there was just punk—no New Wave. Punk was raw and to the point. Punk was pure spirit. Its message was rebellion. Then, it became popular and branched out, producing a lot of derivative, rip-off music. Now, it's chic, robot-disco. The rebellion was against the millionaire rock stars, but it never took off in America. In England, where socioeconomic conditions were worse, punk ruled. Here, it's chic."

What he means, it turns out, is that American punk is the rebellion of affluent children against their own dependency.

Jack was in two hard-core punk bands on the West Coast. They played club dates, usually ignored by recording companies, who regarded them as not quite sophisticated enough. But a big New York management company noticed Jack and felt that with a little polishing, he would make it in the record business. They offered to back him while he tested his wings in New York, and he made plans to go east. At the airport, he broke down and asked his parents to take him home.

He has remained at home with them for the past year and a half, taking courses at a local community college and living in their home in a staid middle-class suburb. It represents everything he has rebelled against, and he is utterly dependent on it. His father is a semiretired bank executive, and his mother is a housewife. He is still working at his music, and it is his consuming and only interest.

Jack is an extreme example perhaps—both in the form of his rebellion and in his inability to separate from his parents. He had a troubled childhood, and his problem is a clinical one. He is currently under treatment for it. But his story has ripples of social meaning. Psychologically, rebellion is a reaction to dependency. The dependent young person feels angry, acts it out, and then needs to be rescued, thus tying his parents to him. Once again, he is their helpless child.

But in a broader sense, the affluent, perfect parent is the ideal target for rebellion-and-rescue dependency, which may well be the social disease of the eighties. The young adult resents that he has been given so much that he cannot give himself. He has been cared for too well and too conscientiously, but security is never absolute or permanent. So we constantly hear stories of young people who defy their parents, go off on their own, get into hot water and need to be bailed out, sometimes literally. A young man I know set off on a life of wandering, claiming that he would never be home again. The very concept of a permanent residence was anathema to him. Within a month, his parents were getting daily anguished letters and collect telephone calls from all over Asia, Africa, and Europe. He came home a year and half later—at the age of twenty-seven—and moved in with them.

These young adults don't particularly like being home. The young prodigal son complained that his stepmother was uneasy about his new girlfriend, who was very young and quiet. Implied in his complaint was that she had no right to question his judgment. And Jack says, "Living with my parents is tense. They don't approve of my hours or my life-style, and I have no place to bring girls. Biologically, the friction is inevitable when you reach a certain age." Yet he is making no plans to leave. "I have a morbid fear of the nine-to-five world, and I could never be in a real job."

Young people often talk about not being able to tolerate a nine-to-five job. That may be because their parents are in nine-to-five jobs. It is the way they provided their children with the nice things and good times they are now addicted to. Their rebellion may be a way of getting their own back against these omnipotent providers who gave them everything but left them dependent. What they rebel against is the discipline and middle-class life-style, which is after all the source of the parents' power. It is what enables them to hold that job and provide the comfort. When their children deride and reject it, they are saying, "You may have the money and the power around here, but you are ordinary and we are special."

The parents, for their part, are honestly stunned. It never dawned on them that when they gave their children everything, they were withholding independence.

"My father is a self-made man from a farm in the Midwest, and he's very right wing," says twenty-seven-year-old Ann, tugging at a shank of her shaggy blond hair. "I didn't know what I was talking about back then, but I told my father that the domino theory was a bunch of crap. I remember running away from the table yelling at him, 'You don't want the war to end!' He called me a 'stupid ninny.' God, I hated him then."

At the time, she was thirteen, and she had learned bits and pieces of anti-war ideology and expressions like "domino theory" from the other kids in her junior high. They lived near a university town, and she had new friends, who had liberal, activist parents. It was a tantalizing, mischievous change from home, and she joined them in protesting the war in Vietnam and supporting the farm workers. "I dropped out of Girl Scouts and stopped taking piano lessons. Mostly, I was against the Vietnam War. That was the big thing in my life."

Before all that, she was the family pet, a feminine little girl in hair bows and dresses, and very different from her tomboy sister. As she remembers it, being a little girl was utter heaven. It was evenings at home with the family, eating dinner on a little snack table in front of the television set. It was family camp in the summer, and going through her father's pockets for chewing gum when he came home from business trips, and the fort he built that made her the envy of the neighborhood.

She was the younger child, and long awaited. "My mother went through a lot to have me. Maybe that's why I was so spoiled," she reflects. "I had everything I wanted. I remember once, I got a green bike from Sears. My mother and some neighbors were assembling it in the front yard, and they were having a hard time. I came over and said, 'When's lunch? I'm hungry.' The neighbors couldn't believe it. I was also a hypochondriac. Something always hurt—my ears, my throat, my head."

Her father was a successful insurance executive, but her parents remained frugal farm people. They bought their own clothes at Monkey Ward's or Sears, but Ann was taken to expensive, trendy shops by her grandmother. "If I couldn't decide between two dresses, I got both."

The price of it all, at least in her mind, was that she had to stay a little girl. "My mother never wanted me to grow up. She was upset when my first boyfriend asked me to go steady. I was excited. I got my first period when we went to see the Royal Canadian Ballet. I told my mom when we got home. She said, 'How do you know?' She just refused to believe I was growing up."

But she was, and, in order to test whether they would still love her in her new metamorphosis, she let them know with a vengeance. "I gave this party when I was in junior high. My mother thought it would be like my older sister's parties—kids drinking Cokes and dancing to 45 records. Well, she came home in the middle of this party and couldn't believe what was going on. Kids were using drugs. Some of them were hyperventilating till they passed out. That was a favorite thing to do. Two kids were in bed kissing. That's when my mother knew that I used drugs.

"She was very naïve. When I was in junior high, I knew that friends of hers were alcoholics or having affairs, and she never suspected. So she never suspected that I was using drugs or smoking cigarettes. Or later on, that I was doing mescaline and acid.

"My sister was the model teen—the cheerleader who did healthy, American things. Then there was me."

It was all part of the great protest—marching, boycotting, doing drugs, and defying your parents. "I used to cut school a lot. My teachers said I was involved with the wrong crowd. And every night at dinner, I fought with my parents, and I'd leave the table crying. I hated my father then. He knew so much. He read everything. But all he said to me was, 'The Communists are taking over the world.' Or, 'Shut up. The government knows what it's doing.' My mother could believe in the government in the face of nuclear disaster.

"But what I really wanted was that they notice and appreciate that I had ideas of my own, that I wasn't a cute little kid anymore. I was becoming a person on my own."

At the time, that meant being exactly the opposite of what her parents might like. Her high school days began with a ritual meeting with her friends in the hills behind the school, where they kept a secret stash. "I was always stoned. I had reached a point where I didn't know when I was straight. In high school, I was doing nothing that my parents would approve of. I would sneak out, drop acid, go out shoplifting. The worst part of my day was when my father drove me to the bus stop in the morning. I didn't know what to say to him. My mother said, 'Talk to him about his insurance.' I didn't know what to say about insurance.

"But they gave me everything. One weekend, we were going away to the lake. I was supposed to take a friend, but she couldn't come because she was in jail. So I brought another friend. My parents never asked about it. We had a horrible relationship then. But it was worse when we talked.

"One Easter, we went to Mexico on a private plane with two other families. We kids had the greatest time. We all did mescaline and a lot of pot. On the plane home, my mother asked, 'Were those kids smoking pot? Were you?'

" 'Yes,' I said, 'but it wasn't the first time.' I thought we were relating, and I told her everything. She forbade me to see my best friend or to go to parties. It didn't do any good. I just learned I couldn't tell her things. What finally scared me off drugs, I think, was my hypochondria."

The family spent summers at a cabin near a lakeside resort. It is a famous and beautiful area and it attracted a lot of teenagers. The woods, the lake, the beaches teemed with unsupervised kids, like pampered denizens of Never-Never Land. "It was where I learned about music, poetry, drugs, independence, and lying. I lost my virginity there when I was sixteen. My mother was there all summer, but we totally ignored her. I don't know what she did all day. I was just into my friends. Every night, we'd be on the beach, playing the guitar and getting stoned. We had a guest cabin on the property, and I'd sneak guys in there. Or I'd do bizarre things, like wash dishes in a restaurant instead of paying when I had the money. I had boyfriends my mother hated. She forbade me to drive to the city with one of them. She said his car wasn't reliable. I did it anyway, and he had two flats.

"I would say, 'Trust me.' I can't think what I meant by trust. I think I meant, 'Trust me not to blow it all.' "

After graduation from high school—where she had done surprisingly well, all things considered—she headed back to the lake. "It had always been my dream to live there," she says. With adulthood pending, the resort town took on a mythic quality. It was the place where the children played. She lived in the summer cabin, worked the night shift at a hotel, and drank too much. Her good friends of the magic summers weren't there, and she hadn't much money.

What she learned that year was that dreams also die in the dark. In the wee hours one morning, she stepped out into the hotel parking lot and found her car on fire. "Some freak discovered that you could rig VW's to catch fire, and he rigged all the VW's in the lot." She was at the end of her fraying rope.

Sobbing, she called her parents in the middle of the night. "I'm lost," she pleaded. "Please come get me." They did, and she spent a few angry, depressed months at home. Her friends were gone, except for one boy who kept pressuring her for a sexual involvement, which she didn't want. "That was the worst," she says.

But another friend lived on Maui, a mecca for lost kids, so she drifted there and promptly set up housekeeping with a boyfriend in Lahaina, a sleepy, former whaling village halfway converted into an indifferent tourist town. She told her parents that she was just sharing a house with the boy while she looked for her own place. She never made any effort to find her own place, of course, and she confided all of this deception in a letter to a friend. For some reason, the friend showed the letter to her mother, who was already upset and concerned about her.

Her parents pressured her to come home and go to college, and eventually she succumbed. There is, after all, only so much that a bright young woman can do in a town surrounded by pineapple fields, and where the purchase of a newspaper is a major transaction, likely to confuse the clerk. So she applied to one school, having decided, Russian roulette style, that if she was admitted, she would go.

She was admitted and reluctantly left the boyfriend and Maui behind her and flew home to get ready for student life. Her mother met her at the airport alone.

"I told Dad that you were just sharing a place with David," she announced. Then she asked worriedly, "What kind of birth control are you using?" It was an unnecessary worry, a measure of the gap between the two generations. "I had been using birth control since I was fifteen," says Ann. "I had used pills and IUD's. I was so organized about it, I was on pills when I was still a virgin." It was one of those confusing confrontations in which Ann felt that her mother still saw her as a little girl, and it left her feeling angry and guilty.

By the time she unpacked at school, she was thoroughly miserable and longing for Hawaii and her boyfriend, who kept pressing her to come back. She stayed at school for a year and had such depression symptoms that campus doctors thought she might have a brain tumor. She saw a therapist who told her to take control of her life; she thought about his advice and decided to leave school.

Taking control of her life was something else, something she wasn't quite ready for. Once again she phoned her parents for an emergency rescue. "I made my parents pay for me to fly home—even though it was very expensive." Since they were thrifty people, she would make them prove they loved her by being costly. And once she arrived, she had to justify the cost. "They picked me up at the airport, and all the way home I didn't talk. I had to let them know how depressed I was."

She began seeing a private therapist, even though her father worried that "it would be on my record." Therapists, to him, were part of the permissive, liberal world that his daughter had so perversely chosen. When the therapist sent a handwritten note as a bill, he saw it as proof that it was all counterculture flimflam. A real doctor's bill was typewritten, on a form. "How can I send this to my insurance company?" he protested.

Perhaps it was the therapy, but the following fall, she returned to school, this time to another, more academically demanding campus. Miraculously, she was ready. She liked it and she did well. "But I was still a rebel," she insists. The Vietnam War was over and the farm workers were fending for themselves. She and other sixties teenagers were reduced to annoying, hollow protests against good grooming. "For instance, I didn't shave under my arms, and that bothered my mother. We went shopping once, and in the dressing room, she complained of the odor."

She also regressed sometimes to the little girl who got whatever she wanted. "One semester at Berkeley, I fell in love and didn't go to class. I missed finals because I was in bed with my boyfriend. I wasted the quarter." She managed to make Phi Beta Kappa despite this because university rules allowed students to seal off one bad quarter. But she sees it as a tainted achievement. "As far as I'm concerned, the real people are the ones who worked at jobs and went to school and made Phi Bet. The ones who struggled to do it. There's never been any inconvenience in my life."

But to her parents' great relief, Ann continued to do well. And they had a graduation to go to. "My father doesn't know how to say 'I love you.' After graduation, he squeezed my hand and said he'd take care of my car insurance."

And suddenly, like a kaleidoscope turning, an adult relationship began to emerge. It was like the sky clearing, and it was just as inexplicable as the storm of the adolescent years. "You reach a point where you can't just do these things to your parents anymore. You want them to like you, not just be your parents. So you show them what you want them to see."

Much of her life since then has been very viewable, and some of it is the stuttering mix of false starts and jobs that don't work out that seem to be de rigueur for young adults now. She moved to another part of the state to go to graduate school in linguistics, and decided she didn't like it. "It was boring. I have a problem with commitment. If I'm not in love with something, I can't do it. I hope I find something I really love."

She does not love difficulty. "We have the idea that things should be easy. We don't want to struggle. Go to a class at seven P.M.? I like to run in the early evening. Eat cafeteria food? I can't stand it.

"So here I am, twenty-seven, and without real direction," she says with painful honesty. But she is beginning to find her bearings. She now has a boyfriend she feels committed to and they have plans to marry. And career plans are finally emerging from the smoke of rebellion. She tried an internship with a magazine and decided she liked journalism. A subsequent newspaper job turned out to be depressing and she quit after three weeks, but then landed on her feet at another magazine job, which she likes better.

Her relationship with her parents is mostly courteous and warm now, but there are flashes of the old friction. She is still a rebel who doesn't like their middle-class life-style. "In ways, their lives irritate me. I try to let them know that I do things differently. I make coffee from fresh ground beans. They have instant. I think they watch too much television and drink too many martinis. They set up their breakfast bowls at night. They buy at Monkey Ward's. I have to have expensive things. Their thriftiness bothers me. I'll call them three minutes before the rates go down just to make that point."

She would also like her parents to go on rescuing her, but they have simply quit that job. Her father retired, and her parents moved to a small house in the country that has no extra bedrooms. There is a trailer in the garage for guests, but that is hardly coming home to the nest. Sometimes they help her out with money, but at other times, she calls and mentions that she is having car trouble—her tires are shot, her windshield wipers don't work—and her mother doesn't make any offers. "She wants me to be independent. When I talk about moving back up north, she tells me I'm better off here. When I visit, I sleep in the trailer in the garage. I feel they've cut themselves off from the kids."

What is perhaps more accurate is that they have cut Ann off from being a kid. By changing the relationship, they are nudging her into adulthood. At any rate, if she wants to be a child, they won't participate. It seems to be working.

"She wants to be my mother," Ann complains, "but on her own terms. She wants to plan my wedding, but she doesn't care about other things I tell her. My father only wants to know concrete things. They don't participate in anything but official parent things.

"I know I ruined my relationship with my father during the Vietnam years. I wish kids could just say, 'I'm in my rebellious stage now. This must be the time when I establish my identity.' And I wish parents could say, 'They're going through the rebellious stage. The issue isn't the Safeway boycott or the war. Just the right to have their own opinions.'

"I still sometimes want to call them and say, 'I'm me. This is what I'm really like. I'm not your good little girl.' But I don't want that daughter's license anymore. I care what they think about me. And I try to assert my independence."

11

Serious Hanging Out

"This town is like the black hole in space. It sucks you in and it gets harder and harder to leave. It becomes your mother," says Walt.

Walt is tall and lanky, with punk-cut red hair. He wears regulation Levi's, a plaid shirt, and one gold earring. He is twenty-seven years old, a professional musician, but he still lives in the little town where he went to college even though he graduated two years ago. We'll call the town and the college Haverville instead of using their real names because it's a small place and Walt feels he can speak more freely about it that way.

Walt—like a lot of other young adults who have lived independent, even adventurous lives—has a new kind of dependency. He needs to live among the youth tribe, his new family. His youth tribe is in his college town. He isn't a professional student or aspiring academic. He doesn't work at school or have any remaining official connection with the institution or anything else that passes as a reason to stay. His music jobs are mostly in trendier places an hour or more away. He just stays in Haverville because . . . he stays in Haverville.

It is a little like ghetto life. The ghetto is the student community surrounding campus, and postgraduate hangers-on, like Walt, are self-confined, not yet ready for the complex, alien, adult world outside. In another time, they might have gone to graduate school and become professors, but everyone knows that you can't do that anymore. There are no jobs. So some delay graduation by "stopping out" for a year, or go to graduate school halfheartedly, or get clerical jobs on campus or menial jobs in town as an excuse to stay. But a lot, like Walt, don't bother with excuses. School without school is okay now.

Being a student has its ups and downs, but the student life-style is seductive: communal living, casual camaraderie, keg parties, espresso bars, bookstores, the easy flow from work to play. It used to be that student life ended with graduation. It was embarrassing to stay if you had no business there. But in the sixties, the nature of student business changed. The campus became an organizing ground for the movement and "student" became a generic term, signifying age and background, but not necessarily enrollment. The demonstrations ended, and the gas lines and the unemployment lines took their place. The nonstudent student now had other reasons to stay around. He was scared of what was out there in the great beyond. The economy got better and worse and better again, but hanging around college had become a way of life.

Walt and I are supposed to meet for lunch, but when I arrive, he is already seated at a table, deep in conversation. "I'm in this coffeeshop every day," he explains. "I come here and wander around and talk to people. I know everybody."

Alex's Coffee Shop is the focal point of social life in Haverville. It is not exactly an ordinary coffeeshop, even though it has a counter with stools and Formica tables and serves breakfast all day. It would not exist except in a town built around an elite liberal arts college. It is designed in the rustic dark wood and stone English cottage style that pervades the town. Most of the tables are outside on a patio, like a European sidewalk café. There are no hamburgers or cheeseburgers on the menu, but you can get a ratatouille omelet, roast lamb and Swiss cheese on pita bread, turkey salad on a croissant, crab and avocado salad, and four kinds of quiche. The salad bar offers pâtés. The hostess is Middle Eastern, perhaps Persian or Afghan. The waitress is English. The cashier is a local girl who subtracts the tip instead of adding when she totals a charge card slip.

Haverville College is small, a little progressive, and not very well endowed. The tuition is high, and most of the students come from families who can afford it. Before that, they had gone to prep schools. Walt is one of the scholarship students. He is from an ordinary middle-class family and he went to public schools that were sometimes less than ordinary. He had problems in his first semester because he wasn't as well prepared as the graduates of prep schools and affluent suburban high schools. "I didn't know how to study or make an outline or take notes," he recalls. "I couldn't even keep up with the reading. It was frustrating at first because I was interested in the work and I wanted to do well." He had a bad first semester academically. But socially, he found that he fit in well with the rich kids. They had the same ethos.

"People at Haverville aren't concerned about careers," he explains. "They realize the intrinsic value of a good education. They're not upwardly mobile. They're content that when the time comes, they'll cross the bridge of success."

Which is pretty much the way Walt looks at it, though with less realism. He had knocked around a bit. In high school, he was often depressed and medicated himself with a variety of drugs. After high school, he went to an experimental college for a year and a half, and then left because he had decided that he wanted to be a musician. He played for a while, worked as a waiter, then got into a top 40 band and started making money. But after a year or so, the music business lost its luster, at least temporarily. His girlfriend broke up with him, his best friend got fired, and the pressure to survive and succeed at all cost was wearing him down. "I got disenchanted with the music business," is the way he puts it. ("Disenchanted" is a word used a lot by his generation, which takes the loss of enchantment hard. According to psychoanalyst Eric Ericson, it is normal to see life as magical until we are eight or nine. Yet young adults routinely use the word "disenchanted" when they mean "disappointed" or just bored.)

So he decided to go back to college. He got into Haverville because a friend's father was on the faculty and "I was pretty together then. I was sure of myself at the interview, and I wrote a good application essay."

By his second semester, he had adjusted academically. He learned to include some easy courses in his schedule, and he was acquiring study habits. He was also acquiring social graces. "There's almost a cocktail party atmosphere here. There are lots of parties. We drink beer and make small talk. Not about anything really important. We talked about art and music. We talked about the future a lot. Mostly, we just played around. Socially, I became an adult here. I dated mostly Haverville girls. It's a contained environment. You never have to leave. There's dancing, music, parties, beer. There's drugs." Haverville had become his place of power.

One of his girlfriends was the daughter of the owner of a large metropolitan sports arena, and they got along just fine. "She had an inexhaustible supply of money, but she didn't take herself too seriously because of it. 'I'm just spending Daddy's money' was her attitude. I didn't envy the rich kids."

He didn't have to. Except for the fact that they had money and he didn't, he had become just like them. "I've become real casual and relaxed.

I'm at home with myself. I'm a laid-back, musician-type guy. That's what I am. I've come to terms with myself."

It's all right not to be ambitious in Haverville. It's an expensive town, but it's best not to seem too interested in money here. It would probably violate a zoning ordinance. In the village surrounding the campus, there are no large signs and no neon. Neither are there any fast-food places. Every structure is tastefully understated, slightly English, and, in fact, conforms to a strict architectural code. Walt acts as a tour guide on the main street, illustrating why the place has such a hold on him. He points out a clothing boutique with quietly avant-garde items in the window, all unpriced. They are made of linen and other natural fibers, in subtle colors, grayish green, dusty rose, taupe. "You don't find stores like this in most towns," he says. He leads me into a large shop that sells ethnic art and specialty music products, like rare Indian flutes and hurdy-gurdies, clever puppets with zippers that convert into purses. There are several art galleries, and a used record shop and a gourmet restaurant with an elegantly simple menu and decor. Walt seems to know everyone— the shopkeepers, the salespeople, other students, pretty girls, other hangers-on, miscellaneous young men whom he has business with. He hasn't the money to be a customer in Haverville's stores, but he enjoys them, as if he were in a museum.

He points to a structure down the street—a big, reasonably ugly modern office complex in tan stone with a red horizontal band and rounded corners. It looks a little like a fortress, but so do many shopping centers and office complexes that in other places get swallowed up in suburban sprawl. In Haverville it is a great sore thumb of commercialism. "This was a big controversy here," Walt explains. "I don't know how you feel about it," he says, politely deferring to the possibility that an outsider might share the developer's taste, "but I hate it. It's very unpopular here. It even has a disco, which just isn't Haverville. I hope it does badly."

At the end of the walk, we stop at an espresso bar in a converted theater and take our drinks to another pleasant outdoor patio. He tries to explain why he stays here. He plays with a band and most of their club dates are in beach towns fifty or sixty miles from here. "The beach cities are more fun," he agrees. "But I guess it's partly laziness, partly economics." He rents a run-down frame bungalow here in the old part of town, and it's cheap. "I hate apartment hunting. I don't have the energy for it," he goes on. "But mostly, I like life here. Haverville is an intellectual oasis. It's a casual, do-your-own-thing town. It's tolerant. It's hard to leave. It's like a nest but after a while, you start to resent the comfort."

At college, he had a radical art professor who got him interested in the environment as a functional and aesthetic entity, a work of art and science rather than an accident of bureaucracy and nature. "He made me think about the room I was sitting in. I would think, 'This is a stupid building. With different exposure, it could use passive solar energy.'" Walt found the ideas so intriguing that he majored in environmental studies and did an internship with the city's energy department. After graduation, he took a temporary job with the city retrofitting homes with energy-saving devices, such as insulation for water heaters and window sealing. It was a temporary job because it was part of a state program and it ended when the state funds ran out. And Walt went back to making music with his friends. But the job was, technically, Walt's first reason for staying in Haverville.

I ask him then for a professional analysis of the Haverville environment. What makes it so appealing that students want to stay?

He thinks for a while, liking the problem. "First," he says, preparing an outline in his mind, "it's familiarity. There are a lot of landmarks here. You know where you are, and I know the streets, the places where I go and how to get there. The familiarity makes me confident.

"Second, there are boundaries here. Everything around here is different from here. To the south it's minority and working class. North is very different—light industry and farming. And the west is absolutely horrible— suburban and polluted. People with Datsun 280-Z's and tract houses. *Discos.* Haverville gives definition. I know who I am because I'm not those other places."

In other words, as long as he stays in Haverville, he has class status. He wasn't born with it, and he doesn't have to go out among the tract houses and the 280-Z's and earn it. All he has to do is stay here. The art galleries and the bookstores render a special status that can't be measured against other kinds of status. Things are tough out there, and he may never be part of this kind of life-style again. A lopsided bungalow in Haverville is fun, a sign of indifference to the disco and Datsun culture. A singles apartment in an ordinary town is depressing and definitive.

The fact that Haverville is fantasy status only enhances its appeal. I suspect that if Walt made enough money to afford Haverville, to buy a nice house here and to eat at the understated, gourmet restaurant and to buy ethnic art and linen shirts, it would quickly lose its cachet. It would be real and he would be a grown-up here. It would *count.* The fun of staying around college is that it isn't grown-up and it doesn't count. And for a lot of young people, struggling against the unequal odds of succeeding in chimeric enterprises, the only way to keep going is to pretend that you're not there yet. This doesn't count. It's only temporary. I'm still a kid and I'm just hanging around with the other kids. The black hole in space that Walt talks about is the reluctance to grow up and be defined.

So Haverville becomes a new home and its tribe of students and former students become a new family. The separation process is just as difficult as with any family. "What I hope," says Walt, "is that my band will go on the road. Then I'll be traveling six or ten months a year and spend only four months or so here. I'll be able to make the break that way."

Jim and Ian are friends of Walt's, and they are trying to make the break another way. They both graduated from Haverville—Ian last year and Jim two years ago—and they lived there until two weeks ago. Unlike Walt, they come from the kind of families that *belong* in Haverville. Their families aren't rich, but they have the background and the values that fit in a liberal arts college town. In a different decade, Jim and Ian might have followed their fathers and become academics or socially active ministers. But those choices seem anemic and unrealistic in the eighties. So what the boys have inherited is the vision of a life-style, shards of a value structure, and a longing that makes it hard to grow up in the real world.

Right now, they are seventy miles away in a seedy, yellow stucco building a few blocks from the beach. The air is better and cooler here, but the shops sell tourist T-shirts, bikinis, and cheap rattan furniture. Their apartment is in the rear, up a flight of unsteady stairs with peeling paint. The door opens into a small kitchen that has no signs of food or cooking. There are no dishes around the sink but some Styrofoam take-out containers are in the trash, proof of human habitation.

The furniture in the living room is vintage Goodwill and the thin carpet is an awful orange. But the walls are plastered with interesting artwork from Asia and Latin America, and one wall is lined with shelves filled with records. And beyond the window, the town falls away into a silver strip of ocean.

Jim and Ian moved here because they have a job with a bank in the next town, which is more expensive, a town with tract houses and discos. Or rather, they think they have a job. They were hired by a bank chartered in another state to sell certificates of deposit over the phone to other financial institutions. They think they will be getting a monthly salary, not a draw against commissions, and that everything is firm. They started training two weeks ago without a doubt in the world, but lately they have begun to feel uneasy. Today's training session was canceled, and the bank keeps pushing ahead the date that they will actually start work. One of the other trainees wondered aloud if management might be having second thoughts about having hired eight salesmen. Jim's relatives suggested that he and Ian check out the bank through the banking commission in its home state. They haven't done it nor have they tried to clarify their salary arrangement. "They hired us. They must mean it," says Ian. He and Jim don't mind leaving things vague.

They need the job of course. It's the linchpin of their plans. But their main task right now seems to be finding out whether there is life after Haverville, and the beach is an interesting place to explore the question. An ocean breeze gusts through the window, fluttering a poster on the wall, and they look at each other half-pleased, like people who have been sent on vacation for their own good and think they might like it. Haverville has class but no ocean breeze, the look says.

Ian is blond and square-jawed, with very good, deep-set blue eyes; he wears standard issue student-hanging-around clothes—jeans, unironed 100 percent cotton shirt, topsiders. Jim is a little shorter and stockier, with a friendly face and a good tan that gives him a certain crispness. It is hard to say why they seem out of place on this sand-strewn town streaked in a gouache of yellow light. Like almost everyone else around, they are young and fit and tan. But they are decidedly different, almost foreign here in their rumpled preppy clothes. This is a funky, slightly seedy place devoted to body worship. The girls wear gauze blouses and slit shorts that ride up over a crescent of buttock, and the men shuffle around in rubber thongs on evenly tanned feet, wearing surf trunks, and print shirts unbuttoned over stomachs flattened by hours in the gym. The pungent smell of coconut tanning oil hangs in the air, along with the odors of sea salt and fast-food grease.

Jim and Ian stroll around slowly, trying to take it all in and like it. The houses on the beach are small and jerry-built; zoning seems to be as haphazard here as it is rigid in Haverville. And the residents are utterly oblivious of Haverville's values and standards of taste. One of the beach-front houses has a giant Advent television screen blocking the front window that looks out over the ocean. They point it out as we pass. It has become one of their jokes. Another is the neighbor who dropped in one night and talked about himself for hours. Implied but unsaid was that the neighbor wasn't their sort anyway.

Luckily, Haverville is only an hour or so away, and they can go back on weekends. Last weekend there was an art show. Next week, there's a party. "We'll spend less time there as time goes by," says Ian. "We miss Haverville, but we'll make the break."

The beach town and the new job are a withdrawal treatment. They have given up the milieu and the status of Haverville, but they are still safe in a youth environment. This isn't the grown-up world yet. "The beach is a new lounge," says Ian.

They are also making the break together, as a team, so they not only have each other as moral support but they have a piece of Haverville along, like a smooth stone in their pockets. They have known each other since they were freshmen. By coincidence, both are the youngest sons of ministers and traveled a lot while they were young. In college, they shared a taste for rock music and parties, and took courses in environmental studies with the same provocative art professor who attracted Walt to the field.

In other ways, they are quite different, but they both found a home in Haverville. The town and its youth tribe inhabitants fit snugly around each of them like foam, molding to the shape of their needs.

Jim loved the sheer coziness of it. It was small and familiar and friendly, and full of like-minded people, just like the world he grew up in. He was, in fact, born there. He is the youngest of five sons, and his father was college chaplain and an instructor in theology and classics when Jim was born. Except for a year that the family spent in England, Jim lived happily in the shadow of Haverville College until he was eleven, when his father had an assignment in India, and Jim went to boarding school there. He loved that too. By dint of the way his world worked, his best friend from Haverville was his roommate in India. At the end of the year, the whole family traveled to Israel, Greece, and Western Europe, and Jim liked that too.

The *wanderjahr* ended, they settled in a small town in Kentucky, where his father was to be provost of a liberal arts college. It was Jim's first experience of a place he didn't like. "It was more of a culture shock than India," he says. It was hicksville, and he hated it so much that his family sent him back to Haverville to live with his uncle—who was, at the time, president of the college. He spent half a year there and then came home and magically adjusted to Kentucky. Some of the kids were country bumpkins and most of the teachers were football coaches struggling with academic subjects they had to teach to fill out their day. But the area was beautiful and green, and he liked playing the guitar in a rock band, and even the football coach teachers couldn't spoil history and biology for him. And of course he made friends because Jim makes friends everywhere.

He went to Haverville more or less automatically. Academically, it was tough for him because he was also playing in a band and he wasn't well prepared enough for the rigors of a real school. But it didn't bother him all that much. "I was much more interested in social things, in friendships I was making and relationships with the faculty. In that sense, I couldn't have been happier anywhere else. Haverville is a real community. I like the small-town aspect of it. Everyone is very accessible. I like the espresso bar and Alex's."

He lived in the dorms every year except one, when he shared a house with several other students. The house had a pool, and it became a resort for everybody else. "We drank too much beer and there were always visitors and I wasn't getting anything done. It was always playtime. Besides, I missed my friends from the dorms and campus life." So he moved back to the dorms the following year.

"I'm a private person," he explains, "and people there respected locked doors. But if you wanted company, you could leave your door open and someone would come in and chat." Dorm life was the perfect existence, with the ideal family; it provided easy, supportive, stimulating relationships without responsibility or commitment. You closed your door when you'd had enough.

Jim was involved in a variety of campus activities—the dorm council, the arts festival, student government. He majored in history and environmental studies. "I was intrigued by the idea of passive solar design." During the summers, he went back to Kentucky and worked on maintenance crews on his father's campus. One summer, he traveled around the country. For a while he thought about joining the Peace Corps or teaching in Kentucky after graduation, but he abandoned those ideas as "unrealistic."

By the time he was a senior, he hadn't come up with anything more realistic. "What I really wanted to do was some serious hanging out in Haverville," is his honest assessment of his plans for the future at the age of twenty-two. "I wanted to play the guitar and do whatever came along. I wanted to stop over at the coffee shop and talk to eight or more people." I remark that it sounds like a good day's work, and he deadpans, "Day? That's two weeks." He is only half-kidding, since it is what he more or less did. "I hang around hard and seriously," he says, with a charming smile.

But since he had to pay his rent and his espresso bills, he and a friend got jobs as go-fers on an art promotion project. They got the job through the friend's father, and in the course of it, made contacts with an advertising company that hired them to do promotional work on the women's golf tour. The golf tour job came along after a year of serious hanging out. The job lasted for most of the next year, and it ended because of problems within the company. But while it lasted, it was perfect. The two of them traveled with the tour a lot, and the rest of the time, they hung out in Haverville, with each other and with the other kids. When the job ended and the money ran out, the father of another friend connected Ian and Jim with the bank job they may or may not have.

Ian is a darker, more restless version of the eternal American boy. He is Huck Finn a century later, affluent, educated, but still searching the river for adventure and rebelling against the Widow Douglas's attempts to civilize him. He liked Haverville because it allowed him to be Huck Finn, without any Widow Douglases or other adult pressure to act like a grown-up.

He is not the first wanderer in his family. He was born in New York, where his minister father had a congregation. Mostly, he grew up in various towns in New England, where his father had other congregations. Right now, his family lives in Texas. His father, who is an activist minister, involved in a variety of social causes, was a Presbyterian pastor, then a Congregationalist, and now a Unitarian. "I think he just liked moving around," Ian says, as if it were self-explanatory.

At fourteen, he went off to prep school—an elite, academically demanding New England school—and adjusted without a wrinkle. It was just another move. Asked if he was homesick at boarding school, he says, "Yeah, for the first two weeks." He liked school the way a seasoned tourist likes a country's second-best city. It had a few good features. Soccer and lacrosse. Some good friends, whom he's kept in touch with over the years. Good Spanish classes. He worked hard, especially at the Spanish because he thought he'd use it. When anyone asked if he had any career plans back then, he said he was thinking about the foreign service.

He chose Haverville because it's not on the East Coast. He felt he had been there long enough and it was time to move on. "The Eastern Ivy circuit would be just like high school all over again. I didn't get into Stanford, and the rep from Haverville made a good sell at my high school." Ian spent his freshman year "being aimless. I drank a lot of beer." By summer, he was restless again and he and a prep school buddy headed for Alaska, where they got jobs on a fishing boat. "It was something we always talked about doing." In the fall, the friend went back to school, but Ian liked fishing and Alaska and stayed on. He came back to Haverville a year later only because he had a vague notion that "it would be a good idea to finish school."

When he returned, he took school more seriously. He got reasonably good grades—"A's, B's, one or two C's. It wasn't genuine interest. But it was a strong interest." During the summers, he worked on a hay crew on a ranch in Nevada and chased mustangs. "Why work in some office?" he had asked himself. "You have your whole life for that." He continued to perfect his Spanish, and spent a quarter in Spain and a semester in Bogotá, Colombia, living with a local family.

He believes that his interest in Latin culture is something that rubbed off from his activist father. "I'm aware of other cultures that didn't have the advantages we did," he says. In many ways, he is an eighties incarnation of his father. His father acted out his wanderlust by changing jobs, but he did it with a family and under the aegis of profession and duty, the way grown men in his day did it. Ian just does it, the way eternal boys do. And while his father expressed his awareness of less privileged people by getting involved with social causes, Ian sees them as another chance for travel and adventure. Asked if he's worried about the potential for another Vietnam in Central America, he is vaguely optimistic. "There are too many bright people in Washington for that to happen. Things will stabilize and we'll leave them alone." He is not interested in causes or issues. He likes places and experiences for their own sake. He isn't avoiding commitment. The concept just hasn't occurred to him yet.

So he too went into his senior year without any plans for the future. His only real interest was traveling to Spanish-speaking countries, and he made a desultory effort to turn it into a job. Haverville was proud of both its Spanish department and its foreign studies program, but it had no study program in a Spanish-speaking country. Ian had to do his semester in Colombia under the auspices of another college, and it cost him his financial aid, since technically he was not a student at Haverville that semester. So he proposed that the college set up a program in Ecuador and offered to run it. "This vice-president stroked me along. Then he resigned. He knew all along that he was going to resign, so he wouldn't commit to anything." Ian was disappointed, but he had no other plans. The day before graduation, he had a conversation with the president of the college, who made encouraging noises. On that slim basis, Ian decided to stay in Haverville and work toward starting the program.

But encouraging conversations are free, new programs are expensive, and things move slowly in academia, especially in colleges without large endowments. After two months of hanging around waiting, Ian was broke. So he went down the street, beyond the fancy part of Haverville, and got a job driving a delivery truck for a cheap furniture store. Sometimes he sold on the floor, but he wasn't very good at it. "I had a hard time selling crap to people who couldn't afford it. What I liked most was picking up deliveries at the docks and jawing in Spanish with the other workers." It was the closest the job came to being a foreign adventure.

Otherwise, it was not much of a job for someone with Ian's ability and background, but it did allow him to stay in Haverville. "I just liked being there. People are friendly. They're interested in the world. It's an academic town, and there are a lot of bright people. The college makes it a hub for music and art."

He has a girlfriend, and, characteristically, it is a loose, long-distance relationship. They met at Haverville, but she graduated two years before he did (she is a year older, and she didn't "stop out" for a year, as Ian did) and went on to get an M.B.A. She now lives in New York and works on the commodities exchange. He doesn't mind that she is so directed, and she doesn't mind his lack of direction. "I think what she does is great," he says, surprised that anyone would ask. They have been together, in their way, for the past five years, and see each other during summer vacations. Ian was thinking of moving east, since he had no particular plans, but it just didn't happen. "The timing was wrong. This job came through, and I thought I'd rather spend the summer at the beach. Maybe she'll move here."

He is enthusiastic about this new job and hopes it doesn't fall through. The salespeople will prepare their own contact lists from various directories. "It's like doing a bibliography," he says, confident that a good liberal arts education is preparation for most things. Does he see a future for himself in banking? "I don't know. Maybe. *International* banking would be nice. Basically this job is high-pressure sales. But I think any experience is good for you. I believe in learning for its own sake. I'm not sure about a career. If I have to imagine myself in the future, I see myself sitting in the Galápagos Islands, watching the tortoises. I'm not kidding, really. I'm going to hit Haverville again about a program in Ecuador."

For Ian, that would be perfect, just as dorm life was for Jim. Like his father, he would have a reason to travel. He would be off on an exotic adventure far from the boredom of offices and routine, but still securely connected to Haverville. To student life. To being young.

I ask him who was more mature at his age, he or his father. He is slow to answer. "It's hard to say who was more mature. My dad grew up in a different time. He was a father when he was twenty-seven, and I'm certain that I'm not going to be a father in three years. But I've had more experiences than he had at that age. I don't think you have to be so directed when you're young. I think there's plenty of time for that. I guess that's eighties thinking. Or sixties or seventies. But it's how I grew up thinking."

So he and Ian are here at the beach, in limbo between college and whatever is beyond. It isn't half bad. Most of this talk has gone on over lunch at a pleasantly funky restaurant near the beach, and it takes about three hours. They don't mind. They are world-class sitters. Back at their apartment later, they check the messages on their new telephone answering machine. Their supervisor has called, and there is a training session scheduled for tomorrow. They are relieved. So far, they still have a job. But that's tomorrow at eleven. Now they can put some music on and look out at the waves and decide whether to go to a party in Haverville this weekend.

Jane—whom we met in the chapter on super students—went to the University of Rochester because the campus looked nice when she visited with her mother and because the psychology department was supposed to be good. It is not an intimate school by any standards, but even big, impersonal schools have a way of becoming home. Jane didn't hang out very long after graduation, but she hung on to the life-style and to the youth tribe she joined there, and that is just a slight variation. Perhaps it is a woman's variation, since women seem to like more structure in their lives, and they can't get jobs delivering furniture when the money runs out.

One reason that Jane may have been a little haphazard in her choice of college is that she was already in love with high school. Academically, she was a good student at an experimental New York City public school, but her real attachment was to the activities and her friends. She was in repertory theater and dance, she volunteered as an art therapist at a hospital, and she worked in the English department. She had a strong sense of her identity there. "There were clear lines at our school. There were hippies and hitters."

So college was a letdown at first. She lived in a dorm full of "JAP's, cheerleaders, and hoseheads." (Translation: Jewish American princesses, pretty but conventional girls, and computer science majors, so named for the hosing that connects the hardware.) She made only one friend that year. "It was all cliques," she recalls. The following year, she and her new friend moved into a dorm with suites and got involved with the student politics group. "We stirred up a little," she remembers, proudly. They demonstrated against increases in tuition and one friend ran for student body president. She and a few others ran for the student Senate, and they all won. It was an intoxicating victory, and they set out to use their power in behalf of their favorite causes. "We were psyched. We thought we had it all."

It turned out they had very little. A favorite left-leaning professor was up for tenure and didn't get it, despite their militant support—or because of it. There was a raise in tuition, and they never saw the budget. University funds continued to be invested in companies that had interests in South Africa. They were still the kids, and the administration were the grown-ups. "It was all very frustrating and disillusioning. We had won nothing. We were an inconvenience to them, but they knew we'd be gone in four years."

Nor did they get support from other students, even on the tuition increase. "My father can afford it," was the common response, and their peers went about the collegiate business of having a good time or preparing for a career. So once again, there were clear lines. An *us* and a *them*. The *us* became an ideal family, all of the same generation, united against the parents and the rival siblings.

The next year—her junior year—her group of eight friends shared two adjacent houses. One of the group was Jane's boyfriend, and her best friend also had a boyfriend. "The two households were so communal, we were almost incestuous," Jane says. Her voice has more than nostalgia in it. She is not talking about an old love, safely consigned to the past. If she had her choice, she would still be there, with all of them.

They lived that way for two years, staying in Rochester with assorted jobs or courses through the summers. "My life was at school. We were like a family. Sometimes we talked about buying a farm together." But inevitably, they graduated, and being bright, academically oriented students, they graduated on time. They stayed in Rochester all summer, working at any jobs they could. "We just couldn't bear to leave." But even the graduate summer ended. They had lived by the academic calendar all of their lives, and they knew it was time to go. "We had an all-night yard sale before we broke up. The last forty-eight hours were traumatic. It was all very sad. We couldn't say good-bye, so we just trickled away, one by one."

Jane had no plans at all. Her boyfriend went home to New England and a job. She had a brother in Boston, so she and one of the other women in the group headed there so she could be closer to her boyfriend. The two young women, a fragment of the old group, shared an apartment and worked in a day-care center. In February, her boyfriend joined them, but by then things weren't the same. He found a job driving a truck for a linen supply company, but he felt restless and crowded. After a while, he took his own apartment around the corner. Jane would have preferred to live with him, but he was ambivalent about the relationship.

"He needed space," Jane says. "He was afraid of commitment and dependency. I used to wonder, 'Why don't I just end this?' But I was willing to go with the relationship till it ended. I'd be going out the door for work in the morning, and he'd say, 'I feel trapped.' I was tired of the relationship also, but he was all I had left. It was like splitting up the family.

"Finally, I told him to take the weekend and think it over. He called me Sunday night, and we had a nice conversation, and he asked if he could come over. It was all very casual, and I thought everything was fine. But he was standing in my doorway with a paper bag in his hand. I knew it was over. He was giving me back my clothes."

" 'Do you think I'm doing the right thing?' he asked me.

" 'You're doing the wrong thing,' I said, and I got his things. We didn't stay friends. For one thing, I was taking the Graduate Records Exam the next weekend, and I don't think he ever considered me. I wouldn't have done it that way. He got in touch with me around Christmas just to talk. We were worried about our friends. Would they have to take sides? It was all very uncomfortable. I know my friends see him even though they said they wouldn't.

"I'm still in the process of reconstructing my life. First the safe communal group went. Then Bob and I broke up. There was always a 'we.' I've just started thinking about me."

It is two and a half years since she graduated from college. She is back in New York now, living alone in a little apartment in Greenwich Village. She has a part-time job as a secretary and is in a master's program in psychology. She has a supportive family and a lot of friends. But it doesn't quite add up to a life. "I feel that I'm in a holding pattern now. I'm waiting for something to happen. I feel lonely and displaced."

What she is waiting for is a husband and a biological family, for her college family to fade into painless memory. She is warm and nurturing and bright. She will probably be a good wife and mother. But real families are the grown-up world. Mortgage payments and visits to the doctor and baby-sitters and a hatchback full of grocery bags don't have the incandescence of eight students in adjoining houses. That was true love.

PART IV

THE CHANGING LANDSCAPE

12

High Tech

I will start this chapter with a confession. I like high-tech people: systems engineers, electrical engineers, programmers, analysts, and a lot of the others who work for those companies with new-language names like Datadyne or Qualitec. I did not like them before I started this book. I would pass those low-slung concrete buildings surrounded by parking lots and spindly trees and imagine the people working inside. They were precise, paper-skinned, white-shirted. They spent their days crunching numbers, and even that activity seemed too muscular, too voracious for them. The college kids called them hoseheads, as if they were part of the machinery they worked with.

I saw them as the people who "took literature in college but didn't read the book." They were, in short, boring, one-dimensional people who had good jobs but little capacity to enjoy life.

I set out to interview them to confirm my prejudices and the prejudices of various psychologists and counselors (all of us onetime liberal arts majors) who also saw them as narrow people who leaped to security and were doomed to misery. "Essentially, these people are oriented to security and once they get that, they say, 'Yeah, okay. Now where's my fulfillment?' " said Berkeley psychologist Richard Beery to the Los Angeles *Times*. Beery was the main source of a 1981 article about young people who chose "hot jobs" and ended up miserable.

Career and placement counselors at other campuses also worry a lot

about "square pegs in round holes." "Our worst cases are those who try
to make something of themselves that they are not," says Robert Ehrmann,
director of the career development unit at UCLA. "They're disasters—
emotional and physical wrecks." I ask the worried counselors if they can
connect me with one of the square pegs in the round hole of high tech,
but no one can think of anyone in particular. I attend a Career Change
Workshop that the University of California offers its alummni, and there
are no engineers or computer scientists there who want to change their
lives. But there are teachers and social workers and other broadly educated
people who wish they were engineers or computer scientists.

"Engineers and scientists don't change," says Ehrmann. "They have
linear minds. They see life differently from the liberal arts people. The
split occurs in the seventh grade." But I begin to suspect that the unhappy
engineer is a figment of the liberal arts imagination.

I do not know why we equate economic security with lack of fulfillment.
It mystifies me. Some of the computer people I met were restless, so
they made a few phone calls and moved on. Compared to their peers
in other fields of endeavor, they seemed to be the soul of contentment.
There is something about being valued, rewarded, sought after, courted,
and treated well that tends to make people happy. When you throw in
interesting work and considerable job independence, it is not a package
that breeds misery.

Tom Wolfe, in a marvelous *Esquire* profile of Robert Noyce, the inven-
tor of the silicon chip, attributes our prejudice against technology to east-
erners' snobbery about engineers (they are glorified manual laborers) and
to a bit of sixties reasoning that equated science with the military-industrial
complex.

But our current misconceptions about computer people may have another origin. They are doing well, and the rest of us are jealous. This is
especially true among young adults. For young adults in high tech are
different from others of their generation in one very significant way: Their
expectations of the good life are being amply met. Computer science
majors graduate from college with a handful of job offers at starting salaries
of about twenty-five thousand dollars a year. In fact, the starting salary
is almost taken for granted, and these college seniors sift through their
options in a nice, systematic way, hefting fine points such as location,
perks, the compatibility of their co-workers, the priorities of the company,
and most of all, how interesting their work would be. Their friends in
less privileged fields work as waiters or secretaries while they wait—often
for a year or more—for opportunities in their field. It explains a lot of
hostility.

In fact, the young people in high tech that I met were not narrow
or boring. In many ways, they were more interesting than their peers,

since self-absorption and depression are not really very broadening. More important to the point of this book, the young engineers seemed to be growing up rather nicely, according to the old, pre-eighties schedule. And it is not hard to see why. Life is being kind to them instead of throwing them into a tailspin of confused expectations. And for that reason, they are strong support for the thesis of this book, which might be summarized—only a little facetiously—as: It takes an extra decade to grow up in the eighties, unless you're in high tech.

Some of the hoseheads were just lucky. They had the right talents and inclinations, like math and science, and after that everything fell into place easily. The jobs found them. A second type of computer people were just practical by nature. Many of them are the children of immigrants or hardworking people who didn't take affluence for granted. When they were told that there was money in computers, they signed up for computer science courses and struggled through. They might not become great creative forces in the field, but they could work their way into management. At worst, they would never have to see the inside of an unemployment office.

Perhaps because there is no gaping chasm between their expectations and reality, these two types have no problem growing up. They are focused, independent, and realistic, almost a different generation from their disappointed peers. They seem like transplants from the fifties, when almost everyone grew up on schedule. They are upwardly mobile, optimistic, secure in their values and their hopes for the future. They work with logical systems and they see life as a logical business, albeit a little less logical than a computer system. Most intend to marry (or are already married), have children, and own their homes. There have been some scandals about widespread cocaine use in the upper echelons of the Silicon Valley, but the young adults that I met in high tech seemed far less interested in drugs or heavy drinking than others of their generation. "I need all the brain cells I can get," said one engineering student. "I'm always in training," said another.

There is a third type of high-tech person, and they almost don't need to grow up. They live on the planet differently. These are the computer freaks who love their work and don't much care about anything else. They are at land's end, looking out at uncharted water, and nothing else, not the money or the title or the company health club, matters. They fit in on their own terms, and at that even, they have a touch of the fifties about them. If they are alienated or rebellious it is within a structure of attainable goals and a belief in scientific progress.

I am about to give the young adults in high tech rather long shrift because the contrast between them and their less lucky peers may shed some light on what has gone wrong for the rest of us. It is, of course, the contention of this book that the high technicians are well adjusted because their expectations of the good life are being met. It is also possible that the people who choose fields in which their expectations will be met were realistic and well adjusted to begin with. There is probably some truth in both, and I am presenting a good many of these young people in order to explore the question. It's clear that some of these young engineers would have gravitated naturally to whatever was most sensible. It's also obvious that others would not have landed on their feet were it not for the grace of high-tech talent.

Carol, a twenty-year-old senior at the University of Tennessee, is a good example of the lucky engineer. She happened to have talent in math. In high school, she loved English and history and assumed that she would continue in the liberal arts in college. But she scored unusually high in the math ACT's. "I thought they'd mixed me up with someone else," she said. But the dean of engineering wrote her a letter suggesting that she might want to major in engineering, and perhaps she'd like to come in and talk to him anyway. She did go to see him, just to clear up the misunderstanding. She explained that she had no chemistry, no physics, no calculus, and no trigonometry—all the subjects that engineers took in high school. The dean took that lightly. She'd catch up, he assured her, and besides, the job prospects were good.

"I was only sixteen when I started college, so I decided that I had a year to kill trying engineering." She found that she liked it and that despite the pressures she could take one nontechnical class each quarter, usually English, her early love.

"There are two types of engineers" is her theory. "The first was born. Since day one, they were engineers. They were rewiring houses when they were three. The second is in it mainly for the money, and they have to struggle. I guess I'm the third kind. I'm not just in it for the money, and I'm also interested in people." She is now twenty and a senior. She is in a co-op program, spending one quarter at school and one quarter on the job with a Florida computer company, earning $310 a week. When she graduates, she expects a starting salary between $24,000 and $27,000 a year and a wide choice of jobs. Thanks to the co-op program she already has some firm ideas about what she is looking for in an employer. "I want a place that doesn't have a high turnover rate and where there is opportunity for advancement. I'd like to get into management eventually."

Without that letter from the recruiting dean, she thinks she would have majored in liberal arts and gotten an M.A. in planning—and been considerably less employable. She does not seem the least bit unhappy.

Her brother, who did major in liberal arts and even went on to a master's at Oxford, is now working in a bookstore.

"I never signed on for any four-year plan," says Greg, a twenty-seven-year-old, lanky, bearded computer science major at the University of Tennessee. Greg is the kind of engineer who doesn't have to grow up because even if he remains a child, he is useful to the world. His skills are in demand, and will probably continue to be in demand for the foreseeable future. So immaturity doesn't have the same consequences, which is a little unfair.

He has been an undergraduate for nine years and he is in no hurry to change his status. He isn't even tempted by job offers. "I just had three," he says grimly. "But I don't like these high-pressure, high technology environments. What I'm doing here means more to me than some thirty-thousand-dollar-a-year job. I like the university environment, the hardware, the minds, the system I'm working with. I can work on my own projects without worrying that they will be canceled for commercial reasons."

What he would like to do eventually is work for a small systems house in computer graphics, with applications in terrain modeling or manufacturing three-dimensional things, like aircraft wings or games. He will probably get what he wants. "The field hasn't developed much because of limitations in hardware," he notes with relish.

Meanwhile, he lives as comfortably as he cares to on assorted university grants. "A job won't change my life very much. I won't be making any major purchases or anything. What I most want is control over my work environment." He now lives in a house with three other students, and he admits that he would like to change that. He will also probably leave Knoxville and move to the Silicon Valley or Seattle. He doesn't see that as a big change. His life happens at work, and he will go where the work is most interesting. "The turnover rate in high tech is one year or less," he explains. I suspect that he is talking about turnover among people like himself, the creative, restless, alienated types who inhabit his favorite place, the leading edge of technology.

"A design group finishes, gets the product out, and people leave. The headhunters take over. It's a mobile crowd. But companies aren't looking for long-term employees. They are offering perks and the basic job environment," he explains. If they are also talking about retirement plans or a future in top management, he isn't listening. That's for the dark side of computer science, "the transfers from business. They get degrees in computer science, but they don't have a thorough understanding of the leading edge of technology. They know sales and markets," he says, not so much with contempt as utter lack of interest.

Greg sounds like a superannuated whiz kid, a six-foot version of the small boy with a large digital watch who spent his afternoons peering into his computer monitor in a room full of wires and tubes. In fact, he is too good-looking, too hip for that stereotype. He wasn't an intellectual child, just an outsider, an Air Force brat who lived everywhere and, as a result, has no accent at all. If anyplace was home, it was Nashville, and his interest in the town's most famous industry is neither musical nor social. It is technical. "The country music stations had such strong signals that the music came out of the water pipes," is his telling comment on the closest thing he has to a hometown.

Greg's high school was dominated by cliques, but Greg wasn't in any of them. He liked science, languages, and music, and was in the school band and two outside rock bands. He drove a motorcycle. When he graduated, he'd had enough school for a while. "I considered going to college, but I was unwilling to consider another strenuous academic program." So he hitched across the country to California, and then up to Oregon, Washington, and back across Idaho, Colorado, and Wyoming. He started out with a high school friend, whom he left behind in Berkeley, and he continued on his own.

"I enjoyed it," he says of his wandering. "My mental state was right. I met people. I felt free, and I had a sense of total control over my life. I could go anywhere I wanted to." It was the ultimate, untrammeled adolescent ramble. Hitching was cheap, and he covered his expenses—about a hundred dollars a month—with money he had saved from high school jobs. His parents, he says, were "understanding. It wasn't quite what they had in mind for me."

He started the odyssey in June and returned in time for Christmas. Not even loners want to hitchhike on Christmas day. "Being back home was a big readjustment period," he recalls. He had odd jobs, and he lived with his family. It wasn't bad, but he was no longer king of the road. It was time to think about the future, and that meant college.

The following fall found him at Georgia Tech in Atlanta, majoring in electrical engineering. It was another big adjustment, to life in a big city and to a tough engineering program. It was here that he had his first, fateful encounter with a computer. He and some other people chipped in for a MITS-ALTAIR, which they assembled from a kit. What he most liked about it was the feeling that he had finally found his clique—the other computer people. "They were sharp, clever, quick to grasp things and on the leading edge of technology." The last is the great litmus test.

But his encounter with the MITS-ALTAIR, the first widely marketed microcomputer, didn't keep him at Georgia Tech. He didn't like staying places. After three quarters, he transferred to Tennessee Tech in Cookville. "The program was easier and I didn't have to pay out-of-state tuition." Besides, "I wanted to take advantage of my college years. I see the experience differently than most people. It's not just a quick four-year route to a degree. It should include good times—women, beer, backpacking, skiing, snowcamping. I wasn't in a hurry." During this time, his parents were paying his tuition, and he paid his other expenses by working as a computer programmer. Since then, his father has retired, and Greg pays his own way entirely.

But Tennessee Tech brought new changes. "They had a mainframe system from Xerox, and my interests started to shift away from hardware engineering and into software."

So he no longer wanted that electrical engineering degree. Computer science was new as an academic field then, and a lot of people were learning it by puttering in cinder-block sheds. The official difference between electrical engineers and computer scientists (or systems engineers, as IBM named them) is that electrical engineers work with the hardware—the actual machines—and computer scientists work with the software, or programs. The electrical engineer is a notch or so higher on the status charts, and he's also makes a little more money. A 1984 survey of employers by Michigan State University's Placement Services had electrical engineers with bachelor's degrees starting at $26,643 and computer science majors at $25,849.

What Greg was interested in was "making hardware talk to software." So he moved again, this time back to Nashville, where he worked for a small systems house configuring hardware and software. He didn't exactly leave school during this period. "I just saw a chance to make money in Nashville and go to U.T. Nashville at night." He also worked on computer systems for a bank and was operator of a system at U.T. Nashville. During some of this time, he was in the San Francisco Bay area, but he is vague about why. He spent two years in this work-study program of his own design, and then he decided to transfer to U.T. Knoxville where the computer facilities were better.

That was five years ago, and he has been there ever since. "I may graduate next June," he says glumly, as if he were talking about going into the Soviet Army for twenty years. He is in no particular hurry to grow up, marry, and do the expected. He has lived with two girlfriends and has done "a fair amount of drugs and drinking, but more drugs than alcohol. I've tried grass, speed, cocaine, and LSD recreationally," he says in answer to a question. "But nothing extreme." His real addiction is to the hardware and software, and that will keep him out of harm's way. His skills will support him anywhere, and even his once-concerned parents know that. "For a while, they were worried that I would never graduate, that I'm just on a long, high-tech adventure. But now, they're very happy that I've found something that's profitable and interesting." It is the modern equivalent of being a rich kid.

There are a lot of well-equipped, modern, poured concrete buildings at Ohio State, but Caldwell Labs isn't one of them. Caldwell Labs is the kind of building that goes with rain. It is an old brick building with wooden floors and swaying bannisters, and the smell of wet wood and the drip from umbrellas in the slatted corridors seem conjured from another era. Even the women's bathroom has a time warp. It seems to have been made out of something else, a piece of classroom or an old storeroom, from before a time when women worked in labs. The offices are small and bare, with battered old furniture of the kind that is usually made by prisoners. It is the kind of building that speaks of penny-pinching by taxpayers or the legislature, perhaps even collusion by building code inspectors. It is the kind of building where a university would house its least-favored department.

It is puzzling, then, that OSU keeps its graduate students in Computer Information Sciences here. And C.I.S., as it is known, is hardly a stepchild. I know too much about universities to ask how office space is assigned. It is an arcane, often cryptic business. So I have come up with two theories of my own. One is that the department grew quickly, beyond all predictions. When it overflowed its assigned space in some nicer building, the graduate students were moved here. The other theory is that C.I.S. graduate students were too happy contemplating their prospects to complain. They would have their whole lives to spend in nice, modern offices.

Ohio State's department is known in the field as solid, but not first rank. It is a big department; computer science is popular among midwesterners, who seem to learn at an early age that they have to be useful, like farm machinery. The graduate student-teaching assistants, known as TA's, teach lower-division sections and grade papers. These damp fourth-floor cubicles—not furnished so much as littered with scarred desks and chairs—are their offices. They gather here most afternoons to see confused undergraduates, work on their own projects, and shoot the shit with each other. They are here more or less in force today, despite the rain, because they have appointments. The recruiters are in town. Representatives of high-tech companies are here to interview, to tout their company, to size up talent, and, they hope, to hire.

The job market is not as strong this year as it has been in other years, but in computer science, that means three offers for each graduate instead of six. In fact, it would take a very sharp eye here to spot those who have interviews. None of the men are wearing suits or even sport coats or ties, nor are any of the women wearing dresses or skirts. A clean V-necked sweater over a sport shirt and jeans seems to be the maximum concession to making a good impression. They know what the interviewers want to see: grade point average, progress toward degree, and rudimentary pleasantness. Some of the recruiters have set up shop in borrowed offices on campus and keep a formal schedule. Others stroll the corridors, drop in, chat, take phone numbers, and host pizza dinners. I get the feeling that the recruiters' style doesn't matter any more than the interviewees' clothes. The students also know what they are looking for.

Consider for instance the following conversation between two OSU graduate students. Deborah has just returned from an interview. "I liked the recruiter, and I liked their offer. I'm just not sure how committed the company is to the modifiability and versatility of software," she says.

Steve apparently knows something about this company. I learn later that he worked there for a year. "These aerospace people are basically interested in onetime use. They're not going to modify anything, and you just have to get used to that," he explains.

She nods. Now she understands and can enter the data. No one will dazzle her with pizza and beer, or a description of the company gym. She wants to know what kind of work she will be doing and what the company values.

I meet these courted young midwesterners haphazardly, as they are available between classes and job interviews.

Don is twenty-three, gentle and bookish looking, with dark, curly hair and glasses. He is in computers because he is lucky enough to have talent in math and because he grew up in a home where the good life wasn't taken for granted. The oldest of five children, he was raised on a farm in western Ohio. He grew up understanding that you had to be useful in the world. His father is a high school teacher as well as a farmer. He moved the family to a farm because he wanted his children to grow up in the country with plenty of room and because he was uneasy about some of the things he saw in the small-town Ohio high school where he had taught before. Things like drugs.

Don was active in the Future Farmers of America and the 4–H Club. He did soil judging, agronomy contests, and wool and livestock judging.

It was not a community that valued education or intellectual achievement, and Don's ambitions to go to college were suspect. Even a high school diploma was seen as a threat to the status quo. "Parents were afraid that their kids would be smarter than they were and leave them behind," Don realized. "I was a triple threat to them. I was an outsider. I was ambitious. And I was college-bound. Of the seventy-four students in my high school, only seven or eight went to college, and they were also outsiders or exceptional students. The others got pregnant, married, and went to work for International Harvester."

In a way, the community defined him. It told him what he was *not*. He won almost a full scholarship to Ohio Wesleyan University, a private liberal arts school where tuition was between nine and ten thousand dollars a year. The scholarship was his main consideration in choosing the school, since his father was then earning twenty thousand dollars a year.

He started college knowing that he wanted to study computer science. "I can't say why I did. I'd never even been around a micro and there was no talk of computers at home. I'm not sure I knew what I wanted. I didn't know there would be jobs. But it was an interesting field, and I liked math and science."

Ohio Wesleyan is liberal arts oriented, and he took a sampling of courses. Mainly, he took math, science, and French, which he minored in. (Computer people seem to have an affinity for foreign languages.) He also managed three trips to France during high school and college thanks to his farming. He raised veal calves to pay for one trip to England and France and paid for the other two by selling sows at a livestock sale.

He loved college; it encouraged him to expand and do things. "I thrived," is his farmer's way of putting it. He also graduated magna cum laude and Phi Beta Kappa, with special honors in both math and French. He ran into one slight wrinkle just before graduation. The school had an unwritten rule that a student's combined units in math and science could not exceed the rest of his program. Don's did, and he received a note informing him that there was a problem. "I just resolved it somehow," he says. Colleges seldom want to put major obstacles in the path of magna cum laude graduates.

He has been at Ohio State for the past year, working on a master's degree, and he expects to finish within six months. He is a teaching assistant here, and it is the first job he has held, since his college scholarship covered all of his expenses. He is now interviewing for jobs, and he realizes, with rueful pride, that his starting salary—around thirty thousand dollars— will be more than his father now earns after a long career in teaching.

He tosses around the names of several companies and cities, but thinks that eventually he would like to come back to Ohio. "I'd like to live out of the city, in a rural area, like the one I grew up in. A lot of people make me nervous." Since most high-tech companies are generous about paying for education, he expects to get a Ph.D. in the course of time. He is modest about all of this good fortune, but not unmindful. He knows what it's like to stretch to make ends meet, and he has had enough. He would like to marry and have a family, but also, *eventually*. Not now. "When I'm thirty. My parents married young. They were twenty-one when I was born. They keep warning me not to rush out and get married. I think they may have regretted doing that themselves."

Deborah, the young woman who was concerned about a company's "commitment to the modifiability and versatility of software" is a tall, soft-spoken blonde dressed—even for job interviews—like Annie Hall, in gray trousers, striped vest, and baggy sweaters. Her long, wheat-colored hair is neatly barretted back off her face, and she wears no makeup. She is twenty-six, and expects to have her master's in hand by next summer.

When I find her, she is sitting at a particularly battered maple desk re-explaining the morning's lecture to an apparently dense undergraduate. She does this kindly and logically, but when her student leaves, she shakes her head in dismay. "He shouldn't be a computer science major if he doesn't understand the basics."

Deborah is a second generation scientist. Her father is a research physicist. Since she is three or four years older than most of the other teaching assistants on the floor, it would seem that she has done a little exploring. She has. It turned out self-exploration rather than drifting because of two factors: her own strength and intelligence and the luck of having the right kind of talent for the time.

A bored, bright, rebellious teenager, she hated high school enough to leave at sixteen and enter Ohio State on an early admission program. She stormed through six straight quarters, majoring in math and French, and then decided she was tired, and needed to get away. "I had to clear out the cobwebs a little. I wasn't escaping a love affair and I wasn't confused."

A physical education teacher told her about an Outward Bound program in which juvenile delinquents were taught to survive in the wilderness, and she signed up for a year as a counselor in Massachusetts. "I got training on the job. I had done some backpacking and climbing, but I wasn't an expert." She was seventeen years old at the time. "They were *my kids.*" They were, perhaps, a little younger than she was, and in their way, better versed in survival techniques. "They knew how to survive in the city. They stole when they were hungry, so this was an extension, a way to feel good about the skills they already had." The program had its successes, but it was also exhausting. "I constantly had to rally my energy."

Her parents didn't mind her leave from school. "I was a difficult adolescent—difficult in the relationship with them and rebellious against authority. They were glad about anything I did that was reasonably okay."

Her year with less privileged difficult adolescents turned out therapeutic, a little like recovering alcoholics helping new members in AA. She returned to school the following year with a new sense of herself and plowed straight through for the next three years. Her grade point average was a stunning 3.95. "If I hadn't gotten a *B* in my first quarter, it would have been a solid 4.0."

Her life-style, however, remained unconventional, a reflection of her other side. She never lived in the dorms, but in a series of off-campus houses shared with men and women. When she graduated in the summer of 1978, she gave full rein to her other side. She took off for Wyoming, where she worked on a construction crew building cabins. She spent the next three years in Wyoming, Colorado, and Utah, holding down low-paying jobs. She did construction work, pumped gas, and worked as a ranch hand and a mechanic. "There's a dichotomy in me. A part of me needs wilderness and physical work, a change from the academic and intellectual."

It was a hand-to-mouth existence, but in the course of it, her future began to take shape. "I was working as a mechanic on a ranch in Colorado. My hands were rotting in the cold holding metal wrenches, and I realized that I lacked the kind of intuition that real mechanics had, the mechanics who had been doing that kind of work since they were kids, when I was doing math. I would need four years just to catch up with them. And meanwhile, I had a four-year head start in thinking. In intellectual pursuits, I could contribute a higher level of expertise than I could here with a wrench in my hand." She had, in other words, reached an age where she had to go with her best shot. She couldn't be everything, and it was time to say, "This is what I am, and this is what I am not." It's not an easy lesson for her generation.

She enrolled in a Fortran course at Colorado State and was instantly smitten. Sixteen months later, she was back at Ohio State in the Computer Information Sciences department as a graduate student and teaching assistant—teaching Fortran. She never thought about the disadvantages of not having had undergraduate computer courses because the subject was never difficult for her. "It was easier than math, and I was fascinated with the logic. It was like a game and it was creative." When she finishes this summer, she plans to work in industry for one or two years and then complete her Ph.D. and either teach or return to industry. She points out, as others do, that high-tech companies are flexible about allowing employees to go to school while working.

She also plans to get married this June, to a civil engineer she met in Utah, where she was working on a construction project. They have continued the relationship by flying back and forth between quarters, and both are floating their career plans until they can find a way to be in the same place. "He builds power plants, so one of us may have to commute a little distance." She doesn't care about owning property, but she does intend to have children, despite the complication they would bring to an already complicated two-career household.

"I remember when I was a lot of trouble. I don't feel guilty about it. It's part of growing up."

Steve is the young man who explained to Deborah that aerospace companies weren't interested in modified software. After he graduated from Ohio State, with a major in computer science, he worked for an aerospace company in Southern California, which makes him the resident expert on that very large company, on aerospace, and on California. He is twenty-four, and about to get his master's. He has done it a little slowly because he also coaches a soccer team.

Like Greg, Steve was a military brat. His father was in the army, and he lived in at least five states, about a year apiece. But instead of becoming alienated, a permanent outsider, he became adaptable. "It was a bummer," he says, without self-pity. "I have no old friends. But I learned to make friends fast." He is helped by the fact that he is easygoing and nice-looking.

Steve has his generation's strong sense of entitlement, but it will probably not trouble him very much. As long as there is a high demand for computer scientists, he will get most of what he feels he is entitled to.

When he was fourteen, his father retired from the army and went to work for the state of Ohio, and the family moved to a comfortable suburb north of Columbus. Steve went to a local public school, which was then an experimental "school without walls." Steve was a member of the first class, starting when the cement was hardly dry. If the curriculum or the teaching was unusual, it didn't bother him. He had already done a little of everything, and he continued to. He got good grades, played soccer, and was a member of the Thespians and the speech team.

He also met his first computer there at a campus demonstration by Battelle, a Columbus-based think tank. "I was impressed because the machine could do so much—games, equations. And it could do things so quickly, it appeared to have intelligence." He has since learned that "machines do what they're told. A computer isn't any smarter than a toaster or a refrigerator light. It's just faster."

He went to Ohio State on a Naval Reserve Officers Training Corps scholarship, which he gave up after his sophomore year "because I decided I didn't want to spend four years on a ship." His parents—the great safety net—paid his tuition for his third year, but after that he paid his own bills by working on computer jobs.

He likes what he does academically, but he is anxious to get out and work. The job title he expects is software developer or operating system developer. "I like the field. You work with people who are rather bright, and you can dress informally." He rattles off a list of companies he is considering: TRW, Texas Instruments, IBM, DEC, Hewlett–Packard. He might want to go back to his old job in Southern California, which is waiting for him. "Los Angeles is the best sports town in the world," he ruminates. On the other hand, he can't afford to buy a house there, and he could easily buy one in Ohio. But he's tired of Ohio. Perhaps Utah or Colorado might be perfect, since he likes driving around the mountains and the desert in a four-wheel-drive truck.

"Computer companies are usually in nice areas. They have to be to get good people," he observes. "Bright people want to be in nice areas. In California, they offer perks—tennis courts, health clubs. I almost feel guilty. A friend of mine has a degree in business/marketing, and he finally got a job a year after graduation."

This low concrete building surrounded by new little trees, square patches of grass, and an acre or so of concrete parking lot is part of a large and famous aerospace/high-technology company. We'll call the company Tronics Corporation. This location houses a project to build a satellite-operated ground station, and it is set in a quiet industrial park in Southern California, among other neat rectangles of grass and concrete. Another well-known aerospace company has a facility down the street, and opposite is a company with a name like DATCOM. Neat shapes on a board, orderly and peaceful in the vivid winter sun. Off in the distance are mountains, tactfully shrouded in mist. Now and then someone leaves or arrives, but very little disturbs the quiet geometry of the street. There are a few men in three-piece suits, a young woman in faded jeans, a bearded, shaggy-looking young man in a down jacket. It is as if the air has been soundproofed.

I am here because this is the kind of place where computer-science majors work after they graduate.

I can go as far as an entry lobby on my own recognizance, and then a receptionist dials Chuck, a systems engineer who was one of the recruiters at Ohio State that rainy week. Chuck got his own master's degree at OSU eight years ago and remains his company's ambassador to the university's computer-science department. On that last trip, he recruited six new people for this project. But now he is back in Southern California and I am waiting for him to come down to the lobby.

"Are you ready for lunch or do you want to look around first?" says a voice above me. I finally locate the voice as coming from a futuristic mezzanine overhead. A minute later Chuck materializes in the lobby, dressed in jeans, a terry shirt, and a very good-looking leather jacket that never comes off. (I learn later that the jacket is not an affectation. The computer room is kept at about sixty degrees because heat damages the silicon chips.)

Over a Chinese lunch, he tells me what it's like to work at Tronics. The fact that he can take as long as he likes for lunch tells me even more. "We have no dress codes and no set hours. As long as you get the job done, you work when you want to. There's pressure, but most people don't mind. They're turned on by what they do. We don't have any of the famous Silicon Valley perks here, but there's a ski club, a volleyball club, a skin-diving club, and a lot of parties."

He lists all these with practiced ease. It is the pitch he has made to dozens of potential recruits on his annual trip back to Ohio. His project needs ten new people as "technical staff," the entry-level professional position. And they will be wresting all ten from the jaws of other, more aggressive companies. "We interviewed fifty people and forty passed muster. The ones we rejected came off too flat and unresponsive in the interview. But most of the ones we want will have other offers. We'll be getting the ones with GPA's between 2.8—our lowest—and 3.4. We're too laid back to get the ones with the really high GPA's."

So the people at this facility are the happy medium, the norm in the profession. They are not the geniuses or the baby millionaires but the representative mainstream. As such, they provide a valuable glimpse into the industry that dominates both the economy and imagination of the eighties. They give us a chance to find out how their world works and how good their lives really are.

"Mostly we recruit from the California campuses and the Midwest: OSU, Purdue, Michigan, Illinois, Carnegie Mellon," Chuck continues. We try to sell them on California, which is both a sales point and a liability. They like the climate and it sounds glamorous, but a lot of them don't want to get close, partly because housing is so high here.

"One year, when we were having trouble hiring, I took the list of everyone I interviewed and called them up. Thirty percent wanted to get out of Ohio and go anywhere, and the rest wanted to stay because they had ties there."

That, by the way, is about as close as high tech gets to scientific personnel practice. Although Chuck and his counterparts in other companies have made a profession of developing sophisticated, logical systems, their approach to hiring is as personal and random as the garment industry's. High-tech jobs are gotten through a network of contacts. Sometimes a staffer has a friend or classmate who wants to move on, and he passes on the résumé. Mostly, Chuck and other veterans take time out from their own work every year and go back to the schools where they got their degrees. They "maintain a relationship with that department." For instance, on his last trip, Chuck presented the OSU department with a three-thousand-dollar contribution from Tronics. They hear about candidates for degrees, they interview them on campus, and if all goes well, fly them out to the site to meet the rest of the work group. But a letter and a résumé from a 4.0 student at MIT or Cal Tech would probably go unanswered. More likely, it would go unread. "It is too much trouble to go to the personnel office and leaf through paper and then phone or write and fly the person out."

This is still a young industry, impatient with procedures and amenities. I ask him what matters most to potential hires. "The question they ask most is 'What do I do?' The most important thing to job candidates is the kind of work they will do. They want technical challenges."

The offices that house this project are a maze of cubicles and work bays, all equipped with computer terminals. The carpeting is gray, the ceilings are soundproof, and it all seems clean, even when the desks—like Chuck's—are cluttered with interoffice memorandums and manuals. Staffers lower on the hierarchy have almost no paper at all around. Everything they need is in the computer. The men are mostly in jeans or khakis, but the young women tend to dress more formally, in silk or linen blouses and skirts. I suspect that they just like to.

The atmosphere seems relaxed, casual, as if this were a university lab with decor. The difference here is that a visitor has to be escorted everywhere, even to the bathroom, because this is a high-security government project. Chuck, who is my escort, searches out people for me to meet. I have asked for young employees, recently out of school. He sticks his head in doors to see who is available. As far as I can tell, the selection is random. A drill evolves. Chuck sets me up with an interviewee and then returns to his own office. When the interview is over, the young staffer accompanies me back to Chuck's office. And we start all over.

The first one, a chunky, studious-looking Asian woman, agrees to be interviewed and then suddenly changes her mind after the first, innocuous question. She is a private person, she explains. "The thought of talking about myself makes the hackles rise on the back of my neck." Chuck conjectures that she is nervous about security checks, and I begin to wonder how the rest of the day will go. Is this a paranoid, tight-lipped industry? I needn't have worried. The young woman with the risen hackles, it seemed, had problems that were entirely her own. All of the others were like young people everywhere—quite happy that someone was interested in them.

Twenty-three-year-old Marla has been at Tronics for a year and a half, since she graduated from the University of Illinois with a major in computer science. She is in the field for practical reasons. She doesn't love computer work, and she is aware that in choosing security, she gave up certain kinds of excitement. "I was always math oriented," she explains, "and when I was in high school, I saw an article in the paper about computers being the career of the future. I wasn't exactly fascinated in college. Computer science was very theoretical. But I went into it for the opportunity. I thought, 'It will pay off.' "

She is married to her high school boyfriend, a graphic artist, and they came to California because he had a job offer here. "I had a lot of offers," she says frankly.

Her practicality, Marla says, comes from her immigrant parents. It is a subject she has given a lot of thought to. "They always stressed money— too much so at times." She grew up in a suburb of Chicago and her parents owned a retail clothing store. They are now retired, but her mother still works part-time in another shop "because she can't sit still. They wanted me to have an easier life than they did. And it's my nature to want to be independent. In my mind, money equals independence. And money always has strings attached. There was always pressure on me to do well in school because that meant a good job and money."

It was assumed that she would be a professional. Her only sister is a teacher. "My parents don't understand what I do, but they are pleased that I'm doing well." It is the way things used to be, thirty years ago, when a lot more of us were first generation Americans and our parents remembered the Depression. Children grew up knowing that they had to find a useful place for themselves in the world, and if they had marketable talents, they put them to work.

But are people like Marla happy? The answer, I suppose, is more or less, considering the circumstances. She likes her work but readily admits that "I don't see myself here forever." The good thing is that she doesn't have to be. Since they have been in California, her husband has gone into medical graphics and learned computers on the job. "We'd like to start a computer graphics business of our own. He has no strength in math. I'd like to learn graphics. But I'm confused right now about how to go about it. Should I go into management and learn those skills or should I acquire more technical knowledge?" These seem to me to be good questions rather than the questions of a confused person. But people who have been very focused all of their lives have little practice in dealing with ambiguity.

She makes no bones about the fact that computers are her work, not her life. She is not taking graduate courses in computer science because "it would infringe on my time too much." What she wants is more time with her husband and time to read for pleasure instead of for technical

182 THE POSTPONED GENERATION

information. "Also, I like to write poetry," she says matter-of-factly. These work bays are full of surprises.

She and her husband live in an apartment located between both jobs, and she has a forty-five minute commute every morning. "Our social life is humdrum," she says. "It's not as easy to meet people as when we were in school. Everyone is too busy, including ourselves. And it's hard to socialize when you live so far from the people you work with."

She would like children eventually, but can't say when. "We have to postpone that for economic and career reasons." But they do hope to buy a home of their own as soon as possible. "We're anxious to come up with the money by next year. If we don't, we face a big tax bite."

Relatively speaking, it is a nice problem for a twenty-three-year-old.

Beth is a very pretty, slender blonde, properly turned out for the office in plaid skirt, silk shirt, dark pumps. She is twenty-seven and has been at Tronics for four and a half years—since she graduated from the University of California, Irvine, where she was a math major. Comfortably traditional, she too has practical immigrant parents. But she is luckier than Marla. She doesn't write poetry or have any inchoate longings. She has found exactly what she wants here at Tronics.

For one thing, she learned about computers here. "The logic is a lot like math. I've taken a few computer courses since then, but each job is different, and it's best to learn it on the job."

Math and science were always her strong subjects at school. "English was my worst. It's really important for engineers because we need basics in writing. The hardest thing for us is describing and communicating what we are doing or what we want to others. My writing isn't bad. It was the creative writing that I didn't like. I didn't mind research papers. My strengths were always numbers and writing."

Beth grew up in Orange County and went to public high schools. Her parents were both born in Germany; her father, now retired, was an accountant, and her mother was a bookkeeper, so she feels that she comes by her affinity for numbers naturally.

But throughout college, she had no idea how she would use her education afterward. "School is so isolated," she reflects now. "It offers no ideas about what jobs are available. In my senior year, I researched the job possibilities for math majors. The math club had career lectures, but the department didn't tell us about these opportunities. Mostly, I just worried about getting my degree. I took things like chemistry because I liked it."

She graduated from college in 1979, the worst of the recession, and was warned that, despite her 3.9 grade point average, she would have to sell herself on the job market. But it was the peak of the engineering boom, and before she could work up a résumé, she had four job offers.

Was she just lucky then that she was in the right field at the right time? Partly. If she had been, say, a history major who waited until her senior year to check out the job possibilities in her field, she might well have come up empty. But I suspect that Beth always understood, subliminally at least, that math majors don't go hungry. "I had always wanted to be in a field that would make me employable," she says, revealing a practical turn of mind. "I was brought up to work hard, to get a good job. My parents are very practical and ambitious."

Her husband, an electrical engineer whom she met at college, also works for Tronics. He started at another large aerospace company, but she convinced him that Tronics was a much better company. "It's good to its people and treats us professionally. We set our own hours. We have noontime exercise classes right here. And there are other perks."

She would like to have children, but feels she couldn't stay home all day. "On the other hand, I wouldn't like the pressure of a full-time job. I'd like to work part-time, and you can do that here if you have a good reputation. The project might not be so interesting, but what I mainly want is to be out of the house and have the social life of the office."

She would like to own a home, since she grew up in one. Right now, she has to work just to keep up the payments on their condo. "If we want to buy a house, my husband will have to get promoted and we will have to make good investments."

She has never done drugs or serious drinking. She goes to church occasionally, out of tradition rather than feeling. She swims, jogs, plays tennis, and works out regularly at a health club. She sews and she bakes.

Karin is a classic beauty—tall, with an arrowlike waist, tawny hair, and translucent skin. She is elegantly dressed in an interesting dark-red linen blouse and navy skirt.

She is twenty-five, and she has been with Tronics for three and a half years. Now an assistant manager, she started as a programmer.

She too was a math major—at Vanderbilt University in Nashville— and she too has German parents. In fact, German was her first language. Perhaps it is just an inherited gift for math that brings so many children of Germans to this company. But I suspect that there is another reason. The children of immigrants feel less secure, less entitled, and therefore are more likely to make sensible choices.

Karin's father is an aerospace engineer for NASA in Huntsville, Alabama, where she grew up. Her mother never worked outside the home, perhaps because she was timid about being foreign and speaking English imperfectly.

"I never got any clear message from my parents about working or being independent." They stressed academics more than careers, thinking that one naturally led to the other. Karin majored in math because she liked it. "I wasn't being practical and I didn't have anything specific in mind. I've since found that computer logic is like math." And yet, she confesses, "I've always known that I'd be in engineering and work for a company like this."

She is married, to a resident in surgery whom she met at college. Both of them liked Southern California and decided to look for jobs here. Tronics offered her part-time work while she went to graduate school in computer science at UCLA, where she met her first computer.

Unlike most of her peers, she can have the American Dream now. She and her husband have just bought a house in an expensive beach community. "It's a quarter of a million dollars, and we are heavily in debt. I know that we were approved for the loan because my husband is a doctor." She plans to have children, but doesn't want them raised by someone else, so she and her husband hope to arrange a split work schedule. "I don't want to just drop out and stay home for a few years because the field is changing so rapidly that it would make me nervous." She is confident that this company—or some other company—would be amenable to her split schedule. Life in high tech offers a lot of options.

Mark isn't a numbers person. Five years ago, he was teaching social studies at a high school in Queens. He is now twenty-nine and a program designer. "I work on man-machine interface," he explains. "I'm one of the few people here who does better in verbal tests than in math."

He got into computer work because it was where the jobs were. He had been bounced around a bit, and he learned that he had no magic protection from reality. So he decided to be practical. He is also interesting to us because he is an outsider, not really an engineer in talent or temperament, and he is trying—with considerable if less than perfect success— to make it work.

He is from Brooklyn; his mother is a librarian, and his father, now retired, owned a delicatessen on the West Side of Manhattan. When he graduated from Brooklyn College, he did what college graduates used to do: He started teaching. This was 1977, and he was earning ten thousand dollars a year. He liked it well enough, but after two years, he was laid off because of budget cuts.

"I realized that there was no future in teaching and it was time to get into something with prospects." He had taken a few computer courses and enjoyed them, and his brother worked for Tronics in New Mexico. So he went off to New Mexico State in Las Cruces and lived with his brother while he got another bachelor's degree in computer science and twelve credits toward his master's. Two and half years later, he began work for Tronics in Las Cruces and was soon transferred to another project in Socorro.

As a bachelor, he found it lonely in that remote community. But the job allowed him to keep in touch with some of the people he met on trips and at conferences. "There's a network in this business. The section heads and department heads take care of us." Within a short time, he landed his present job in Southern California.

He is very glad that he left teaching. For one thing, he is making more money. He started at twenty thousand dollars a year and now earns twenty-nine thousand after three years and a promotion from programmer to designer. But mostly he feels that "teaching was a dead end. There was no change or growth and the bureaucracy was stifling. Teachers aren't appreciated or considered professional," he says, echoing the women who also left human services jobs. "For instance, we had to punch time cards. Here, we're respected. The days are different from each other, and I have a sense of progress rather than stagnation. And I feel different about myself. I'm appreciated, I get a pat on the back once in a while. I think most of us feel that way. You can see progress in the work. It's visual."

But he feels that teaching has been a help to him. He can verbalize his thoughts, make points, and do presentations, things that numbers people often have difficulty with. "I conduct a presentation just like a lesson in the classroom."

He has only a few complaints. Housing is expensive in Southern California. He would like to own a home, and he also misses the East and the change of seasons.

His problem may solve itself. The high cost of real estate—both housing and office space—is in fact one of the reasons why Tronics is gradually moving its operations to other parts of the country. His project may move to Washington, D.C., and he would like to move with it. He also finds that teachers and New Yorkers are more social, more gregarious, more aware of the world than his present colleagues.

"I'd like to marry and have a family, but it's hard to meet people here. I go to a lot of parties, but there's something very isolated about L.A. The company is that way too. I mean, I'd never know if we were at war until I went home and watched the news. Teachers always listened to the radio during free periods or lunch breaks and major news got around. But here things are very enclosed, isolated."

Since Mark isn't one of the mathematical/scientific types, he has less independence and tends to see his future with the company. He would like to work his way up in management. The career steps for him are programmer, designer (his present job), manager, section head, department head, software project manager, assistant project manager, and project manager. "The company likes you to move up into the managerial ranks," he explains. "They expect it, in fact."

Because I am curious about what life holds for these young people ten years down the road, I ask Chuck—who is thirty-eight—about his own career. He also introduces me to Alex, who is forty-one and also a systems engineer/software developer. The two men are interesting and worth including in a book about young adults because they tell us not only where these young people may be going but where the field has been and how it is changing.

Alex is where it came from. He learned about computers before universities all had computer science departments. This now sounds primordial but it was only the mid-sixties.

He was a cadet at the Naval Academy at Annapolis when he fell in love with computers. He used the office machine to do ballistic missile equations. "It was just a calculator function, but I always knew it could do more."

What happened next is one of the great stories of the technology revolution. Alex never graduated from Annapolis. "The navy and I had a falling out. They're usually pretty anxious to have you go on to graduate school. I wanted to go to graduate school in computers, but they wouldn't allow that because they couldn't see what use the military would have for computers." This was 1965, and he swears that it is a true story. I have told it to several Navy men I know, and they smile. "Sounds like the navy," said one.

"They thought those things were just calculators, good for the payroll," says Alex. "All they cared about were guns and boilers. It wasn't until the seventies that they saw the value of high tech." But Alex was the old style, high-tech radical, a true believer. He left Annapolis without a degree and went looking for a job that would provide an opportunity to learn about the new machines. "In those days, the company that hired you to work with their computers sent you to a course conducted by the manufacturers. There was very little formal education then."

His first job was with Blue Cross Insurance, where he spent a year and a half. "I was greedy. I learned all they could teach me and I didn't stay." He did the same thing in stints at RCA and four or five other jobs. He would spend a year or so, learn all he could, and then move on to someplace that could teach him more. He landed at Tronics ten years ago and has been there ever since. "I've never had to look for a job, and I've always been well paid. I still love what I do, and it's getting even better." Despite his long sojourn at Tronics, his loyalty isn't to any company but to what he's doing. He stays because "there are lots of good projects within this company."

But he likes the luxury of independence. "You don't have to deal with the problems of making a living. In high tech, there's always another job. I've been with five or six companies and every conference I go to, I meet people I know and have worked with. When I want a job, I just call friends. It's a family."

If there is a problem in this kind of work, it is the middle-age career crisis. Technically young people seem to be better and more enthusiastic engineers. Alex admits that computer people do their best work when they are in their twenties and thirties. "I did better work when I was younger," he says, undisturbed. He seems to have made his peace with this fact, and he is ready for the middle-aged man's role in this business— as manager or coordinator, as the overseer of the brilliant young technicians. "Now, I get paid to deal with problems that can't be handled by the young geniuses. There are a lot of parts to the puzzle. The younger guy gets separate problems. I make sure the right decisions are being made on all the pieces.

"Maybe that's why these young people put so much time into their outside interests—hiking, skiing, sailing. The work is narrow. A businessman has a variety of activities and contacts on the job, but here people talk high tech eight or ten hours a day."

Alex also tells me about another type in the high-tech cast of characters—the nomad. A nomad is not a guy like himself who follows the interesting projects around the country. The high-tech nomad is an engineer who works for a year, saves his money, and travels around the world, usually to exotic places. "They even have these newsletters about things like where to live cheap in Nepal. They come back when they run out of money. Then they call and ask for a job, and there's always one waiting." Tronics, he says, has two nomads but they're not here right now. I call him some months later, and there still aren't any around, and no one else I ask knows of any. Perhaps they are just a myth, the opposite and counterpart of the unhappy square peg in the round hole.

While we are on the subject of mythology, I suppose I should also mention that there is a rumor at Tronics that Alex, who is a very respectable-looking man with short brown hair and frame glasses, was once a hippie in Haight-Ashbury. He just smiles when I mention this. It tells us the space he occupies in the sociogram. He is an original computer freak, and by now the field has evolved, to become conventional and corporate. Everyone has advanced degrees now. Alex is an eccentric, a relic from the distant past, which in high tech is ten years ago.

Chuck is more like an older version of the young staffers he hires. He was practical, not a high-tech adventurer. And unlike Alex, he has not resolved the crisis of the middle-aged engineer. He likes tinkering, but it's time now to leave that to the new people and move up. But moving up means management, and that sounds, well, middle-aged.

Chuck grew up in a semi-rural suburb of Chicago, where his father was a carpenter and his mother, a secretary. He was good in math, and in high school he wanted to be a math teacher. "But my mother was a realist and she told me that teachers didn't make enough money." Chuck evidently was also a realist; he dropped the idea.

His parents were not very education-minded, but he went to a tiny private college in Wisconsin. He started out as a math major, but found it too abstract and switched to physics, which also had few practical applications. He liked his math and science on a tinkering level. When the school bought a small computer for payroll and grades, science majors were allowed to use it when it wasn't otherwise occupied. This too was 1965, when the navy and Alex were coming to a parting of the ways. Chuck fiddled with the machine, but still had no idea what he wanted to do with his life.

So after graduation, he joined the air force, which generously gave its recruits a choice of occupation and area. Chuck asked for a technical field and the Southwest, which was much nicer at the time than Vietnam. He was sent to New Mexico where he programmed computers for seat belts, air bag studies, and missile testing. In 1973, his duty to his country done in this safe and interesting way, he went to graduate school in computer science at Ohio State. Two years later he went to work for Tronics as a member of the technical staff. That was eight years ago. He now earns fifty-two thousand dollars a year and drives a white BMW with red leather seats. Like Alex, his job concerns have shifted from the merely technical problems. "As you get older, you have the more realistic concerns—budgets and schedules. Am I spending too much money? Will I get it done on time?"

He is still single, and I guess that he is a little restless. "I'm at a crossroads," he admits. "There are no new faces here except for the new hires, and they're twenty-two years old." He would like to spend some time in Europe, where the company has operations. "The projects there aren't very interesting or important. I would just like the personal change." He applied for one opening, but his present salary is far more than the job merits. "I wouldn't mind going into some computer-related business of my own. The company encourages us to go into management. It sort of expects us to. It doesn't turn me on. I don't want to count beans all day."

It seems as if now—at thirty-eight—he is asking questions about what he would like to do with the rest of his life. He is just one person, not Every Engineer, yet he raises a question about the future of the bright twenty-five-year-olds in his department. Perhaps because life is so easy when they are young and just out of school, they don't do quite enough adolescent wondering. Self-exploration remains a bit of unfinished business that they get to in mid-life.

On the other hand, it is not so bad to wonder where your life is headed when your options include a job in Europe, a management spot at home, and starting your own computer software business.

At the end of the day, as the work bays and cubicles are slowly emptying, I offer to buy him a drink. "A drink sounds fine," he says, "but nobody has to buy." He shuffles through the papers on his desk and comes up with a mimeographed sheet. "Let's see where today's party is," he mutters, holding up what turns out to be an invitation. After-work parties are part of the culture at Tronics. They keep people in the fold long after the faces and the technical work aren't new anymore. They remind them that they belong, that they're part of the high-tech elect.

I follow him to a tract house on a treelined street in a suburb about fifteen minutes from the office. It is a nice, fifties-style tract house with a lot of wood paneling, disproportionately large because it has been added on to several times by the owner. There are phones everywhere, of all sizes and styles. Buying them at yard sales and installing them is one of the owner's hobbies. He too, it seems, is a tinkerer. There are crackers and cheese and corn chips and dips and franks in barbecue sauce on the dining-room table, but everyone seems to be in the kitchen with pretzels and a bottle of Carlo Rossi wine, hovering around the built-in electric range. It is not just the house that has a fifties feel.

The party is in honor of an engineer who used to be on their project. He is passing through Southern California on his way back to Saipan, where he now works. I speak briefly with the guest of honor, and he tells me that he is in Saipan as a result of a dare. A friend of his wife's is a headhunter, and he always told her that she could place him if she could find him a job on an island in the South Pacific. She did. He now manages the data processing for the trust territory government and loves it. When he stops loving it, he will come back.

This is an older crowd at first, mainly secretaries and office managers. The engineers trickle in later, having stayed behind to finish up just one more thing. One of them—a recent transplant from New Jersey and still in love with his work—is supposed to meet his wife here. "She's a dentist," he explains. "When we're at parties together, people sort of yawn when she tells them what she does. But when I tell them that I'm building a computer-operated ground station, they gaze in wonder."

Mark, the teacher turned programmer, is one of the last to arrive. Perhaps he has been at another party first. He is with a young woman colleague, and he circulates tentatively for a while. He doesn't stay long, probably because he has noticed the absence of unattached young women.

I leave a little later. It is now eight o'clock, but the party is still going strong. They have begun to talk shop and no one is in any hurry to leave.

13
Business Kids

Slightly amused, he peers out at us from behind heavy, plastic-frame glasses. He seems to be wondering why he is on the cover of *Time* in his V-necked sweater and rumpled button-down shirt, open at the collar. Perhaps it is the pose that he finds funny. A floppy disk is magically balanced on one corner of his index finger. The disk, of course, is a symbolic explanation of why he is on the cover of *Time*. He is Bill Gates, chairman and co-founder of Microsoft, a computer software company whose 1984 revenues, according to *Time*, were one hundred million dollars.

Time also estimates Gates's personal worth at a hundred million dollars and tells us he has a $750,000 home with a thirty-foot indoor swimming pool and a view of Lake Washington. Gates is twenty-eight years old.

Of all the things that computers have contributed to this generation, one of the more significant must be the image of the new breed of business-man, the under-thirty entrepreneur who became a millionaire on his own. High-tech enterprises, especially software, required brains but very little capital investment—a few machines and a garage to work in. It was a business in which a graduate student—or a college dropout—with a good idea could become a millionaire virtually overnight.

Bill Gates is a hero for our time. Just when large organizations—major corporations, universities, government—stopped hiring and even started firing as part of the lean, mean approach of the eighties, we have a vision of a head unbowed, someone who isn't shining his shoes and kowtowing to his boss to keep his job, someone independent, even eccentric, *getting rich on his own.* The new hero came from high tech, but he spread to other fields like ink on a dry blotter. Young adults who couldn't find jobs began a romance with entrepreneurship, and it didn't have to be in high tech. *Business* was no longer the office, with its coffee machine and overdue reports and clacking typewriters. It was now a world of high adventure, of moves and countermoves, of macho plays and hardball. It was a glamorous world of expensive suits in power colors, sometimes worn with running shoes (a perfect symbol of the athletic new business personality), and American Express cards and sudden plane trips to distant cities.

This new businessperson was not a company man, a functionary loyally shuffling papers or working a territory till it was time to retire. He was self-propelled and blatantly self-interested, and he approached what he did as if it were the Big Game and he were the quarterback. He had strategies and tactics. He bought books on power lunching and learned to eat raw steak. And more and more often, he was a she. For women were breaking into the business world in record numbers, and they talked just as much about playing hardball and wielding power, even when what they were actually doing was retail sales or secretarial work glorified by another title, like executive assistant.

The hot new degree became the master's in business administration. The M.B.A. programs became so popular that the more prestigious ones stopped admitting students right after college graduation. They had to have "significant business experience" first so that they "brought something to the table." Undergraduate business departments became impacted as eighteen-year-olds eagerly signed up for a future in making money. In 1966, 11.6 percent of entering freshmen planned to major in business. In 1982, the percentage had risen to 20.2. Similarly, 38,900 bachelor's degrees in business were conferred in 1975. By 1980, the number had soared to 61,600. In the past few years, the value of the M.B.A. has fluctuated downward slightly as corporations question whether the degree is worth the salary it commands. But it is still very much the degree to get.

Much of this change was clearly practical. Learning for its own sake is a privilege of fatter times. Yet necessity seems to create its own myths. Some business majors—those who specialized in finance or accounting— had indeed made a practical choice. But those who studied softer business subjects, like marketing and business administration, turned out to be among the least employable of college graduates. According to a Chicago *Sun Times* series examining the "job gap" (the widespread underemployment of the nation's college graduates), majors in business administration and marketing were among those least likely to be in college-level jobs three years after graduation. Just 42.9 percent of them were in jobs that required their degrees; only communications (journalism) majors fared worse. And in Michigan State University's Placement Services survey of the 1984 job market, starting salaries for marketing and business administration majors were in the bottom half of a list topped by engineers.

Perhaps these young people, like the Humphrey Bogart character who came to Casablanca for the waters, were just misinformed. I think they were also caught up in the blossoming romanticization of business. When they couldn't get jobs or when the jobs they got turned out to be dead ends, they started thinking about going off on their own. Publications like *Venture: The Magazine for Entrepreneurs* and *Inc.: The Magazine for Growing Companies* started to appear on the newsstands. There were feature stories on small businesses that prospered and service pieces on how to buy software or choose a bank. Mainly, they conveyed a sense of excitement about small business. The big stories were profiles of successful entrepreneurs, often pictured schussing down the ski slopes or standing, arms akimbo, on a hill covered with scrub oak.

The highest calling in this brave new world was to be a risk-taker, to leave the security of the company and become an *entrepreneur*.

"There's no definition for that word," says Tom Omalia, a financial consultant who teaches in the University of Southern California's Entrepreneur Program. "The entrepreneur is the one who makes things happen." Of course, there is a definition for the word. *The Concise Oxford Dictionary* offers "Person in effective control of commercial undertaking; contractor acting as intermediary." The word also has a certain resonance. If you say it quickly, it sounds a little like "intrepid." It has a definite panache, and it is unlikely to be used by the owners of mom and pop grocery stores, at least for a while.

A good many of the young people coming out of business schools these days think of themselves as entrepreneurs. They were inspired by the glamour of the high-tech millionaires and the subsequent portrayal of the businessperson as the Lone Ranger. They had to live with the fact that large corporations, once the employer of choice for college graduates, were no longer offering jobs, security, or opportunity for advancement. They might give you a job after college, but middle management positions were disappearing and top management spots and partnerships were distant stars.

Moreover, these young people weren't cut out to be cogs in the corporate wheel. They are all former special children, brought up in the culture of individualism. And when they found themselves approaching adulthood in a buyer's employment market, they longed for some sense of control over their lives and a way to be unique again.

Entrepreneurship is a way of adapting to the eighties. It is not a romance as much as it is a way of coping with lowered expectations. In ways, it works, but it is an adaptation, not a custom fit, and life isn't as easy for these young people as it is for the high-tech professionals. Unlike the engineers, they are not the keepers of the keys to the modern kingdom, and their lives are tenser, more ambiguous. Unlike Bill Gates, they have to worry about how they look and what they wear. They have to work hard, not because they have an obsessive fascination with a problem they must solve, but often at unrequited drudgery. Most of them live lives that are far more anxiety-ridden than glamorous. They have adopted a way of life that is not so much maturing as just aging. Personal growth isn't part of the business agenda. All that matters is the bottom line, in dollars and cents. It is an ideology utterly at odds with their history and with the sense of entitlement of their generation. For some of them, it is a confusing and intense struggle, and the way they are working it out is changing the social landscape.

Some of the young entrepreneurs start out by working for large companies, but think of themselves as either in training for the day when they will go out on their own or as independent contractors using the company as a facility. Others leap right into the fire of their own enterprises. Some of them were born to be in business; they were the eight-year-old kids who picked their neighbors' trees and sold the peaches. Others had to learn it as adults. Some of them are fiercely realistic, and others live in fantasy, just like their peers who aren't in business.

Mike is twenty-nine, and he is not floundering or drifting, like some of his peers. He is a stockbroker with the Los Angeles office of a large Wall Street brokerage firm. But he does have a sense of entitlement, to a life that is materially comfortable, adventurous, but also spiritually fulfilling. He is learning that he will have to earn it with hard work. It will not be handed to him on the basis of his impressive résumé. To his considerable credit, he has accepted that reality.

He has been with his firm for less than a year, since he got his M.B.A. in finance. Before that, he was an accountant with a Big Eight firm for four years. He left that because it was too limiting.

Mike was the kind of kid who thought about money. The trick to making it, he learned early, was to position yourself right. Leave the drudgery to others. When he was in junior high in Memphis, he had the best paper route in the city. He didn't work it particularly hard. "It was just a great route because it had all the high rise apartment houses." He had spotted it as the best route, and he got himself into position to get it by filling in for someone who was on vacation.

It paid off well. "At sixteen, I could have bought a new car for cash. I didn't. Instead, I bought a used car and saved money for college." He kept such meticulous records on the route that everyone thought he had to be an accountant. He gave up the paper route only because something better came along. He got a job as a checker in a supermarket, where, thanks to union scale, "I made three times as much money as a kid should. My parents complained that families couldn't buy milk and here was this kid who was paid so much."

He went to Memphis State, where he belonged to a fraternity and majored in accounting, as everyone thought he should. He interned with a Big Eight firm, knowing that internships were part of positioning. When he graduated, the Big Eight firm offered him a job in Memphis and in Los Angeles. He accepted the Los Angeles spot, knowing that he could always come back to Memphis.

"Accounting was great experience," he explains, "but it wasn't stimulating enough. I prepared a lot of information, but I couldn't use it." He was one of the accountants for a company involved in a famous and disastrous shareholder lawsuit, and he worked seven days a week, most days from eight in the morning until eleven at night. "It was a lot of pressure, but it was fascinating. I don't regret doing it."

What he did mind was his powerlessness. "As an accountant, I knew a lot, prepared a lot of information, but I couldn't make money on what I knew. I couldn't even buy stock in clients' companies. I knew more about the company being sued by its shareholders than any analyst, but I couldn't even discuss it with other accountants in the office."

Frustrated, he decided to retool, and he went back to school full-time. He had loved college and decided that he wanted the campus experience again. "I felt that going part-time would hurt my work performance and my schoolwork." He had savings and a fellowship, enough for unruffled enjoyment of the academic environment, made even sweeter by his years out in the real world. "I would never have gotten as much out of graduate school without the work experience. I could sit in class and say to the professor, 'This is what happened at the such-and-such company. It was a real advantage."

His work experience also turned out to be an advantage when he was ready to look for a job. "I got fifty interviews," he says modestly. "I took this job because it's a good springboard position. It looks good on my résumé. This is a keystone job, and the name of the firm will benefit me. I don't intend to leave soon, but very few brokers stay and become partners. My attitude is, I'm in business for myself. I watch out for myself. Technically, I'm an employee. But really, I'm a one-man corporation. What I sell is my expertise, my knowledge." He doesn't envision being technically on his own. "I need the office, the research, the secretaries that a big firm provides. But I couldn't be with one company for years. I would get bored."

His job is to sell stocks, bonds, options, and tax shelters to individuals and small corporations. "But I don't push product. I'm a businessman, and I think of myself as a professional adviser to other businessmen, like a lawyer or accountant. What I'd like to be able to do with clients is sit down at lunch and say, 'What do you need? An investment, a tax shelter? Let's talk about your needs.' "

Right now, he is just starting out, and he is a long way from two-drink lunches with a string of regular clients. "I'm discovering the difference between sales and accounting," he explains. "As an accountant, the client needed me and he knew it. Now I have to prospect, be aggressive instead of passive." What that means is that he makes cold calls from lists of potential clients. Mostly, they don't return his calls. "I'm just a voice on the phone, and it's frustrating." He is on salary for his first eighteen months, and he is earning less than he was as an accountant. He hopes that by the time he is thirty-five, he will have a strong client base and deal only with his own clients and referrals. But right now he is spelling his name for secretaries.

He works a long day, starting soon after the opening of the New York market at six-thirty in the morning, Los Angeles time. He usually leaves the office at four to work out at the gym and then returns at six or seven to make evening calls to prospects who can't be reached during the day. But on weekends and vacations, he treats himself well. He has been to Europe and traveled around the United States, and he hikes, skis, and rides his bike along the beach. He loves living in California, and though he misses his family and friends, he seldom longs for Memphis. "It's hot, flat, and it has no beach."

He is on most counts a contented bachelor. He lives in a rented apartment in a neighborhood where there are a lot of other single people in rental apartments, popping Stouffers in the Toast-R-Oven in the evenings and taking their shirts to the laundry on Saturdays. But about a year ago, it began to feel somehow less complete. "My life was *me, me, me.* It was all about what *I* wanted, and what *I* was doing. But I guess I was looking for something else, and about six or eight months ago, I saw an item in the church bulletin about the detention ministry—volunteering at juvenile hall."

He now spends two evenings a week and Sundays at juvenile hall, visiting with young detainees, offering friendship, counsel, and the benefit of his example. It has been satisfying work. During those visits, he met one of the other volunteers, a pretty, dark-haired young woman who is a college senior and a psychology major. They have been seeing each other for the past two months. She plans to do youth ministry work as her profession, and he finds that the relationship with her adds balance to his life. "Linda doesn't know the prime rate from prime beef, and I like that. When I was in graduate school, I had a girlfriend who would call me up to talk about an article in *The Wall Street Journal.*"

Linda's interests, he explains, are not so much more feminine as more humanistic. They are considering marriage, but not right away. "I have too many other things to do. I need to be financially settled, settled with clients. Being a two-income couple is great if your wife is an attorney or a C.P.A. But Linda won't make a lot of money. But I'm a firm believer in doing what's right for you. I could have made more money as an analyst, but I wanted to work with people and their investments because it's more varied."

If he and Linda do marry, they will be a slightly modernized version of his own parents. His mother worked "until the children came along. Then my dad laid down the law." Since then she has been an active volunteer, especially in the church.

Mike is a traditional young man in many ways. He is religious and responsible, and he wants a marriage like his parents. Yet even he is struggling with role models. In certain ways, he has to break away from the past and be different from his father. The times are different. His father accepted life's burdens with few questions. Mike feels entitled to much more. At twenty-nine, he has changed professions and he is ready to change jobs as opportunity strikes. He wants to see the world. He would like to own a home, as his parents do, but only because he hates paying rent. "It's money thrown away." He wants the equity more than a place to raise a family. "A condo would be fine," he says. He would like to have children, but, again, someday, not right away. He is thinking about marriage, but he is not quite ready.

By contrast, his parents married at twenty-one, and his father worked for the same life insurance company for twenty years, his only job after leaving the Marine Corps. So his father doesn't entirely approve of him. "My dad is someone you can never please, no matter what you do. He wishes I were in Memphis. He doesn't know why I left a good job in accounting. He has a Depression-era mentality. I explained to him that I work hard so I can play hard."

I ask him who he thinks was more mature at this age, himself or his father. He is the one interviewee who answers without hesitation. "My father. Absolutely. I ride a bike and go to the beach. I'm horsing around. He had the responsibility of a family."

The reception lobby at a firm we'll call "Crane and Scott" has wall-to-wall carpeting in a dark green and bone pattern. It is not the kind of thick, foam-cushioned carpeting that your shoes sink into with each step. It is fine quality wool that doesn't show wear or footprints. The furniture and the wall paneling are dull-finished oak, and solid but unobtrusive. The large oil portraits of the firm's founders are in dark brass frames. It all speaks of solidity, experience, and money.

Crane and Scott is, in fact, an old firm and a prosperous one. This lobby is in one of the many regional offices of a nationwide consulting empire that provides business advice for organizations all over the country. This office, however, is fairly new, despite the turn-of-the-century tradition suggested by the decor. And the advice given by the consultants is often to computerize, modernize, get rid of dead weight and outmoded procedures.

Those who give such advice, of course, must seem impeccably conservative and reliable. Robin steps through one of the heavy oak doors that are barely discernible breaks in the wall paneling and enters the corridor off the lobby. She is a pretty young woman with short, wheat-colored hair, even features, and clear skin untouched by makeup. She wears a dark-gray wool suit, an Oxford shirt with a maroon stock tie, and low-heeled black pumps. She wears no jewelry, except for a small gold ring. In this context, she doesn't look unduly severe. She seems instead natural, composed, centered on her low-heeled shoes, thoughtful, and trustworthy. It is exactly the note the decorator was trying to strike, but it is not a decorator look.

She speaks in the nicely modulated, unaccented tones of an educated, upper-middle-class professional woman accustomed to considering her words carefully. She would seem perfectly at ease and in control if it weren't for the way she shreds bits of paper into fierce little pieces.

Robin is twenty-seven and a senior consultant at Crane and Scott, where she has been for almost two years. She has an M.B.A. in accounting and information systems and she is also a C.P.A., a title she just earned a month ago. Like Mike, she is a business adviser who sells her skills, and she is beginning to think of herself as a business entity, rather than a company employee. She likes that. But she is finding that success in business is all-consuming, draining, and she is starting to question her goals. She wants the big brass ring, but she has discovered that she also wants inner growth. And at the same time, she is dealing with what it means to be a woman in business. The corporate world is designed for men, for old boys with few other responsibilities. They haven't yet made room for women at the top. It is also personally confusing for her because her real role model is her father, who encouraged her to go into business, but was himself ambivalent about the demands of corporate life. Ultimately, she has no role models, no maps. She is working her way toward adulthood entirely on her own, and all things considered, she is doing it very well. But it takes time.

She majored in marketing in college and spent two years as a supervisor of clerks with the telephone company. Deciding that was a dead-end job, she applied to graduate school in a city some distance from home. "I was tired of the weather and the same old faces. I also thought it was time to get away from my family, much as I loved them." She specialized in accounting because she kept hearing her father's voice saying, "Wouldn't it be great to be a C.P.A.?" And she added a specialty in computer systems, she explains with characteristic understatement, because "I thought it was a growth area."

Her job is to tell other companies how to run their business. She works with the chief financial officer and the president of client organizations that range from tiny start-up companies to companies with two billion dollars in assets. Having analyzed their operation, she sits down at lunch with the top managers and advises them on what kind of computer system they need, what kind of books and records they ought to keep, and what other problems she thinks they have, such as an incompetent executive. She also prepares a somewhat sanitized written report that doesn't usually include mention of incompetent employees. That kind of thing is for the *intime* lunch. "I try to get them in a different environment," she says, "away from the office."

It is a lot of responsibility for a twenty-six-year-old. "I'm the expert, but sometimes it's scary. I keep in mind that my value to them is my objectivity. They need someone who will validate the existence of a problem they already know about. Often, they can't implement a solution until an outsider acts as hatchet and spells it out."

She likes her work and finds it rewarding, especially when a client implements her advice and it works. At one firm, a daily sales report was required by noon. Bookkeepers had to come in at 4:00 A.M. to start manually prepared spreadsheets. She showed them how to computerize the operation, and it allowed employees to work a normal day and be more productive.

What she chafes at is the bureaucracy of a large organization and the special problems that a woman has in a basically masculine structure. Crane and Scott has about two thousand partners, and only partners develop clients and authorize resources. Robin has just had her annual review and was told that she is on top at her level. "But beyond that, it's an old boys' network. Only three of the partners are women. The firm is run by and for the partners and there aren't enough women to pull for the others. The firm's first woman partner left recently to go to another firm because she felt she wasn't moving up fast enough within the structure."

But more deeply, she worries about the price of success and the even steeper price that women still have to pay. The first worry is a legacy. Her father was an executive who quit his job with a large, multinational corporation when Robin and her younger brother were children. "The job left no time for the family or fishing, which he loves," Robin relates. "He began wondering about the value of success. He'd be vice-president of the company, but so what? He had no time to do the things he liked." So he became a teacher, and had summers and school vacations to himself. Her mother, a nurse, pitched in and worked one or two days a week.

Despite her father's misgivings about corporate life, he tried to channel his children's interests into business. He also saw to it that they were very directed and focused, as good business executives must be. "Dad always made sure we had a plan. 'What will you take this year?' he'd ask. In February, he'd start asking us what job we had for the summer. He never pressured us to excel, but we always wanted to."

Robin also took on another aspect of the personality her father tried to shed—his competitiveness. "My teachers found me almost too competitive. I always had to turn in projects first. I had to win. I had to control everything."

It was that side of her that made her an A student in college and in graduate school. "My parents often wondered why I pushed so much. My mother isn't competitive at all."

When Robin started with the firm, she worked relentlessly. "My drive has broken up relationships with men. They didn't understand that I can't leave at five-thirty and meet them. I've had to break dates because of the demands of the job.

"Society isn't very supportive of ambitious women. The partners in the firm are male and married. Their wives don't work. They look after their lives for them. They run the house, pick up the dry cleaning, arrange their social life. For a single woman those things are a problem.

"I feel more secure now after two years. I understand the limits—what I can get away with on expense accounts and things like that. I have confidence when I interview clients. You have to be 'on.' I'm more comfortable about it. I used to wake up in the middle of the night worried about projects. I worried that I'd make a fool of myself with the client.

"I'm more relaxed now. The job requires at least fifty or sixty hours a week, but so many other things seem important to me now besides work. Passing the C.P.A. exam was my last big goal, and right now I'm more focused on personal relationships than I used to be. I don't want to work all the time. But still, I see my peers putting in all these hours, and I feel that I should be."

She alludes often to "other things in my life." One of them predictably turns out to be a man, an investment banker who has just been transferred to a city four hundred miles away. They now commute on weekends to see each other, and it is frustrating. He is urging her to move there, but she is reluctant. "I'm secure here. I like my living arrangement and my job. I would do it if we were married or engaged. I think we'll either get serious or break up. If we don't communicate on a day-to-day basis, it's hard to keep it up. For me, out of sight is out of mind."

But she has reached a point where she would like to be in a relationship. "I wasn't lonely before we met, but I would like one person to confide in." She also hears her biological clock ticking and knows that if she wants a family, she ought to marry soon. She has been in other relationships, but she wasn't ready to make a commitment. "It's easier and safer to commit to a job. You don't ask yourself questions. The goal is legitimate. It's frightening to give yourself away, and it's easy to find reasons to break up. I was so busy with work.

"Now, I feel I can take the time for a relationship. I'm more secure. But in the long term, I can see myself as happily single. I can also see myself married, but it would involve a big change. Right now, I don't have to put up with someone else asking questions or messing up my living space. I really cherish my space and my flexibility."

Her "space" is a rented guest house on an estate property in an old, socially exclusive part of the city. It is a very pleasant arrangement; it allows her privacy, security, charm, and a prestigious address. "I have it fixed up just the way I want it," she says, and it is hard to hear wedding music in the way she says it.

The other recent change in her life is a little more surprising. "In the last six months to a year, I've become significantly more religious." Her mother was religious, and the family went to church when she was a child, but she had been away from it during the years on her own. About a year ago, the firm had a church as its client, and Robin was asked to set up its computer information systems. She found she liked spending time there. "I listened to some tapes by the pastor on the importance of the Bible, and it awakened me spiritually and personally. Religion colors the way I handle myself personally and professionally now. In business, I won't overcharge customers or overpromise. In my personal life, I think about the way I treat others. I make sacrifices. I'm less selfish. The tape on materialism has been important to me. I'm in business, which is about making money. I've been into cars, hanging out at the right places, travel, clothes. Ultimately, those aren't the important things. It's nice to make money, but it's not everything. I'm still materialistic, but I'm working on it. Money is the measuring stick in this society, and I'm goal oriented. They pay me well if I do well."

She is now a member of a Presbyterian church in an exclusive community near the one she lives in. It is a church that is proud of its outreach to the less fortunate. She is involved with the church's fellowship and youth ministry and has volunteered to help with the finances. "Religion," she says, "brings you back after money and deals. I have been self-centered all my life. It's been me, me. It's boring. It's time to give back. Maybe I feel guilty about having a privileged life. Mom and Dad paid for my education. I have a body that works. I have money and a job. I'd like to help others now."

She and Mike do not know each other. Their names came off lists provided by their graduate schools. Yet each acted on the same need and expressed it in almost the same language. It may well be a coincidence that both of these young business professionals—goal-oriented, self-absorbed, directed—turned to religion in their late twenties, on their way up the ladder. Perhaps it is a substitute for marriage and family, which they aren't quite ready for. It may also be that they are now doing the personal exploration that they didn't do when they were younger.

But it also sounds as if a business career in the eighties can be obsessive, that it can produce stress that needs the grace of perspective. There is the pressure of the job itself—making the deal, succeeding, moving up in the chart—and that creates another problem: The career can be so all-consuming that it shuts out the activities and other relationships that normally provide growth and support, leaving the successful professional feeling deprived and empty.

"I'd like to be a partner," says Robin, still struggling to find a personal center. "But I have misgivings. There's a lot of money in it, but it's a harrowing life-style. The pressure on the partners is to develop new business, and they're forever traveling and entertaining potential customers. It's fun, but it leaves you with very little time for your own life. That was my father's complaint."

So she is considering going off and starting her own consulting firm. She has even discussed it with a potential partner, another consultant at the firm. The benefit would be control over their own enterprise. "There'd be no bureaucracy to deal with. But the downside would be that we're both driven by the need to do better and better. I'm afraid that we'd work weekends and vacations when it's our own money on the line. The blinders go on when I have a goal. I see nothing else. It's hard on my personal life and my body. But it's all so rewarding.

Dr. Richard Buskirk is director of the Entrepreneur Program at the University of Southern California, which he claims is the oldest such program in the country. He started it ten years ago, for graduate students only; it lapsed for a while when he was at another campus, and it was revived back up again four years ago when he returned. The program now has 130 undergraduate majors and 30 graduate majors. The majors take ten courses and develop their own business plan. A good many of them leap immediately from the comfort of school to the fire of their own business enterprises, very often the ones they planned in school.

It is quite a leap. The middle-aged employee who leaves his company to go out on his own takes with him years of experience, some savings, connections, and often, a few major clients. The young graduate of an entrepreneurs program has a fancy business plan, a loan from a relative, and a belief in the efficacy of prayer. He is taking this leap confidently because he has been infused with the new faith in entrepreneurship.

Buskirk, who describes himself as a product of the corporate age, sets forth the tenets of the faith. "Once, you got a job with IBM or some other big company and you worked there till you were sixty-five, cradle to the grave. But now with layoffs, kids see that the emperor has no clothes. The table of organization narrows at the top and you tend to plateau out at forty. There's nothing sadder than that. And you don't accomplish very much in a corporate job. I asked a guy at Westinghouse what he had achieved that year, and he said he negotiated a deal for one product. That's a year's work?

"Also, people are tired of moving around at the will of the company. They want roots. Entrepreneurs can stay put.

"But most of all, the only way to get rich is to be in business for yourself. A guy at IBM who did high-level work on the PC Jr. made a hundred fifty thousand dollars a year. He could have been a millionaire if he'd been on his own. Corporate clones never get rich. Their salary is all taxable and it stops when they stop working."

Asked if entrepreneurs don't sacrifice the security of a large corporation, Buskirk sputters angrily, "What security do you have in a large corporation? Your only security in business is your talent and you provide that yourself. If there's a merger, you're out at forty-five or fifty and what do you do then? An entrepreneur has more security. Dun and Bradstreet says so many businesses fail. What they don't tell you is that the people made money. There was a deal. Statistics are phony. If you have the brains and the initiative, you make it, even if not with the first business. Failure is another word for education."

For what the statistics are worth, Dun and Bradstreet sees businesses failing at a rapidly increasing rate. Their index of business starts, which charts new businesses on which a credit inquiry has been made, shows an 11 percent increase between 1982 and 1983 alone, and their numbers do not include farmers or those who have incorporated their businesses.

Still, Buskirk favors diving in, head first. He does not encourage would-be entrepreneurs to get their feet wet working for someone else. "We've preached, 'Go right into your own business. Corporate experience doesn't give you an education in anything except sales and marketing. Go off on your own and you learn rapidly or you hire someone.' "

It is an inspiring sermon, and few people sitting in the pews would not come forward for full immersion baptism. Tom Omalia, who also teaches in the USC Entrepreneur Program, is a little less of a true believer. "When our students come back after graduation, the one thing we hear most often is, 'You didn't tell us it would be so hard. You made it all sound so easy.' It isn't easy. It's drudgery. We talk about financing, and they think of meeting with bankers. For most of these kids, financing is ten thousand dollars from Uncle Joe. We talk about risk, and it sounds very dramatic. If you can't come up with the money by five o'clock, the bank will foreclose. That's not the way it is. Risk means you sold twenty-three dollars forty-seven cents worth all day and you're sitting there wondering if it's working."

This is a fairly accurate picture of the USC entrepreneur a year or two after graduation. Like his grandparents, he is getting started the hard way. He may someday be a millionaire, but at the moment he is working very hard in not-so-glamorous surroundings and doing a fair amount of worrying.

The Pizza Club is tucked in the corner of an L-shaped shopping center on a quiet suburban intersection. It is open for business, but it still has the earmarks of a new business—construction work around the doorway, paper signs taped to the window announcing application for a state license to sell wine and beer, the newness of the vinyl benches and the blond wood tables. The interior is done in a fifties theme. The fake brick wall is covered with old ads for Wheaties and shiny cars with fins and pictures of Elvis Presley, James Dean, and Marlon Brando. The main room seems spacious, at least when it is empty at ten o'clock in the morning. Off to the left, there is a small "private" room furnished with low tables and benches for Little League banquets and birthday parties.

The owner of this establishment is Dick, a twenty-three-year-old graduate of the USC Entrepreneur Program and winner of its Highest Achievement Award in 1984. Dick was especially recommended by Buskirk, who predicts that he will soon turn the Pizza Club into a major franchise operation. Like many in his generation, he wants a lot of things and he wants them soon. Mostly, they are material things. He isn't given to cosmic rambles in search of fulfillment. But he is different from his peers in that he never felt entitled to have what he wanted. He always knew that he would have to work for it. And even at that, it is harder than he ever dreamed.

Dick owns two other pizza places that do takeout and delivery, but this is his first restaurant. It has just opened, and he has had only three hours of sleep because he and his partner worked on "systemizing" the place after closing at ten last night. He takes me on a tour of the kitchen to see the result of his labor, which is that his kitchen is more orderly than most hospital operating rooms. There is a place, marked with plastic label, for every ingredient bin and utensil. "Melted margarine," "grated cheese," "sauce," "spatulas," "rollers" say the neat rows of labels above the covered bins, and each one is true to its word. There are even wall hooks for big colored plastic drinking mugs for employees, all labeled with names. Posted on the walls are lists of instructions headed "Opening Procedures," "Closing Procedures," and "4:00 Procedures." They are all handwritten, by Dick. This place is his masterpiece, so far, and he is leaving nothing to chance or employee vagary.

"I can do unlimited business here," he says excitedly. "I have the facilities and the location. This is an area of young families, with an average income between twenty and thirty-five thousand dollars a year, and I'm near a college campus. Young families and college students eat a lot of pizza, and I deliver also. I'll get them better food and I'll do it faster."

He is interrupted at this point by a visitor, an investigator from Alcoholic Beverage Control who tells him that he can now take down the sign announcing his intentions to sell wine and beer. Dick handles this conversation in a friendly, businesslike way, but he is a little crushed when the investigator tells him that his application for a license is moving along smoothly. "This is just like every pizza place I've ever seen."

"I thought it was unique," he says ruefully, after the man leaves. But he also heaves a sigh of relief and admits, "I'd kiss his feet to have that license."

Dick was the kind of kid who always made money. He wasn't in trouble or slow, but he never liked school much. "I just wasn't interested. I was always thinking about how to make a buck." He found aluminum cans and sold them when he was a little boy, and by the time he was thirteen, he had a lawn service, worked in gas stations, and sold Fuller brushes door-to-door by lying about his age. In high school, he had a job delivering pizza for a tiny counter-and-kitchen operation owned by a slightly older young man. Dick saw that money could be made in the business and began talking to his employer. "We tossed ideas back and forth, sometimes all night long." Often he barhopped with his boss. "I had a full beard when I was seventeen, and I didn't look my age. I grew up fast. I had plenty of women. I wasn't comfortable doing it. I just did it to be with him and talk to him about the business"

He came up with an idea for a door-to-door ad that doubled sales, and soon the tiny kitchen expanded to six locations, later whittled down to three very good ones. Dick was made a 25 percent partner in exchange for doing all the work. At seventeen, he had a beach house, a Porsche—soon replaced by a BMW—plus a surfboard and a windsurfer.

"My family were middle class," he says. "My father made thirty-five thousand a year ten years ago, and they had a tract house and a motor home for vacations. They didn't feel any pinch, but I always wanted a better life. I like Porsches. I want the means and the freedom to have five houses if I feel like it. It isn't that I need five houses. I just want the ability to do it.

"My mother always talked about how ambitious I was. I guess I am. Now I'm almost a snob. I want the good life."

He can't actually say why he sold out his interest in the pizza business and went to USC. His parents had divorced and his mother had gotten a job at USC just so he and his sister could have free tuition. What may have convinced him to make a change was that his partner—freed from the day-to-day business of making a living—got into real estate and became a millionaire. Dick was just a kid with a little money, and he began to see the limits of his status.

It goes without saying that he majored in business and was a star in the Entrepreneur Program. But meanwhile, he had his own apartment and his BMW, and his income from the sale of his share in the business didn't quite crack the nut. "So I went back into the pizza business because it was what I knew." He started the two takeout and delivery places, and developed the restaurant as his business plan—the program's equivalent of a thesis.

While he was at USC, he met the young woman whom he is about to marry. "I knew what I was looking for," he says decisively. "I had my fill of bar women. I wanted brains, beauty, and a Jewish girl who had high goals in life for herself. I want a family and connections so my business victories aren't hollow."

Stephanie, his fiancée, meets all of those requirements. A prelaw student, she is from a solidly wealthy family, immersed in suburban temple life. His father-in-law, now a successful real estate syndicator, started his business career with a single hamburger stand and is Dick's most fervent admirer and supporter.

He and Stephanie are having a very large, traditional wedding in less than three weeks. They have already bought a house in an expensive suburb near her family's home. The down payment was a wedding present from his father-in-law. But the monthly payments will be Dick's responsibility, along with the three pizza places and his current luxury car.

He is beginning to feel the pressure. "I'm tired. I average six hours of sleep a night, but I never get the average. It's three hours or nine. I think I'd like an easier life," he muses. "This is hard work and I don't want to work my tail off forever. I have to decide what I want to do with the cash flow. If I stay in this, I'll try to package and franchise. I'd like to see ten more places. But if I franchise, I'm in this business to stay."

He could also use the business as a source of cash for property investments, like his father-in-law, and he is buffeted by conflict. "This store could be a gold mine. I could use it and find real estate deals. It depends on how much I make and how much I take out. I want to enjoy myself too. But I feel I've missed some opportunities, and I'm discontented with my progress. On the other hand, I'm always a step beyond my means. I'm buying a house too early, I realize that. I guess I like pressure, but I don't relax enough. I'm a little burnt on these businesses."

But the morning is vaporizing in the hot California sun, and the early lunchers are drifting in. His cook hasn't arrived, so he mans the counter and takes their orders, and then goes into his perfectly organized kitchen, rolls out the dough, spreads it with melted margarine, sauce, and two kinds of cheese, puts pepperoni slices on half, and pops it in the oven. He does it expertly.

Peter is not a born businessman. He now has an M.B.A. from the Entrepreneur Program, and he too is one of Buskirk's star pupils. But basically, he is a liberal arts major who needed a job. The opportunities to do the kinds of things he had always wanted to do had shrunk, and besides, somewhere along the way, his values had changed and he didn't really want to do those things after all. Entrepreneurship suddenly appeared out of the mist. In its romantic new incarnation, it was something an educated, upper-middle-class young man could do.

A heavyset, jowly young man who looks older than his twenty-six years, he is struggling to learn the art of making money in this gray industrial park. Park here is a euphemism. This is not a grassy, landscaped compound. It is a few acres of concrete with rows of squat, one-story buildings and strips of parking spaces marked by diagonal white lines and puddles of crankcase oil. Work yards are in the rear, hidden from the street view.

Peter's cluttered office looks like it belongs in a gas station. The tiny, dark woman working the computer is his wife, Narda, several months pregnant. Behind the office is a long, dark room housing products awaiting shipment. The product is a small, lightweight boat with a bright-colored fiberglass hull surrounded by a stout rubber tube. There is a well for a motor and an optional canopy. It is a nice boat for unadventurous putting around on lakes or slow rivers, for fishing widows and children, for solitary, patient fishermen. "It's the water version of a 'Moped," says Peter. It is called the Boot Boat, and it is the child of Peter's USC business plan. A dozen or so are lying around the storeroom in various stages of completion, and Peter displays them with a father's pride.

He and Narda have arrived at this industrial park by a circuitous route. It was not what anyone would have predicted for either of them. Life somehow took them here.

Peter was born in New York but moved to Holland when he was a baby. His Dutch-born, Stanford-educated father is an executive with a multinational engineering company headquartered in The Hague. His mother is a native Californian who raised three children in the Netherlands. Peter, the middle child, enjoyed growing up in the international ambience of The Hague. He went to an American school and most of his friends spoke English. He loved sports because when his school teams traveled to "away" games, they went to Geneva, London, Paris, and Brussels. Unlike the other young entrepreneurs, he never thought about business in those days. What he liked was archaeology, an interest inspired by a family trip to Greece.

He returned to the States to go to Pomona College, a highly selective, academically demanding private school in California. His older sister went to Scripps, a close relation to Pomona, and the Pratt Institute, and is now an expert in Oriental art. His younger sister went to Stanford and is now pursuing an M.B.A. in international business. Peter majored in international relations, planning a romantic career in the foreign service. He had no adjustment problems when he came back to the United States, except that his exotic background sometimes awed his classmates. "I learned not to talk about it. It created a gulf."

When he graduated, his father set him up with an internship in the Washington office of a popular congressman who was also a family friend. Peter worked on a project to send aid to Cambodia during the famine and he also worked on a constituent case that became a cause célèbre. The constituent was a soldier who had been given drugs by the army as part of an experiment. "It was all very exciting and dynamic. But I began wondering about my future and whether this was the right direction to go in." This was not an age for an idealistic, public-sector career. There were few government jobs to be had, and salaries were low. He started thinking about business and asked his father for help.

His father sent him to audit one of his firm's companies in New Delhi.

He spent seven months in India, and he did three important things there. He wrote a report on the company that was very well received. He met Narda, who worked on advertising and layout for the company, and they became engaged. And he had an idea for a business. He wanted to import fine India crafts into the United States.

He did one more auditing job for his father, in Mexico City, and then married Narda in India in a Hindu ceremony and again in a church in California, where his parents are now living half the year. And he entered the USC graduate program in business because he wanted some business education before starting his import house.

To support himself and his new wife, he managed a small manufacturing business affiliated with his father's company. The little outfit made plastic fruit dehydrators in the location that now houses the Boot Boat operation. It didn't make many fruit dehydrators because they weren't selling well. A neighbor in the industrial park liked to play around with designs for new products, and on slow afternoons, he would show them to Peter, who was taking a new products course at USC. The Boot Boat captured Peter's imagination. He went into partnership with the designer and took unused capital from the fruit dryer operation and started building Boot Boats. Fairly soon, the entire fruit dryer business was converted into a boat business.

Peter also changed his business plan at USC. The craft importing business was shelved, and the Boot Boat became the focus of his life. His partner designed the prototype, and he set about teaching his foreman and workers to make fiberglass boats instead of plastic bowls.

"We've done all this without engineers," says Peter proudly. "We hustle technical advice from the sales reps we buy from. Our employees are all involved, and they use their own common sense when there's a problem. This is a real start-up business."

It has not been easy. First of all, he had a partner. "An entrepreneur shouldn't have a partner," says Omalia. "He can have an investor or a shareholder, but not a partner. The entrepreneur is the guy in control and control can't be shared." They quarreled over control, and Peter invoked default clauses in the contract and bought his partner out.

He then went about the task of putting the business on its feet. He took over production himself, with help from an awesome foreman. Investing eight thousand dollars, he took the Boot Boat to four national boat shows and got boats in dealers' showrooms. Narda, who was an advertising specialist, sent out press releases to the boating magazines. They have sold two hundred of them in the last five months and they have a map of the United States on the wall, with pushpins to indicate where they have dealer representatives. There are a lot of pushpins, mainly in the

South and the Midwest, where there are a lot of lakes and rivers. They have orders for boats now, but very little cash.

"We don't worship money," says Peter. "We want to make enough to get along. A start-up business gobbles up dollars, and you can't say 'no, that's enough.' It's like a hungry baby. Money is tight now. We're on a budget. We hope for a turnaround soon, but we're still in the struggle stage, with a lot of frustrations. There are easier things to do for a living."

"During the partner problems, we didn't sleep very much," says Narda, who would still rather be back in advertising, in an elegant modern office with white lacquer drawing boards and clearly defined responsibility.

"We all do everything here," says Peter. "I dream of the day when we have departments for shipping, accounting, production. We get the wrong size nuts and bolts, and none of the right size can be found anywhere in the county. I spend the day tracking them down and driving to the end of the world to get them. Boats that are ready to go are held up for tiny reasons—a small ring is missing, there's a minor crack in the color coating on the mold. This gets down and dirty. Anyone who works for me now would get the most well-rounded view of business," he sums up euphemistically. "My former college roommate works for me as general expediter. He's a graduate student in political science. At the end of the day, he can't wait to get back to his books. They're so nice and orderly."

Making boats is not so orderly. It is dominated by the roar of the spray guns and the smell of paint and plastic. The shop is in the rear of the concrete park, a long room with a half loft. It is run with a strong, proprietary hand by a Chicano foreman who does all the hiring and firing, mainly out of his neighborhood bar. It is a bar where you can find men strong enough to hold the heavy guns that shoot strands of fiberglass into big black molds, and then press the two parts of the shell between huge metal braces and leave them to dry in the concrete yard behind the shop. "The big colors are red and orange," says Peter. "That's what's selling. It's amazing how much I've learned about making fiberglass boats. I was an international relations major."

Not everyone who was in the Entrepreneur Program lives by the faith. Some of them decide that, despite all the swashbuckle, they don't want life to be such a down-in-the-dirt struggle.

Diane was in the Entrepreneur Program, and her business plan—to set up in-home fashion parties for executive women too busy to shop—was considered one of the best in the class. "It was an exciting program," she says. "You learn to think, to take a concept and build a foundation, to do the financial analysis." But Diane is now a market representative for Xerox. She explains the switch unconvincingly at first. "The more you learn, the more you realize that you don't know anything. I realized that the business world is a swamp, a hornet's nest, and that a large corporation is a great training ground for that world. You learn the ropes. You learn to play hardball. Then you can go out on your own. I'm still an entrepreneur at heart."

We talk a little about what some of her classmates in the program are doing, and it becomes clearer why she is at Xerox. She doesn't want to be spreading sauce in a pizza kitchen or watching workers spraying fiber glass or lying awake nights anxious about whether it will all work. "There's a lot to be said for the prestige of a job. You learn in a structured training program. You have the amenities and dignity of a real office. At Xerox, I have twenty-four-hour typing services and telephone answering. I guess a true entrepreneur doesn't need those things and can just take risks. But I thought it would be more natural to do it part-time, to make the switch into my own business gradually, so that it flows from what I'm doing now. If I had started my own business, I know I'd be working out of my house and I'd hustle everything."

Janet, one of Diane's USC classmates, is less honest about her situation. She considers herself an entrepreneur, and she has a great sense of adventure about it. Yet what she has is a good job as an administrative assistant. A slender blonde with blunt-cut hair tucked behind her ears and an off-season tan, she is wearing a ruffled blue blouse with real pearls and off-white slacks. She also wears a headset phone and sits behind a desk piled high with documents.

In between calls, she is a great booster of the Entrepreneur Program. "My dad flipped out when he heard about it. 'Go to USC,' he said. The program was very intense. Classes met twice a day and each course was eight units. We learned the ins and outs of running a new business from scratch. But spending your first hundred dollars is different from anything in a course. You have a business plan, but will it work? That's the excitement.

"One reason the program was so successful was that they used successful businessmen instead of academics. Professors from other campuses got a bad reception from us. We had no sympathy for their point of view. We walked out or we argued with them. They weren't practical or interesting. We were very anti-bureaucracy."

"Entrepreneurs," says Janet, "are the people of the future." And she goes on to predict that magazines like *Venture* and *Inc.* will surpass *Time* in circulation. "People think entrepreneurs are money-hungry kids. We're not. We don't do it for the money. We do it to build, to make something work. The empire is your brainchild."

Which makes it all the more surprising that Janet isn't an entrepreneur.

At USC, she developed a business plan to be a broker of expensive imported cars, and she started her business out of some extra space in her father's office—an executive-suite arrangement in a brown-stone and gray-glass building, surrounded by rustic wood stairways and attractive ground cover. This office does not look like a gas station's. It has bronze plush carpeting, black chairs, and modern glass and chrome furniture.

Her father is a venturer—his own coined word—who develops computer software businesses, and he tended to call on his daughter for administrative help. She found she liked helping her father and she didn't like the auto brokerage business. "It made me see the worst side of people, and I don't like that. Car dealers lie a lot. They tell me they have the car the customer wants and they don't really. Besides, my father's businesses are much more dynamic and interesting."

They may well be since her father is a real entrepreneur. At the moment, he owns ten companies and has eight limited partnerships. He pays Janet a salary so large that she doesn't want to talk about it. "It's more than most people my age make." Her father is in another room, meeting calmly with an associate. The phone rings incessantly, and most of the calls are for Janet, who takes them all on her headset phone at a pace that can only be called frantic. Something has gone wrong with the printing of covers for an important report, and she has to straighten it out quickly. It takes about six calls.

In between she tells me about herself and her family. "We don't follow rules. Everything we do is off-base. My dad lives by his own rules and even has his own business category—venturer, not venture capitalist. There are no titles in Dad's company. Dad is the CEO, but that's all. We do what has to be done." She loves working with her father. "Dad is a great guy. I want to get mad sometimes, but it's hard to.

"And we're always learning new things. Next year, I'll learn about oil drill bits. Dad likes to do more than just add a product. He likes to change, revolutionize an industry."

One of her father's associates looks in at this point. "Do we have a place to sleep in New York?" he asks. She shakes her head. "Get us reservations at the Stanhope," he says, without breaking stride. I ask when she is going to New York. She isn't. The reservations are for her father and his associate, and she makes a note to herself to take care of it. She has a lot of things to take care of, including finding new office space for her father's burgeoning business.

"I couldn't be in a big corporation," she says later. "I like doing things my way. I like things to be my responsibility. And I treasure flexibility. I'll work eight to six, but not nine to five. For instance, I need a break, so I'm going to Hawaii next week." I suggest that she has an enviable life, and she halfway agrees. "I do, but it's too hectic. My main problem is that I don't have any time for my own ventures. I have an idea for a new breed of horse, and I'd like to think about it and create a business plan. I wanted to start next month, but I'll have to move it back."

She may move it back a few more times. It is much easier to worship the entrepreneur ethic than to live it.

14

Love, Marriage, and Other Unnatural Acts

Kathleen works in the office down the hall from mine. She is twenty-three and pretty, with a kind of Catholic schoolgirl coltishness about her. It's something in the lock of hair that falls over her eye, the sweater wrapped around her waist, the tan, bare legs. She is a recent university graduate, with a degree in accounting, but she is working as a bookkeeper. Sometimes she stops to chat with me. This is a temporary job, she explains in the fall. She has a job lined up with a Big Eight accounting firm that starts in March. Fall fades into the Christmas holidays and Kathleen is as friendly and chatty as ever. She went up north to see her family for the holidays and says she had a good time, though it rained a lot. In the fullness of time, it's spring, and Kathleen still has not moved on.

I ask her what happened to her Big Eight job. "I don't think I'm going to take that," she explains. "I don't know if I told you, but I was going with this guy, and I married him over Christmas. He's going to medical school in the East, so there's no point in my changing jobs."

This is a much bigger mystery than the job change. She wears no rings, except a pearl on her index finger that she has had all along, and marriage in advanced societies leaves no other marks. She has talked to me confidentially about her job situation, trusting that it would not get back to her employers. Yet she has chosen to keep secret a perfectly acceptable marriage to a handsome medical student. She came back after Christmas and talked about the weather and how nice it was to get away, but omitted to mention that she had gotten married.

This is something new, and I ask her about it. "I don't know," she says in her soft voice, pushing the hair out of her very lovely blue eyes. "I just didn't want people to think I had changed or to act different toward me. When you're married, people expect you to act out a certain role, and I don't want a role. I just want to be myself. For instance, my father thinks I ought to be buying furniture and china now that we're married. I have no interest in any of that right now."

"Why did you get married?" I ask.

"Well, I was in this relationship, and I didn't know where it was going. He's going east in the summer, and wanted me to come with him, so he said, 'Let's get married,' and we did. But it doesn't really make anything different."

Marriage, of course, does make things different, but that isn't my point right now. My point is that it seems to be a very different institution than the one Kathleen's parents signed up for, the kind that led to setting up a household, with furniture and tableware as soon as you could afford it, to accepting new family ties and community responsibilities, and to having children. Sometimes these goals had to be postponed while he finished medical school or started a business, but there was no question that these were the goals. It was the program. Sometimes there were questions about whether the wife ought to work, but even then, the unspoken subordinate clause was, "until there are children."

Marriage/Family is no longer the standard program. Right now, in the mid-eighties, it is one possible life-style option in a world of confusing, changing relationships. Kathleen may be unusual in her "nothing much happened, I just married this guy I was going with" attitude, but her confusion, her vagueness, her general willingness to make things up as she goes along are very typical. Her generation is the first to deal with a menu of more or less equal life-styles. You can marry; you can have children or not; you can divorce and remarry; you can live with someone who is or is not a lover; you can live alone, with or without a lover; you can be gay or straight; you can even remain married and live separately. And there are probably a few options I haven't thought of. The choices began in the sixties, but this is the first generation that can view them all as acceptable options, rather than bohemian deviations. According to Bureau of the Census figures, married couples with children constituted only 30.2 percent of the households in this country in 1981. By 1990, demographers project that the percentage will drop to 25.8 percent. Similarly, the share of married couple households is expected to drop from almost 60 percent in 1981 to 55 percent in 1990. The types of household expected to increase most rapidly through the end of this decade are the unmarried couple and the single person living alone.

Committed, lasting relationships are a critical aspect of maturity. To-day's young adults are having more trouble with relationships than with almost any other area of their lives. They are having problems for two reasons: 1) They have trouble with commitment in general, and this is an echo, a subheading of their overall reluctance to define themselves. 2) The menu of choices makes life more confusing. It is different from the kind of lives their parents have lived and have brought them up to expect. Once again, they are in unmapped territory, looking for trails of crumbs.

Despite two decades of liberation, women still see their love relationships as crucially important. Ask a young woman to tell you about herself and she will give you a history of her love affairs. Ask a young man and he will tell you about changing his major or going to Europe. The men are probably experiencing the same problems and the same upheaval, since most relationships still involve two people, but they seldom talk about them even when they are asked. Greg, a twenty-seven-year-old graduate student in computer science, isn't unusual. He talks easily about his trek through four different colleges and a year of hitchhiking across the country, about drugs, about alcohol, about changes in his field. I ask him, at the end of the interview, whether he has been involved in relationships that were important to him. "I've lived with two women, and both relationships ended because of incompatibility."

"Did they affect your values or development in any way?" I ask.

"They made me look more at the 'people side,' at the human rather than the functional," he says, after some thought. That is all he has to say about the two women he lived with.

The sex difference held even among gays. Young men who were clearly gay and had an obviously gay life-style declined to talk about it. For instance, most interviewees were asked if marriage and family were part of their plans for the future. Gay men tended to give closet answers. It's hard to find the right woman. They needed a better job. Or they cherished their independence. Lesbians usually preempted the question. They talked openly about their sexual identity and whatever struggles they had in coming to terms with it. One lesbian—who had incorrectly assumed that I knew about her orientation—was asked the marriage and family question. She answered simply, "Well, I'm involved with another woman right now." And she proceeded to tell me about the woman.

There is a myth that we are in the middle of a marriage boom and a baby boom, that the traditional family is back in force, starting with bridal registries and working its way happily toward baby showers and car pools. The media, looking at marriage data based on a bulge in the young adult population and searching for stories about the new conservatism, have been pouring out a steady stream of pieces about the renaissance of marriage. Local television news programs run five-part features on weddings. The wedding industry, we hear, is healthier than ever. A 1982 *New York Times* piece on a "Bridal Expo" in Long Island showed wedding merchandise, from cutlery to limousines, in high demand. A delighted spokesman talked about "a return to traditionalism, formalism, and quality." Fairs like this one, he said, were drawing thousands of brides every month. The National Center for Health Statistics reported 2.5 million weddings that year, the seventh straight year that the number of marriages increased. Bridal shops seemed to be springing up everywhere, and some brides said that it took as long as three months to get a custom-made bridal gown.

There is, in fact, a wedding boom. But there is no marriage boom.

Jacqueline, whom we met in an earlier chapter, as she was successfully resolving her dependency on her parents and anticipating a proposal from her boyfriend, was married six weeks ago in what she calls a *"Bride's magazine wedding."* It is a little more than a year since that first interview and we meet for another lunch. She and Tom were married in a pretty neighborhood church, and since one of Tom's parents is nominally Jewish, a broad-minded rabbi as well as a minister officiated. Jacqueline wanted it that way. The reception for a hundred and thirty people was in her parents' large, rose-bordered backyard, and Jacqueline was involved in every detail, down to the matchbook covers and the flowers. "It was my day," she says. "It's the only time I was queen for a day since my Sweet Sixteen party, and I could have anything I wanted. If I wanted a purple flower for my hair instead of a pink one, I got it.

"I wanted a traditional wedding, not a statement. Tom and I didn't make any speeches to each other, and I didn't want the minister saying we'd been living together. What I wanted was a beautiful, picture-book wedding, a proclamation to a community of friends and family."

Doing it was not entirely easy. Her father had suffered some business reverses that year, and money was tight. The guest list had to be kept down, and "Tom has at least one hundred thirty cousins, and his mother couldn't understand why we couldn't invite the pediatrician who took care of him when he was a baby and his third grade teacher." Jacqueline was caught between the two families, and she didn't enjoy the pressure, but that vision of the perfect wedding sustained her.

"A lot of my friends are getting married now, and just about all of them are having church weddings with at least an hors d'oeuvres reception. Most have lunch or dinner. In some cases, I'm surprised because they don't seem the type. But there they are, with the ice sculpture and the bridesmaids in matching dresses.

"You know, if you have a big wedding with a hundred people watching and caterers and pictures and presents, you feel it's real and you have to make it work. If you sneak off to Las Vegas for a weekend and get married by a justice of the peace, it's a casual kind of thing, and no one even notices if you get a divorce. It's important to make a statement when you get married. Then you've got to make it work for a while."

That may be one explanation for the traditional wedding boom. It is a ritual to protect against divorce. It conjures up a past when marriage was secure and forever. But young people who marry now are making an almost controversial choice. They are not just doing the expected thing, what everyone else is doing, wrapped in the cotton batting of social support and approval. And they are uneasily aware that they have no guarantee of success. In the year ending in March 1984, the divorce rate was five per one thousand population. The marriage rate—the number of marriages per thousand population—for the same year was 10.5. In other words, there was about one divorce for every two marriages.

What is more surprising is *that the marriage rate did not go up.* In fact, it dropped slightly between March 1983 and March 1984. The wedding industry may be booming because there is a bulge in the young adult population thanks to the postwar baby boom. Demographers attribute the slight upward fluctuations in the marriage rate to the fact that baby-boomers are marrying later, and many are now facing the "biological clock" syndrome. There are also more remarriages as a result of all those divorces. And it seems that a lot of those who are getting married, like Jacqueline, have decided to do it the old-fashioned way. But graphs of the marriage rate show hardly any fluctuation at all in the eighties. Among Jacqueline's peers, it is actually declining. The percentage of both men and women under twenty-five who have been married dropped 6 percent between 1980 and 1984. There is no marriage boom.

There is also no baby boom. There are more people of potential parent age—resulting in more babies—but the average number of children born to each woman of childbearing age is near a record low and so is the average family size.

Still, the media are constantly celebrating our switch from the "me" decade of the seventies to the "us" decade of the eighties. But it just hasn't happened.

What is happening is that we are shifting undeniably and inexorably from a family-oriented society to a society of individuals. It's a shift clearly reflected in the marketplace—in the Lean Cuisine dinners, "apartment-sized" furniture, health spas, singles bars, restaurants with little butcher-block tables that cater to the lone diner, Club Med trips, and adult condominiums. Marriage, with or without children, is one option among many in a world of confusing, rapidly changing kinds of relationships. To make it even harder, marriage is itself being redefined. It doesn't mean what it used to mean, and young couples are pretty much making it up as they go along.

But today's young adults aren't just victims of social change. Their personality as a generation make them very much part of the change. Commitment to a relationship is just as difficult for them as commitment to a career or a point of view. It is one more act that might define them and therefore limit their potential. I ask Ellen, a young actress we met in an earlier chapter, if she plans to marry the boyfriend she is now living with. "I'm still looking for the perfect man and the perfect relationship, even though I know it's a fantasy." She cannot say what is imperfect about this man, and she seems to be in love with him. But to say "this is it" is limiting. It's an admission of adulthood.

Besides, it is difficult to be in a relationship when you still don't know who you are. There is a tendency to demand too much and depend too much and be dissatisfied for vague reasons. What you want from the other person is not company but an identity. Among the people interviewed for this book, good relationships seemed to happen to those who found their own direction first. Love conquered very little.

But most of all, these are special children, brought up to be individuals and valued as individuals. They never felt that they had a role to play in the community or the family, and certainly never believed that they might have to sacrifice their individuality. A twenty-six-year-old financial consultant has a boyfriend she considers "very special," but she hesitates about marrying him. "I have my apartment fixed up just the way I want it." It would mean giving up an environment that expresses her, in exchange for a compromise between her and someone else.

A twenty-nine-year-old stockbroker has a similar problem about a girlfriend. "What about my trips and vacations?" he asks himself. Another young woman was madly in love with a man who was uncertain about her. Suddenly, he did an about face and announced that she was all he wanted on earth. She was ecstatic for a month and then began wondering to her girlfriends what it all meant. Would he be in her apartment all the time, and could she still have evenings to herself?

Some of the confusion of course is a result of the historical ground shift begun by the women's movement. Feminism sent women off to work for personal fulfillment, but the economy and the high cost of housing has kept them working. No man, nowadays, ever says in the old paterfamilias style, "I wouldn't allow any wife of mine to work." Quite the contrary. "Comfortable times generated the feminist movement," says Miriam Meyer, a Los Angeles family therapist who is suddenly seeing a new kind of marital conflict: "The push for women to be independent wage earners comes from *him* right now. In a lot of cases, she's feeling the pressure out there and would just as soon kick off her shoes."

"Economic survival is the name of the game, not feminism," says one recent male graduate, who wishes his own fiancée were less dependent on him. "I'd like to marry a doctor. It would be nice to have a wife with a lot of drive and competence. I'd like support instead of arguments, hassles, and problems."

And from the woman's side: "I used to think you got married a year after college, and that you used college to set it all up," says Joan, a young economics major facing her senior year. "But I'm no longer working for a Mrs. degree. My sister married a dentist and she's working to help pay back thirty or forty thousand dollars in loans for dental school. The way it is now, both the husband and the wife have to work for an upper-middle-class life-style. My friends who are getting married are going on with their career plans. They're covering their ass. You never hear guys say, 'I don't want my wife to work.' "

"Until the late sixties, young women assumed that they would marry and that work was not so important," says Dr. Barbara McGowan, director of counseling and psychological services at UCLA. "But realism has set in. Women know that their career is for twenty-five or thirty years. Young career-bound women must prepare and complete their education before they have children. And in recent years, we've been counseling a lot of women in their late twenties or early thirties because of conflict between marriage and career. Women want everything—a beautiful wedding and a career. And men still want traditional services from a working wife. It all starts to wear thin. 'I can't do it all,' she cries." They can be themselves or they can be the kind of women their mothers were. They can't be both, they learn.

The result of all of this is that young adults are very confused about what their relationships mean and where they are leading. "There are no clear expectations," says Melanie, the social worker turned businesswoman. "We live in a mix of the past and the present. It's okay not to have children and not to marry. Do I want to do those things? I ask myself. It's all so modern. Relationships have no rules, no structure, so there's a lot of anxiety. I'm in a single woman's support group, and we keep talking about the confusion. He hasn't called me in a week. Is it okay if I call him? What about expressing affection? Will it be seen as dependency? Your ego is always on the line. You wonder, 'Would they like me more if I were dumb?' It's like a strange dance, and neither of us know what our roles are. There are no boxes, no labels. It's liberating, but scary."

Even dating is now a confused and not always pleasant business. Says Joan, the young woman looking to her senior year: "The guys on this campus are cautious about commitment, but real quick about sex. There's a lot of looseness here, but there's no set definition about relationships. You can go out for a year and there are no promises. It bothers me that a lot of guys act like you're out to tie the rope. If they've gone out with you a few times, they make a point of letting you know that it doesn't mean anything.

"Anyway, dating isn't as big a thing as it used to be. It's expensive. A movie and a snack around here cost twenty dollars. Usually, you have lunch or study together or take a walk. It's very informal." It is, in other words, something that just happens rather than something anyone takes responsibility for. It's hanging around together.

Beth, a recent college graduate who is about to be married, remembers her dating years without any regret that they are over. "Dating was empty. You couldn't confide or talk freely. There were always questions of who will pay or how much to get involved. And there was always sexual pressure—implied or outright." Sometimes she didn't even know what an invitation meant. Was it a date or a friendly hang around?

"I met a guy on a college ski trip. We were just friendly. He called when we got back and invited me to dinner at this great place he knew. I said 'yes' and talked it over with the girls in the dorm. Are we friends going Dutch treat or is this a date? Everyone said, 'If he called and invited you, it's a date and he'll pay.' Well, we got to the restaurant, and I looked at the menu, and I asked him what he recommended. He said, 'It depends on how much you want to spend on dinner.' I was so flustered, I must have blushed. First of all, I didn't have more than ten dollars with me. We talked it over, and he explained that he used to take girls out, but it got too expensive."

Beth's fiancé finds the new options just as confusing. "When I'm asked out by a woman, I don't know how to act or who will pay. When I ask her out, I run the evening. When it's vice versa I don't know what to expect."

This is not a defense of chivalry. It is just an illustration of the confusion of contemporary social life. Paying the bill is a simple, specific issue, but the cost of dinner can loom large in a student budget and young people are just acquiring social skills. Perhaps Dear Abby or Miss Manners could offer solutions. For instance, Beth could have asked directly, "Is this a date or are we going Dutch treat?" When he responded that it was to be Dutch treat, she could then ask about how much it would cost. If it sounded like more than she could afford, she could suggest a cheaper place. Which isn't at all what he wanted. He wanted company at his favorite restaurant. It is excruciatingly awkward and more trouble than it is worth.

Moreover, it is a pervasive symptom of the fuzziness of their dealings with each other. Nothing is clear and no one is responsible for anything. You can share dinners and bed with someone for months and then, when you ask where it is all leading, get "Huh? What?" for an answer.

So some young people find ways to avoid relationships. One twenty-two-year-old man was in therapy because he couldn't decide whether he was gay or straight. His therapist suggested that his indecision served a purpose. It kept him from relating honestly to men or women. If his sexual identity weren't a problem, he might drink, take drugs, work long hours, or find fatal flaws in every woman—or man—he went out with.

What it all means is that in this very crucial way, he and many of his peers don't want to grow up. A few are passive dependent. They want to remain young children, and they often go from one painful, addictive relationship to another. Two young women—both intelligent, middle-class college graduates—told me about being abused by the men they were living with. Neither saw it as reason to leave the relationship immediately, and they are not alone. Reported domestic violence is on the rise, even though women have more economic independence than ever.

But most aren't infants, neurotically looking for parents. They are just eternal adolescents, and what they want to be is *free* of the ties and responsibilities that not only keep them from doing what they want but *tell them who they are*. They are lonely, but their attempts at relationships fail because they chafe at the thought of commitment or even inconvenience. Their parents did all the giving, and giving is an adult job. One young man complained of having problems with women. "I always got attention from them at the wrong time. I had girlfriends when I was in college and involved with a lot of things. But I wanted to do what I wanted to do when I wanted to do it. I didn't want to be needed when I was busy." Now he isn't a student leader anymore. In fact, he isn't doing much of anything, and women aren't interested in him. "They want more stability, security, money than I can offer," he says bitterly. What they want of course is an adult, not a little boy who can't be counted on.

A few just enjoy the confusion because it allows the fun of relationships without the commitment. A gay woman in her late twenties talks about her present relationship. "It's solid and mature, but not forever. Since passion isn't forever, why stay with one person forever?" Some turn to marriage as a safe haven from the relationship storms, only to find that marriage isn't so safe anymore. And some of the braver ones are struggling to invent new forms of relationships that will work. Marriage among young adults is a brand new institution.

Beth and her fiancé, Brad, will be married in three months in church, in front of 150 people. As a couple, they have decided that they don't want to live in the modern maelstrom of shifting, vague relationships. So they have decided to establish rules and structure for their marriage, using religion and traditional roles. But they can't just will themselves back to a safer time, and the roles and the rules don't cover all of the realities of life in the eighties. Theirs will be a modern marriage, and for some time to come, they will be a young couple finding themselves rather than establishing a family and household, as their parents did at their age. They are strong evidence that the process of growing up has changed, and even with the best will in the world, it just takes longer.

Beth is twenty-one, with a mass of taffy-colored hair and intelligent eyes. She just graduated from a first-rate university with a major in kinesiology and grades good enough for medical school. She will not go to medical school. In the fall, she will look for a job as an aide to a physical therapist. Her fiancé is five years older and is a commercial photographer who just started his own business. He has an A.A. (Associate in Arts) degree from a community college.

They met at the church they both attend, on their own, without their parents. Both refer to themselves as Christians, which means more than being nominally Catholic or Protestant. "Our church is different from our parents'," Beth explains. "Theirs has a lot of ceremony and formalism. Ours is more personal. Your relationship with God should be personal. It's more human. It's about the way you live your daily life."

"It's basic and simple. Jesus Christ is our Lord and savior," adds Brad, her fiancé. "He died so we might be forgiven our sins. God knew we couldn't cut it alone."

He was drawn to religion when he was in high school. He was on the track team and most of his teammates were "born again." At first he went to their church; he found their present one when he was a freshman in college. Beth tagged along to a Bible class with a girl whom she met at work. She found it had meaning for her and started attending the church. (Later, she tells me more about why it had meaning for her.) But her co-worker's church was big and impersonal. "Then I went on a water-ski trip with some kids from this church, and I decided to go there," she explains.

She and Brad began going out a year ago. "We didn't fall madly in love," says Beth. "Love came slowly. I had been infatuated before, and it didn't pan out. This relationship was so clear. I saw Brad for what he was. It wasn't a fantasy. It was real. It could last. We're still two separate people. Independent. I'm still my own person—me. I used to think marriage was domination—like my grandparents. On our third date, Brad and I talked about it, and he disagreed with me. Other guys would just agree. But he said he saw it differently. Life doesn't end with marriage."

Their church is opposed to sex outside of marriage, and they abide by that. "Ours isn't a conservative church. We do drink," she says, pointing to the margarita in front of her. "But sex is a sacrament. Sometimes it seems stupid, but it's worth waiting for. Meanwhile, we're doing our best, which is all God expects. We avoid provocative situations. We use common sense. But I feel that if I can wait now, I'll be able to avoid provocation after we're married.

"Some of my friends live with their boyfriends. I don't judge them or avoid the friendship. I just don't agree. Living together is a limbo. Either you know or you don't know. According to statistics, living together doesn't improve the odds of the marriage succeeding. Some say it's like marriage—it's an exclusive relationship. Others see it as looser. They even see other people. The trouble is the views don't always coincide. Marriage is more understood, but even that takes a lot of discussion. There are different ideas of marriage. The Christian belief is that marriage is forever. It's a gift of God. God blesses it and no one can put it asunder. That's very different from living together."

They have both given a lot of thought to the subject of marriage. It is almost a church activity. Brad attended a dating seminar and thought about relationships a good deal. "I talk to a lot of people. You need common sense and wisdom to make something work. Relationships today are so flaky. There's no commitment. I think it's a cop-out to say you fell out of love. What happened is, you just stopped making it work."

Their church has a group of fourteen couples, recently married or about to be married, and they meet regularly to talk things over. "Problems like handling the checkbook, the budget, doing the household chores," Beth explains. She and Brad have worked out plans for most of these. The housework will be shared. Each will keep a separate checking account and be responsible for certain bills. Nothing is taken for granted anymore. Their parents' marriage—no matter how good it is—isn't a natural model anymore. It is hardly relevant, even to these serious, religious young people who want structure.

First of all, there is the question of money. He has a new business. She expects to earn less than a thousand dollars a month at her job. That affects ideas about home and family. "A house is way out of our range," says Beth. "The only young marrieds who can buy a house now have help from their parents. When my parents bought their first home, my mom worked for two years to make the down payment. Then she got pregnant and quit. A few years later, they bought a bigger house. Now, it's five hundred a month just for an apartment. We expect to wait five years before having kids."

And, of course, Beth is an educated, modern woman, an entirely different creature from her mother or her grandmother. She expects to stay home and care for her children when they are small, but she will go back to work as soon as they are in kindergarten. But one wonders if a home and yard will contain her energy even that long. She has plans to go back to school, to go into public relations and perhaps even bridal consulting on the side. "I definitely want a career. My dad died when I was eight. My mom had secretarial skills, and I got through college on Social Security. If anything happened to Mark, I would want to be able to take care of myself," she says, with blunt lack of sentimentality for a bride. This is definitely modern marriage.

"Sometimes I think her independence goes too far," says Brad. But he doesn't seem to mind very much. He values marriage, family, and certain old ways because they smooth out the hard edges. When a group from the church goes out for ice cream, he pays for the girls who are unescorted. "I do it because I'm a gentleman," he says. Yet he has chosen to marry a very bright, high-powered, independent young woman, who has four years of college to his two—not a Phyllis Schlafly prototype. No young man seems to want that kind of burden anymore.

This conversation so far has taken place over lunch. But Brad has to get back to his business. Beth, who just finished her last set of finals, has time for another cup of coffee.

"If you're interested in young people who are drifting, without any sense of direction, you should call my old boyfriend," she says, smoothing down the edge of her place mat. "He's twenty-six, he's a college graduate, and he has almost a master's in psychology. But he's still a lifeguard. He lives at home, and he just hangs around and does nothing all winter."

She tells me a little about that relationship. It lasted for four years and little of that time was peaceful. He was ambivalent and undependable. They had sex and they used drugs, but since she wasn't a Christian at the time, she doesn't feel guilty about it. In fact, he was the main reason that she turned to the church. She was lonely and hurt, and religion was a good way to get out of the relationship. He didn't share her views, and after a few years of hoping that he would change and they would get back together, she realized that "being a Christian was more important to me than Frank was. The two were incompatible, so I had to wash my hands of that relationship." Her new religion provided a context—a belief system, a supportive group of new friends—that allowed her to avoid the Franks of this world. It also helped her conclude that she wanted a caring, solid partnership instead of the unpredictable push-pull of romance and rejection. "With Frank, I was always the third or fourth priority. 'If the lifeguards don't have a party, I'll see you.' Now I have what I want. For Brad, I'm first."

She does have what she wants. Yet when I ask for Frank's phone number, she rattles it off easily even though it is three years since they broke up. "I ran into him a few weeks ago in a restaurant. I was having lunch with my mother. Just seeing him shook me up. It reminded me how much he had hurt me." Her eyes fill with tears, and then she says that she'd rather I didn't call him after all. It would be a kind of communication with him and she prefers not to have it. She is a wise young woman.

Jacqueline and Tom had an elegant, traditional wedding and a lovely honeymoon, but that was the end of the social support system for their marriage. They are now fumbling their way toward a new kind of marriage—without the help of religion or tradition or even agreement about what it means to be married. They did live together before they were married—for two years, in fact. Yet marriage, they are discovering, is different. It impinges on the self, the most precious possession of the special generation. Prized for their individuality, they have a hard time becoming part of a couple, a family, or a community. Marriage for them is an unnatural act.

"I think I need another project," says Jacqueline. "For months, I was involved in organizing my wedding. Now that it's over I feel let down. I have that 'Now what?' feeling. If I don't get a promotion, I might look for a new job. That's a project."

She needs a project, it turns out, because she has so much time on her hands. It isn't just that the wedding is over and Christmas is so far off. Her problem is that her new husband is never home. He has given up the music business and gone into a new line of work—selling wine. He loves it. For the first time in his life, he has a structured, daytime job. He wears a suit and tie. He interacts with people and has measurable successes. It has made him euphoric. He has so much energy that he works late one night a week, takes a class another night, plays in a rehearsal band a third night, and goes to his therapist a fourth. While Jacqueline spends her evenings alone or meets one of her single friends for dinner.

"I don't know why, but it's just not the same as living together. When we were living together he didn't have to prove that he could have his evenings to himself.

"We quarreled about it this morning. I said that it might be nice if we spent an evening together once in a while. He said that I just resent his new happiness because I'm bored with my job. That's not true," she said, her eyes misting up. "I would just like him to spend one night a week at home. I think that he's experimenting with what being married means."

At this point, neither of them exactly know. Both have parents who have happy, long-term marriages, but it doesn't offer them many clues. Unlike either of their mothers, Jacqueline has kept her own surname. "It's too confusing to change my name at work. The customers know me by that name, and I don't think it's very professional to change. People sometimes read things into that, but actually I just did what seemed easiest. I didn't want to change my driver's license and my Visa card and everything." She has her own checkbook and her own money, and so does he. Yet she was irritated when he spent eighty dollars on a new tennis racket without consulting her. "That's the gas and electric bill," she thought. "It's *our* money he's spending."

She plans to work for the foreseeable future. "We won't have children for some years," she says. Tom, in fact, would be disturbed if she wanted to quit her job and keep house or have babies now. On the other hand, he feels they should be buying a house fairly soon because married couples should own their own home—as his parents did. "That's what marriage means to him," says Jacqueline, who loathes the thought of giving up their pretty, centrally located apartment for a house in the distant suburbs. She isn't ready for commuting or yard work or neighbors.

We talk for a while about the mystique of marriage. It isn't just a relationship. It's status, role, definition. The fact that you are married says something about you—something that Kathleen, the young woman who kept her marriage a secret, didn't want said. And whom you are married to says something else. A boyfriend or girlfriend is another person. A spouse is a fact about you.

"Tom and I had tickets for a play the other night," says Jacqueline, who was a theater arts major in college. "I was practically brought up in the theater. My family went to plays all the time, and I'm very fussy about the theater. Anyway, we were with another couple, and the play was absolutely awful. I knew it and so did the other couple. But Tom just loved it. He kept laughing at all these terrible jokes, and during intermission he said how much he liked it. I was so embarrassed and angry.

"After a while, I stopped and thought about it. Why shouldn't I just be glad he was enjoying himself? When we were living together and not married, I didn't care if he liked the right things. I didn't see him as a reflection of me.

"But the changes go both ways. There are good things too. For instance,

I'm not much of an athlete. When we were living together, he would go out to run or play tennis, and I would stay home and read. But last week he asked me to play tennis with him and I decided to do it. I don't know why, but it had something to do with being married. Some idea that we should do things together. I had a great time. I think I'll take some lessons so I can be a better partner for him."

Neither her mother nor Tom's mother would have felt the slightest pressure to share their husbands' interest in sports. Women of their day would also have carefully calculated just how their husbands' status, income, and behavior reflected on them. They would have done this well before marriage because they knew that marriage would define them. Once married, they were wives. They would soon be mothers, and they knew exactly what it all meant. Tom and Jacqueline are making it up as they go along.

15
The Bigger World

Just before the 1984 Democratic Convention was gaveled to order in San Francisco, a network magazine program did a nostalgic, those-were-the-days flashback to Chicago in 1968. Old footage showed chaos in the convention hall and demonstrators being bloodied in the streets by police.

And in the off-hours of the same convention, the *Today Show* trucked across the bay to Berkeley to do one of those "twenty years later" features. As "The Times They Are A-Changin' " played in the background, film clips showed long-haired students in low-slung jeans and loose, gauzy shirts caught forever in the act of protest—playing guitars, raising their fists, shouting into megaphones, waving placards.

The message of both programs was clear. Things used to be much more exciting. *Today* went on to show Berkeley in 1984: neat, sensible students going about the business of raising their grade point averages and signing up for job interviews. A few diehards were still sitting at tables stacked with political literature, like soldiers stranded on a remote island who never found out that the war was over. But mainly, Berkeley—the spark of a student movement that exploded for a decade—was a quiet place, devoid of the political passions that once seemed so consuming. People's Park—the fulcrum and the symbol of Berkeley activism—was an empty lot, overgrown with weeds and forgotten by all sides in the battle, just a curious bit of local history to the current enrollees. "I just can't see why anyone would fight over that little piece of ground," said one bemused student.

As far as most of us can see, there is not any issue that young people in the eighties would find worth fighting for. They prefer not to have a nuclear war, but they would not march about it. They prefer good government leaders to bad ones, but since it is hard to tell which is which, they tend not to vote. Besides, they just moved, and they're not registered at their new address. They can quote fluctuations in the wholesale price of cocaine but they are uncertain how many senators their state sends to Washington.

That at least is the prevailing view, the one reflected in the media and a battery of polls and voter registration statistics. Young adults care little about politics and know even less. They see the whole business as an irrelevant flurry of numbers every four years, an archaic relic, irrelevant to their own fast-paced, now-oriented lives. Politics is a dividing line between the generations; it belongs to the anhedonic, older people who have the patience for complicated procedures, formal meetings, and institutional responses (resolutions, bills, amendments, and other things that offer no quick gratification and not even visible change). By the time the money is appropriated and the road is built, no one wants to go there anymore.

It is a view that is almost true. In a 1982 Gallup poll, only 49 percent of the respondents under thirty were registered to vote, compared to 73 percent in the thirty to forty-nine age group and 84 percent in the over fifty group. Only 15 percent of the under thirties had given "a lot of thought" to the next election, compared to 24 percent of the thirty to forty-nine age group and 32 percent of those over fifty. And perhaps most revealingly, only 59 percent of the under thirty group knew where their polling place was, compared to 81 percent of the thirty to forty-nine group.

Their lack of interest in the political process is becoming more pronounced. There has been a general slip in voter interest in the last decade, but it is most dramatic among young voters. According to Census Bureau reports, the greatest drop in registration and voter turnout percentages between 1972 and 1982 was among eighteen- to twenty-four-year-olds.

Campus politics has also become a vestigial organ, the preserve of a few hobbyists as rare as lepidopterists. Student government comes alive only when "Greeks" (fraternity and sorority members) try to take over as a diversion. In recent years, they have even controlled student affairs at Berkeley. Other than those sorties, no one much cares. A student leader at Barnard—a campus known for its seriousness—complained that "we had to drag people out of the library to vote in school elections."

Searching for something that would touch their lives directly is no easy matter. The Barnard leader was trying to mobilize a group to persuade the college to keep the dorms open during the Christmas holidays. Once upon a time, it would have been a good issue: Students who can't afford to go home for the holidays have no place to stay. In the sixties, it would have inspired at least a fiery denunciation of campus housing for its insensitivity toward less privileged students. But only a handful of Barnard women have that problem, and, in the spirit of the eighties, they would rather jerry-build a personal solution—like getting themselves invited to a friend's—than involve themselves in an "issue." The student leader herself concedes, "I guess they have more important things on their minds." Even tuition increases fork no lightning. "My father can afford it," students say.

The change is most apparent to someone like Robert Ringler. Ringler has been associate dean for student affairs at UCLA since 1971. His job is to enforce university policy outside of the classroom, and when he first started, he spent his time cooling down hot issues and mediating disputes between warring factions of the Black Students Union or the peace movement. "Students were boisterous and confrontational," he recalls. "My strategy was not to give them the confrontation they wanted, but to wait it out and find a peaceful solution. It was a matter of being realistic and deciding on the size of the sandbox. We had to protect the institution as best we could. We developed teach-ins here. We found space and money for balanced programs. We provided time and space to demonstrate. We allowed for the redress of grievances.

"I remember the rituals then—the signs, the committees, the enthusiasm for the Peace Corps, the Experimental College. There was a lot of political activity, and the pressure was really on us. Bruin Walk (a main path through the campus) was the scene of a lot of political activity and social and community action." For Ringler, Bruin Walk was the war front, the Pacific theater where factions fought for prominent positions to set up their tables and collect signatures and distribute leaflets.

All that is over now. There are no more confrontations and no hot issues. Bruin Walk is a pleasant outdoor mart for professional, ethnic, and religious clubs: the Black Law Students, assorted Christian fellowships, the Asian Engineers Society. Radical groups have become so weak that a fraternity recently gave a "Viva Zapata" party that made fun of Mexicans, and it fell to Ringler's office to correct them.

And Pam Grant, a residence hall dean at UCLA, says, "In the six months I have been here, I have yet to hear the word 'feminism' or hear a feminist perspective on anything. There was one small exception. I was asked to sign a document permitting a rape awareness event. That's as close as I've come to hearing a feminist issue."

When young adults do raise a political finger, they are more conservative than people their age are supposed to be. In 1984, Ronald Reagan was

the overwhelming preference of voters under thirty. It is a puzzling preference since other polls indicate that young adults are the age group most
likely to feel financially worse off because of the Reagan administration's
economic policies. They also oppose Reagan on other issues, such as nuclear
proliferation, abortion, and intervention in Central America. He is in
his seventies, he made his political bones by standing up to student activists,
and his haircut and values are from another era. Why then is he so
popular among young voters? Is he a father figure, long missing in their
lives? One explanation comes from a young volunteer in a presidential
campaign. "Reagan is making money for their parents," he observed
cynically.

It is a telling explanation. The generation that is reluctant to grow
up does not yet think about its own present or future good. The world
is not yet their responsibility. What is good for their parents is what is
good for them. It's their parents' world and their parents' economy; they
are just the kids and nowhere near taking possession of any of it. Voting
is just playing grown-up, dressing up in stuff from the attic. So when
they do it, they might as well do a good imitation of the way grown-
ups act. And they might as well protect their only real interests—their
parents' money.

The total picture seems to be one of blissful self-centeredness, of young
adults who are indifferent not only to politics and political institutions,
but to society as a whole. They appear to have no sense of any community
larger than their own households. A 1979 study of entering freshmen
by the University of Michigan's Institute for Social Research asked students what they considered "extremely important" in life. "Being a leader
in my community" was at the bottom of the list. Sixth on the list of
eight was "making a contribution to society." Number one was "a good
marriage and family life."

And a study of 1,125 college students by David A. Snow and Cynthia
L. Phillips, two University of Texas sociologists, attempted to find out
whether young people were primarily concerned with themselves or society,
"with impulse or institution" as the researchers described it. According
to the results, which were published in 1983 in the Social Science Quarterly,
80 percent saw themselves as guided by their own "feeling, thought,
and experience." Only 20 percent found direction in "institutionalized
roles and statuses."

The authors of the study interpreted this to mean that students were
unaligned individuals, looking out for themselves, without sensitivity or
obligation to society. It is an interpretation certainly borne out by many
things already touched on in this book—the shift in career choices and
subject majors from human services to the private sector, for instance.
Even the bad behavior in college dormitories—the loud music, the slam-

ming of doors—reveals a childish inability to be a citizen of a larger community.

And yet . . . it is a confusing and contradictory picture. Given a little breathing space, they seem to care. In a 1983 Gallup poll on the so-called "fairness" issues, people under thirty were more concerned about the treatment of blacks and women than any other age group was. Most surprising, they were more concerned about treatment of the elderly than the elderly themselves were. Seventy-five percent of the respondents under thirty thought that the elderly were treated unfairly, while only 61 percent of those over sixty-five felt that way.

This unexpected concern for the underdog may express a sense of their vulnerability and of the fragility of their own class status. There but for fortune go I, and who knows how long fortune will be on my side.

This identification with the underdog may explain the prairie fire of protests over South African divestiture. It seems at a glance like an unlikely issue to spark passions among young people who, so far, haven't been aroused by the nuclear arms race, United States involvement in Central America, or cutbacks in student aid. Apartheid is an old issue, South Africa is far away, and the investment of university funds in companies that do business with companies in South Africa is a legalistic issue, at many removes from the bleakness of life in the black homelands. Issues take off for a lot of reasons, not the least of which is the skill and charisma of the organizers. And this issue clearly has justice on its side. Still, it is interesting that politically dormant, allegedly self-centered students have been stirred by the plight of the most downtrodden people on the face of the earth. It is tempting to think that, despite all of their privileges, they too, somehow, feel powerless and oppressed.

And there are other stirrings of political life among the young. Senator Gary Hart pulled off an unexpected victory in the California Democratic primary that surprised even his own strategists. The credit for the upset went to thousands of young volunteers who worked the phone banks. "We showed you could do it," Hart's California chairman, John Emerson, told the Los Angeles *Times*. "We put eighteen thousand people in the field, and they called four hundred thousand people in the last four days. It made the difference for us in a lot of congressional districts." Hart's main opponent, former Vice-President Walter Mondale, depended on "organized labor and prominent citizens" to do his fieldwork. But the kids worked harder.

And a 1984 *New York Times* feature on young activists in Washington began, "A stroll through the Dupont Circle neighborhood suggests that reports of the death of youthful idealism may have been greatly exaggerated.

"Among these tree-lined streets are the headquarters for some of the more than 100 nonprofit organizations that depend on the low-paying labors of thousands of recent graduates of colleges and law schools." Consumer activist Ralph Nader was quoted as saying, "There's a different type of activism today. You don't get the drama of the demonstrations and sit-ins. It's institutionalized—more joining of groups. But in terms of reporting, researching and lobbying, there's much more."

The piece went on to describe bright young professionals—lawyers, editors, researchers—who worked hard at jobs that paid half of what they would earn in the private sector. These young "grunts" lived in tiny, often shared apartments, and had potluck dinners with their friends instead of going out. "There are a lot of committed people in Washington who care about arms control and other issues," said a twenty-five-year-old chief lobbyist for an antinuclear organization. "I think it's different than it was ten years ago. There's more willingness to be in it for the long haul."

It would seem, then, that this is a generation that cares but can't often put that concern into action, even the simple action of voting. One wonders why, and one answer that emerges solves a number of other puzzles about the generation. They have no place to put their idealism. Like young people always, they have a romantic longing for transcendence, for something bigger and better than themselves. Some members of every generation would translate that into a vision of a better country, a better society. But we seem to be in an age that is short on romantic ideals and grand dreams. We have become practical people, turned in on ourselves and our own tangible concerns—the small world, as Ingmar Bergman called it in *Fanny and Alexander*. This is a natural enough swing for the middle-aged, who may regret having given away so much of themselves during the delusional sixties. But people in their twenties never even had a chance to tilt at windmills. They grew up knowing that it was futile and the game was fixed. For many of them, it remains a piece of unfinished business, a glitch in the process of growing up.

Presidential hopeful Gary Hart, who made a specialty of appealing to younger voters, told the *New York Times Magazine* in one of his more reflective moments: "This is a generation that grew up in 20 of the worst years this country has ever seen, starting with Nov. 22, 1963. In that 20-year span, there was a wave of assassinations unprecedented in our nation's history, the most divisive war since the Civil War, the biggest political scandal of our nation's history, and a period of the worst economic crisis since the Great Depression.

"All we've had for 20 years is bad news. I can't tell you psychologically what that's done to a generation, but it's profound. These things linger on. There were reasons for these people not to get involved in politics.

I believe there is a latent idealism in the American people, a need to serve something other than their own interests. When it isn't tapped, people get cynical."

Seymour Martin Lipset, professor of political science and sociology at Stanford University, maintains that political beliefs are formed in the late teens, "particularly if they've gone through a very heavy experience." So these are cynical young people. The ISR's study of entering freshmen revealed that 39 percent believed that Congress was guilty of "considerable dishonesty and immorality," and 37 percent thought the same of the President and his administration.

The twenty years of disillusionment may explain more than cynical indifference to politics. It may be one of the many and complex reasons why young adults are not so eager to grow up and inherit the world. They knew at a much too tender age that it wasn't a nice place. Politics was one more reason to be scared, and this is especially true for someone raised to be special. How can you be special if you haven't the slightest hope of changing or even affecting the world?

And yet, they can't help wishing there were something to be idealistic about. Pollster Patrick H. Caddell talked to the *New York Times* about the politics of the baby-boom generation. "These people are late, but they have been late for everything—late getting married, late settling down. But they're coming. They're rootless, but they're looking for something."

All of this becomes poignantly clear when you meet young adults who have had some brush with the bigger world.

Joe's bad luck is that he has grown up astride two entirely different sets of values about politics. He fell in love with politics when he was a kid, when everyone agreed that it was a way of making the world better. Now, he is twenty-eight, and he can't make sense of that idea—or let go of it.

His family were traditional, first-generation Armenian-American. They were Republicans because a Republican state legislator was also Armenian, and he serviced the ethnic community well. By demographic accident, Joe's family lived in a suburb that, in the sixties and early seventies, was Jewish and liberal, sometimes even radical.

Joe's father was a pipe fitter who made good money. "We were middle-middle class," he says. His mother was an intelligent, ambitious woman who bowed to the old world notion of a woman's role. She didn't go to college because her father forbade her to, and she didn't work because her husband forbade her to. But she liked politics and she volunteered in the local Republican organization.

Joe liked politics too. Even as a child, he collected campaign buttons and followed elections instead of sports. He was a doer, always involved in school projects and activities. In high school during the Vietnam War days, he was the lone conservative pitted against passionate radicals. But it was fun, and he was accepted on his terms as the loyal opposition. It was all part of the froth of being young in interesting times.

His mother, who invested a lot of her own thwarted dreams in her son, found an item in the paper about applications for congressional pages. Joe applied through his congressman, who was a freshman Republican in a Democratic House, and he feels that it must have been a miracle that he was selected for one of the two openings that year. So at sixteen, his parents took him to Washington, helped him find a boarding-house, and left him to the perils of the nation's capital and the House Cloak Room.

His only regret was that they came with him at all instead of letting him have the whole adventure himself at sixteen. He spent the year attending the pages' school at the Library of Congress from six to nine in the morning and then working the cloak room as a page, waiting for the buzzer to sound. He delivered messages to the members and found them when they were needed, and he got a long, inside look at the workings of Congress. He was utterly enthralled, even though it was entirely clear to him that many members of the House (including his sponsor) were half-wits. It wasn't the personalities; it was the institution, the process, the idea of participating in something bigger than himself that he loved. He couldn't wait to finish high school and college, go to the University of Virginia Law School, and return to the Washington arena as soon as possible.

On the day he left Washington, in the summer of 1972, still innocently Republican, five burglars broke into the Democratic National Committee office in the Watergate complex.

None of that mattered right away. It was just a bungled minor crime and no one believed that the President had anything to do with it. Richard Nixon was reelected by a landslide, and Joe returned to high school a celebrity. He had seen Washington and famous politicians up close. Thoroughly lionized, he spent a lot of his senior year making the circuit of all the history and civics classes.

It was quite a moment in the sun, but it made the dark days that followed even harder to take. Nixon's resignation became his own personal disillusionment, his fall from grace. The Republican politicians who had made him a hero in high school history classes turned out to be bad guys. And ironically, it was his cloak room boss, Minority Leader Jerry Ford, who went on to become President and pardon Nixon.

By this time, Joe was a sophomore at a private university. His parents pinched pennies to send him there because his father felt that public universities were breeding grounds for radicals. Joe had a scholarship and a part-time job, but still managed to get A's and be active on campus. Not that there was much for a conservative to be active about back then. Fraternities were weak and so was student government, but Joe belonged to a fraternity and was elected a senator.

He had acted out of habit, but by the time he graduated, he had lost all interest in a political career and a life in Washington. He went to law school near home and took a four-year combined program that gave him both a law degree and an M.B.A.

He is now an associate with a respected law firm. "Because of my accounting and finance training, I've been chosen to look after the accounts receivable of a partner who recently left the firm because his clients turned out to be deadbeats." He shrugs resignedly. "It's okay." He has been with the firm for a little over two years, and he will soon be evaluated for a partnership. But he has no desire to be a partner in that law firm or in any other one. "I never really liked law," he explains. "I know I don't want to do it forever. I'm not sure what I would want to do forever." This is not an overindulged Huck Finn talking. This is a hardworking, goal-oriented, upwardly mobile, conservative young man from a traditional, ethnic family. This is a young man who wears a gray suit, white shirt, and dark-red tie, parts his hair on the side, and shows up for work on time every day.

"I might want to start a management consulting company. A law degree is really a ticket to do what you want. But I don't want to practice law. I'm idealistic. Intellectually, I like law, but I hate reporting back to clients. And lawyers are always the stumbling blocks, the ones who say 'You can't.' I hate that role."

What he does want to do comes out slowly, in veiled hints and buzz words and long pauses, in the interstices of a long conversation. He has just been to his ten-year high school reunion and he has seen his old radical antagonists. "Politically, we've met in the middle and even crossed over. I've moved to the middle and left. They've moved middle and right," he says, amused but as if it all still mattered. He is a member of the redevelopment board of a housing project near his old university, and attends two meetings a week. While he's in the neighborhood, he drops in at his fraternity house, where he is an adviser.

"I guess I still want to save the world. I'm in my third year at the law firm, but it's just not fulfilling. The corporate structure doesn't satisfy me. I want to get things done."

The truth is, he's still in love with politics, and he admits it with a half smile. But politics is now like the kind of girl nice boys don't marry. He worries that a candidate's life is a fishbowl, that holding office destroys family life. Perhaps what he is saying is that holding office is no longer something that would make his immigrant parents proud. It doesn't even sit well with him. "Maybe I'll get back into campaigns sometime and try for an appointive office." Meanwhile, he will spend another year with his law firm, but it's not what he really wants to do. It never was.

It's not the usual storefront office on a main street, with a huge sign advertising the candidate and the windows plastered with placards and bumper stickers. The Hart campaign headquarters in Los Angeles is an old frame house with a porch on a residential street in the north end of Hollywood. You can hardly see the sign because it's hidden by a huge, leafy tree hanging over the front yard. It is an odd choice, but perhaps it is part of what the presidential candidate called "new ideas."

Once you get inside, you see the logic of it. There is a lot of space— even a backyard—and it is cool and pleasant in these high-ceilinged rooms. It is the afternoon of the California primary, and it is bustling here but not frantic. There are a lot of young men in Oxford shirts and Levi's, and if it weren't for the computer print-outs and a profusion of small touch-tone phones, this might be mistaken for university co-op housing.

There are a few older hands in the front room, the usual cabal of political junkies and part-time operatives who show up in some headquarters at every election and work a few phone lists. They are not saying so aloud, but they have all heard that their candidate has lost in New Jersey, and they know that even if he wins here, the race for the nomination is over. One of the old hands boasts that he was in the McCarthy campaign in 1968 and went on to Chicago. Another admits that he worked for Bobby Kennedy that year but supported McCarthy after the assassination. "We were friendly enemies," they agree.

"I've supported some of the best losers," says the first one, the McCarthy supporter. For these old liberals, there is no dishonor in losing.

The young men in the Oxford shirts feel differently. They are still working away at solving precinct problems—voters out in the other end of the county who can't find their polling places or whose registrations have mysteriously lapsed—and phoning identified supporters to remind them to vote. They know about the New Jersey loss, but they are less fond of losing. They also seem to be better workers.

The young people that I meet here are special, certainly in the statistical sense. They are among the tiny minority who have been politically involved. (According to the 1982 Freshman Survey, only 8.2 percent of entering college students had participated in a campaign. Many, I imagine, did it to satisfy a course requirement.) The volunteers here include haves and, relatively speaking, have-nots. They are moderate and liberal, altruistic and personally ambitious. They are from the East, the West, and the Midwest. What they have in common is that they care about the world beyond the borders of their own immediate lives. They feel it is their world and they have assumed some responsibility for it. All by itself, that is a kind of maturity, and it makes them interesting. But what is also interesting about them is their shadow—their friends and peers who don't care. I think of them as shadows because they lurk in the recesses of my mind as a constant, unanswered question. I keep hoping that in asking why these young men are here, I will also find out why the others aren't.

Bill is blond and lanky, with a farm boy's slow, thoughtful way. He is twenty-two and a student at the University of Southern California. He is from the Midwest, and he has been in Los Angeles for a year and a half, going to school part-time, majoring in economics, and working at the university library to pay his way. He chose Los Angeles because it is a "global" city. He has three younger sisters; his father is a college professor, and his mother recently went back to work—selling maintenance contracts for Sears—to help make ends meet.

This is Bill's first political campaign. His first taste of politics was as a volunteer on a project for a John F. Kennedy memorial in Philadelphia. He has no plans for a political career. After he graduates, he thinks he will get a master's in philosophy. "I may go to law school after that, but philosophy interests me, and I want to do something I like even though I'll probably do nothing with it." He is aware that this is an unusual attitude these days. He is a bit of a rebel behind that quiet self-effacing manner.

He is working in the campaign because "I'm scared of a second Reagan term. I'll probably work for whoever is the Democratic nominee, but I like Hart because he has a better plan for the eighties. I like his industrial plan. I've seen unemployed auto workers in Pennsylvania and Ohio, and I think retraining of workers is essential." He also likes Hart's proposed tax reforms. Bill is a logical young man, not a romantic or a hero worshiper.

But still. "I see politics as a solution, but it's easy to get disillusioned. With a lot of politicians, you wonder why they do it. They're just politicians, not leaders. Jerry Brown is just a politician. The Democrats in Congress were just politicians after the 1980 election when they capitulated to Reagan's so-called mandate. Reagan had only twenty-five percent of the eligible electorate, but the Democrats just went with the tide. They gave Reagan carte blanche to destroy this country's social programs and system of government. They're not leaders when they're more interested in opinion polls than the public good."

He admits that he is the only one among his friends or peers at school who is involved in a campaign. "The others just vote." I ask him why his generation is so apolitical, and he pauses and reflects. "The first political event that I remember was Watergate. It interrupted my television watching after school." He was twelve years old at the time. He also remembers seeing George Wallace shot, and he recalls hearing about the assassinations of both Kennedys and Martin Luther King. *"It seemed natural to me and my generation to think that politics was dirty."*

Later in the conversation, he comes back to this theme of his generation's apathy. "I think our generation is complacent and without drive because they don't have that basic drive to go beyond their parents. They know that they can't." Another reason to leave running the world to their parents.

I ask him what issue might mobilize his generation and he shrugs pessimistically. "Maybe if half of them were shipped off to fight in Nicaragua or El Salvador, they might wake up. Or if the Third World defaults on its debts and that creates serious trouble."

Terry is small and neat, with large blue eyes and sharply defined facial bones. He too is from the East, but his family has moved out here, and he shuttles back and forth between Los Angeles and New York University, where he studies acting. His father is a banker and his mother is a psychotherapist; he grew up in Scarsdale and Beverly Hills. He learned about politics from a feminist older sister and an uncle who fought in Vietnam.

His own first political move was registering for the draft. "I registered 'under protest,' whatever that means." Apparently it meant very little, since the draft board considered him duly registered. He also failed to include his Social Security number on the form, and when he was contacted later, he provided it, again "under protest." It is a mild form of protest compared, say, to burning draft cards, or even whole draft boards. "I'll be 4F anyway," he says. "I'm allergic to penicillin and I have displaced kneecaps." He is bright enough to see the humor in it.

He is in this campaign for two reasons. Acting is slow, and he worries about "the absence of intelligence in the Reagan administration." He sounds a little like a sophisticated, eastern liberal, uncomfortable because the people in the White House are not his sort. That may be part of it, but Terry's concerns are more than snobbery. "I am concerned about my future on earth. I know that sounds a little dramatic, but I hate Reagan's foreign policy. He uses the Soviet Union as a scapegoat and social issues like prayer in schools and abortion as a diversionary tactic."

He has been a volunteer for the past three weeks, and he does whatever needs to be done. He picks up the candidate's baggage at the airport. He drives. He licks stamps. He puts up posters. He gives out flyers at rallies. Tomorrow, it will be all over, and he doesn't know what he will do next. It doesn't seem to bother him much. Something will come up.

"I've tried to get some of my friends to volunteer, but I haven't had any luck," he says, talking about the famous apathy of his generation. "They're career-oriented, members of the me-decade. The excuse they give is they have no time. But they're not doing anything. They're just afraid of being committed to anything. Someone might call them next time. It will be inconvenient. God forbid any inconvenience in their lives!"

It may also be that they fear commitment for a different reason. It isn't just time or inconvenience that scares them so much as the threat of definition. If I do this, the unconscious reasons, it means that I know what I stand for. I'm becoming defined and I'm a step closer to being grown up.

David, who is twenty-five, dark, handsome, with ringlets of curly hair, is also from Westchester County and a hyphenate actor/political activist. He and Terry never met before this campaign and the fact that they are working side by side in Los Angeles is either coincidence or an omen. David has no trouble with commitment or enthusiasm, only with natural limits, such as not having enough time to do all the things he has in mind.

He has two main goals. In reverse order, he wants to be President and a "total film maker." He doesn't see the two as at all contradictory. "Movies," he explains, "are an important medium for social and political messages. They're teacher, leader, mirror of America. And acting helps you make a name for yourself. The political parties don't do it for you anymore. And acting helps with television and getting your message across."

He cannot remember a time when he wasn't interested in politics. His father is a doctor and his mother is a housewife, but the family always talked politics at home, and he volunteered for Westchester Congressman Richard L. Ottinger during the oil embargo crisis in 1979, setting up a local energy committee.

But his real political motivation is startlingly old-fashioned: patriotism. He has done a lot of traveling with his family—to the Philippines, Mexico, Spain, and Greece. Travel, he says, "made me love America. This isn't just the greatest country. It's the greatest country that *has ever been*. Sometimes we stumble, but we stumble doing the moral thing." It would be nit-picking to notice that the countries he visited are hardly models of modern democracy. It is enough that the conclusion he drew from his experiences elsewhere was pride, a projection of his own need to be the best.

At the University of Pennsylvania, he majored in political science, was president of his class, and continued acting in campus productions and anything else he could get into. The stress almost gave him colitis, but his pace never slackened. When he ran for class president, he visited each classroom twice.

He has very strong opinions about the direction politics ought to take in the eighties—toward a brand of social and economic liberalism that favors the middle class. "Over a million people showed up in Central Park for a demonstration against nuclear weapons. But that demonstration fell apart because minority-rights speakers got on the platform and scared Middle America away. The demonstration was taken over by fringe groups."

David sees himself as a champion of the underrepresented, overtaxed middle class. "The poor are represented by the benefits system and the rich by Reagan, the worst president of all time. His tax cuts helped the rich, not the middle class. He had a mandate for tax reform, but he just gave breaks to the rich."

On the other end of the political spectrum, he dislikes Jesse Jackson almost as much. "I hate expressions like 'from the outhouse to the White House.' Vulgarity doesn't inspire people." David isn't in politics for the pedestrian or the vulgar. John F. Kennedy, he feels, was eloquent, but a poor president. His idea of a leader is Martin Luther King, who perhaps has the advantage of being dead for many years. "King was eloquent, romantic, beautiful, inspiring."

His own candidate of the moment, Colorado Senator Gary Hart, is also something of a disappointment to him. "Hart has the right positions, but he isn't a good enough communicator. He isn't charismatic or eloquent enough."

Davis is a little grandiose—in his energy, his ambitions, his romanticism—but he provides a good, bigger-than-life clue to what his generation wants in its politics and its leaders, and to our own political future. Young adults want romance, charisma, transcendence. They want heroes. At the same time, they are insecure about their own precarious middle-class status and they want practical leaders who will protect it. It is hard to find inspiring ideals in this agenda of tax restructuring and saying no to the poor, unless, of course, the ideals are manufactured by media wizards, by great communicators. Perhaps in the mode of the Los Angeles Olympics, we will have laser shows and fireworks to announce a bill making private-school tuition tax deductible.

The only thing approaching an ideal expressed by young people is peace. And that may not be idealism so much as sensible fear. This is a generation that has no illusions about war. Asked what issue would mobilize their generation, Bill talks about another Vietnam in Central America. Terry and David quickly respond, "Nukes." "It cuts party and economic lines," says David. "People are scared."

The concerns of the three Hart volunteers may be shared by all ages but are especially intense among their generation. In a 1983 Gallup poll, 76 percent of the respondents under thirty favored a verifiable nuclear freeze. Seventy percent of all of those polled agreed, but the percentage got higher as the age group got younger. Similarly, younger people in the same poll were more likely to see a greater danger of war in the continuation of the arms build-up than in the United States falling behind the Soviet Union in nuclear weaponry.

Clearly, this is a dove generation, but it is hard to say what that means in conventional political terms. In a piece that appeared in several campus newspapers, Pamela Douglas, a teacher of screenwriting at UCLA and USC wrote that her students were obsessed with dread of nuclear war. Of sixty papers turned in for one assignment, 20 percent focused on a character who is among the last human beings alive the day after a nuclear war.

It sounds like the stirrings of political concern. But Douglas went on to explain more about her students. "The majority of young people in my classes are white, from upper-middle-class families in the West. They were born in the sixties and don't remember (or don't understand) the anti-war movement. One might expect them to relate to the Nuclear Freeze Initiative, which had its start in California, but they don't. They don't see the point.

"Instead they collect teddy bears. At USC, undergraduate women keep as many as twenty on their beds. They're happy to tell you about their favorites. 'This is the one my dad got me when I was sixteen.' Or 'He's my favorite because he hugs me back.'

"No male student confesses to hugging teddy bears. But they have their equivalent in prose: Young men are writing stories from children's viewpoints in record numbers. Five this term are about little boys under nine years old. That just hasn't happened in my classes before."

The teddy bears are an apt metaphor for the often childlike avoidance that characterizes the generation. There is just me and Poo and Tigger, but nothing scarier out there. Over a hundred young adults were interviewed for this book. Mostly, these were long, open-ended conversations in which the interviewee had a chance to talk about himself and anything on his mind. Toward the end, I would ask, "How do you see your future?" Only four mentioned—of their own accord—concern about war or other large-scale disaster. (For what it's worth, they were Jack, the punk musician; a very bright Berkeley junior whose father is a history professor; Barbara, the potter in Santa Cruz; and Peggy, the unemployed editor.) Sometimes,

I would bring up the subject, and there would be a flurry of requisite concern. But when they were asked to think about the future, well, that was small and personal. It was about where they would live and how and whether they would marry or travel or own a home. The bigger world still belongs to their parents. Perhaps the attitude was best expressed by Eric, the young artist living in New York. "You know," he said, "I worry about not worrying about the bomb."

16
Ten More Years

Parents have always considered their children of any age immature. It is hard for young people to grow up and for parents to let go. Those of us who are now middle-aged can—if we are honest—remember the ways in which our childishness and inexperience as young adults vexed our parents. As they saw it, we rented when we should have bought or bought when we should have rented. We left jobs we should have kept and kept jobs we should have left. As far as our parents were concerned, we bought the wrong furniture and joined the wrong church and perhaps married the wrong person. We had our children too soon or too late or too far apart. Friction between the generations is a natural part of the struggle to grow up and leave home.

But that isn't the same thing that is happening to this generation. Our quarrels with our parents were about adult decisions. They were advanced adults and we were beginners. Our children, now in their twenties, are not beginner adults, coping well or badly with adult issues, and that is the point of this book. The timetable has changed.

It now takes another decade to grow up in our culture. We can dither about definitions of maturity, but most of us know what we mean by it. We mean having meaningful work and committed relationships, being part of a community, and assuming responsibility. We mean paying your own way, carrying your weight in the world. My father used to talk of it as "getting set in life." Middle-class Americans used to do it in their early twenties. It now seems to happen on either side of thirty.

Many of us, including young adults themselves, are painfully aware of this and feel puzzled and bewildered by it. A lot of "oughts" hang in the air, for them and for their parents. They ought to be on their own, they ought to have more direction, they ought to be able to finish something. They seem like perfectly good engines with mysterious bugs in them. Why are they stuck?

In researching this book, I talked to a lot of young adults. Some of them were stuck and manifested it in a variety of ways, with a variety of rationalizations. Some had been stuck and had gotten themselves moving. And some had been doing fine all along. In examining what they have told me about their lives, I see four basic issues.

The first, of course, is their own burden of expectations, their sense of entitlement. They expect what by most standards would be a privileged life-style in one way or another. Some expect the "good life." Others have subtle variations on entitlement: They want influential positions, freedom from drudgery and frustration, and lasting bliss in this life. As Eric, the young artist in Chapter 5, said, "I have only forty more years to live, and I don't want to spend one minute of it unhappy."

In fact, Eric spends a lot of it unhappy, perhaps because he is so self-absorbed and unproductive. He wants so much, he can't get started on any of it. Like his peers, he has no sense that he has to pay his dues. He was the darling of every school he went to, and he conned and dazzled his way through. Like John, the psychiatrist's son, he wants to have "impact" on the world. It doesn't happen quickly, the way it did in school, and most of his contacts with reality are a jolt to his self-esteem. So he ignores reality a lot. His low-paying, menial job disappears in the fantasy that a beautiful, high-paid co-worker will marry him.

It is hard to say where the fantasy and the sense of entitlement comes from. We are quick to blame the parents, who are guilty mostly of doing too much, of trying too hard, of being too in love with their kids. Yet the expectations seem to be more than the pathology of any family. They seem to be part of the culture. Parents were just acting out the beliefs they shared with the media, the schools, their college classmates, and the child-rearing professionals.

Even children raised by diehards who never spared the rod or spoiled the child looked up in late adolescence and felt entitled. It is an example of the hundredth monkey theory, which begins with one monkey washing the sand off his yams. A few others learn from him, and the practice spreads. Once a hundred monkeys are washing their food, there is no longer any need for direct communication. The idea is in the air, and even monkeys on remote parts of the island and on other islands start to wash their yams. People copy the behavior and the attitudes of their peers, even peers they have never met. "I hate the idea of a nine-to-five job," is a sentence I heard over and over again from young people whose parents all held nine-to-five jobs.

Another of the things they learn from each other is the belief that they have infinite choices and that they can go on choosing until they find perfection. They analyze what is wrong with the company and the industry they work in, the city they live in, and the values of society as a whole. They can tell you what is wrong with Wall Street, the music business, universities, their parents, and the institution of marriage. It is not that they are wrong. It's just that they may not have a choice. They may have to live with these imperfections, at least until they have paid their dues and are in a position to make improvements. Meanwhile, they might learn something in the process. Most of all they might learn about the satisfaction of overcoming difficulties.

But the hardest lesson for this generation seems to be this: Choice is limited. You cannot do everything and be everything in one life. Deborah, the computer science student in Chapter 12, provided the most cogent realization of what I call "the best shot" decision. She decided that she couldn't be a really good mechanic or ranch hand and that she ought to go back to graduate school in some mathematical field because that was what she was already good at. She understood that she had to make a choice and focus. That meant giving up a few dreams, making a commitment, and defining herself. It was hard to do, but she is a happier person than the artist who will do everything but paint. Ironically, nothing is as immobilizing as the need to have everything.

By contrast, the young people who had problems growing up developed an almost reflexive understanding that life was tough. They had practice in struggle that turned out to be their most valuable asset. It was like having an extra gear, an overdrive that they could just slip into.

The belief that they are special and deserve special treatment is the worst possible baggage young people could carry into the hard-nosed eighties. If their first problem is that they are psychologically unprepared for adulthood, their second problem is that they are heading into it in a time of lowered expectation and diminished opportunity. It is important to remember that those young people who are lucky enough to have the right skills for the eighties are doing fine. They are either growing up promptly or not minding that they aren't because they are not facing a crisis of shrinking expectations.

But for the others, the world is just offering less and asking for more than it used to. That is a nasty enough trick for life to have played on them. But there is more.

There is also the change in men's and women's roles and the subsequent change in family life and society. This is the first generation to swallow the changes whole rather than piecemeal. Young women will not be home-makers like their mothers; young men will not be providers like their fathers. It makes finding an identity interesting but confusing. Sorting it out takes time. The existence of all those options also changes life's timetable. If you don't have to marry, settle down, and raise a family, then what is the big rush about growing up?

The fourth reason for delayed adulthood is that young people have found themselves in an eddy of changing values. It once counted for something to help others or to work for ideals. Suddenly, in the eighties, it seemed silly, a job for a patsy, a ne'er-do-well. If you hadn't acquired the skills to make money or complex machines, you weren't special at all. Unfortunately, many young adults just hadn't gotten the word in time. They had already signed up—either emotionally or in the more practical terms of degrees and career commitment—to save the world in some way. When they discovered that we didn't care anymore about politics or education or social work or the less lucrative aspects of health care, they became confused.

Those who were stronger and more determined decided that they wanted to have the best seats in the house, the advertised name brands. They switched to the "hot" fields of high technology and business. Others just withdrew to various Never-Never Lands, like Santa Cruz or "Haver-ville," and stayed confused, loyal to vague ideals they have never developed or tested. Ian, for instance, believes that his college ought to have a foreign studies program in a Spanish-speaking country because he senses that it is a good idea to learn about cultures outside of your own. Yet he has given very little thought to the political and economic predicament of Latin countries or their relationship to the United States. Brian, who left his father's business to be a waiter in Maui and Santa Cruz, had undefined yearnings to make the world better. He settled on massage, polarity, herbology.

To some extent, they have themselves to blame for their lack of intellec-tual discipline. It is possible to develop your values and keep them even in the absence of popular support. But young people find themselves in a context in which that kind of thinking isn't happening. The thinking itself isn't valued. No one is showing them how to do it. And no one is offering them the experiences that they might learn from. In some other time, Haverville College might have decided that it was important, even worth the money, to have a foreign studies program in Ecuador and sent Ian down to get it started. Being naturally open-minded and adventur-ous, he would have met and tangled with Ecuadorians as a grown-up and dealt with those bigger questions.

As it is, Ian stayed in Haverville and then moved to a beach town.

Ian, and many of the others, are to a certain extent victims of class privilege. To be an upper-middle-class American child in the sixties and seventies was almost like being aristocracy. In some unspoken way, these children were raised to privilege and leadership. But it turned out we didn't need so many leaders, or at least we didn't have entry-level jobs for so many of them. What we did need were useful tinkerers—engineers and accountants—and hard-nosed deal makers who understood money. There had been a shift from "soft" to "hard" skills. Often the young people in command of the right skills were the children of foreigners and lower-middle-class Americans who were more ambitious and practical. So once again, we are experiencing a subtle shift in the class structure. The educated, "aristocratic" middle class is involved in old agendas and it is losing ground to groups who are more vigorous, more alert for where the rewards are.

Some of these old agendas are potentially important and interesting. Ian, Walt, Brian, Judy, Eric, Barbara, Nick, John—and thousands like them—were, in their half-formed way, raising questions about the kind of society we are. But none of them are in a position to be heard. I don't mean anything grand by that. Few twenty-five-year-olds are elected to Congress or given syndicated columns. What troubles me is that the young people who are doing the wondering are not connected to the rest of society at all. They are submerged somewhere in the youth culture, in beach towns or college communities or in menial jobs. They are out of sight, like roving herds of black sheep. They are hardly in touch with us and we do not respond to them.

Politicians and product-makers will pay attention to their more successful, more docile counterparts, who are more successful precisely because they didn't waste too much time listening to inner voices. It wasn't a privilege they had. They just wanted to know what society wanted and they happily became it. It is sensible and less troublesome.

It is probably alarmist to see incipient authoritarianism here, but I do see something worrisome. The young people in high tech were not narrow or boring, but they were a little insulated. As one of them noted, "I'd never know we were at war until I went home and watched the news." Deborah, who is one of the more remarkable young women in the world, was concerned about the environmental danger of the chemicals used by her industry. She is the only one of the young people in technology who expressed any concern about the bigger world or about the broader effects of her own industry.

The young business people were more reflective about what their own lives meant, but none of them raised questions about the directions or values of society. Peter, the boat-building entrepreneur, grew up in The

Hague, had a degree in international relations, interned with a Congressman, and had lived in India and Mexico, yet he was entirely preoccupied with making a go of his business. Like a good shoemaker, he was sticking to his last.

Which I suppose is as it should be. In some of the early chapters, I was impatient with some of the bright, introspective young people who have impaled themselves on their questions and can't get their lives going. It seemed to me that they were using their social values as an excuse not to grow.

It is a dilemma. The well-adjusted young people who are getting their own lives in order are a relief. They are more mature. Yet I worry about a world in which the questioners have exiled themselves to Never-Never Land, where they will not bother anyone except an occasional writer. I worry, I suppose, that we will look up and find that we have an economy but not a society, that everyone simply takes care of himself as sensibly as he can. As Martha Green, director of career services at Barnard, put it, "No one is paying anyone to care about other people. In the great society, people could make money *and* care. . . . Responsible young men and women know that they have to make a living."

That, of course, is reality. And I suppose what we need is a magic balance. We need young people who are useful and also thinkers. They need to acquire both "hard" and "soft" skills in a culture in which we have traditionally done one or the other. And the burden to change is greatest for the special children, the young people who expected to have some say in things, since they are most frustrated.

In fact, if I were asked to give specific advice to thoughtful young people it would simply be that they assign themselves two educational tasks: to develop their minds and also to develop ways to make themselves useful. I realize that this is not always easy to do. The departments that offer practical majors—like computer science and business—have become swollen with power and demand an exorbitant number of courses. The good liberal arts subjects—like history—demand a great deal of work. But schools are moving toward "interdisciplinary" mixes, and accommodations can be made for students who are aggressive enough to pester the system. Indeed, if they pester the system, it might change.

But serious students are not betraying themselves or their friends or their favorite professors if they also take courses that will lead to employment. It would be better for them and for us if they could make a living in the mainstream of society and still be around to think about that society. This prosaic advice would definitely include a visit to the career adviser on their campus. (I also think that the advice given by Bernice Russell, the director of placement at Loyola Marymount University, in Chapter 3 ought to be committed to memory.)

This mixing of goals does not preclude young people from becoming thinkers, leaders, creators. And it isn't just advice about having something to fall back on, though that isn't a bad idea. It is a more complex message about discipline and the contradictions of individualism. A political consultant used to tell his idealistic candidates: "Losers don't legislate." The meaning here is that you can be more special if the world works for you and you work for it. It is a way to close the gap between reality and expectations.

In fact, the second suggestion I would offer young adults—and this applies also to the ones who have made themselves useful and are doing well—is that they pay more attention to the mounting national deficit, the arms race, Central America, India, and Poland. They ought to concern themselves more with the possibility that debtor nations will default and about famine in Africa. It will make them better citizens, perhaps better leaders. But even more, it will distract them from their ceaseless preoccupation with themselves. We are moving relentlessly toward a society of individuals, free of family or community ties, and this is not always healthy. We tend to think about ourselves too much. A young alcoholic I know called his AA sponsor (a kind of peer counselor) and complained for some time about what was wrong with his life. His sponsor told him to go clean the bathroom. The bathroom may have needed cleaning, but even more, the young man needed to think about something besides himself.

If I were asked to give advice to the parents of young adults, it would be simply to let go, to accept that adulthood happens a decade later. Your young adult children are facing a different set of problems, even if their own mind-set is one of those problems. There is little point in resenting the fact that your children are still dependent and confused at an age when you had real adult responsibilities. That doesn't mean you have to enable your children to go on that way. You can stop taking care of their unpaid bills or finding new jobs for them when they get bored. But you can also stop thinking about what they ought to be doing and criticizing them and giving them unwanted advice. You can't nag them into adulthood. The very nature of becoming an adult is such that no one can do it for you.

It is also important to keep in mind that they have their own truly special, if not eccentric, kind of strength, precisely because of the history that gave them their vulnerabilities. They deal with uncertainty and ambivalence better than we do because they have had more practice. They have a greater capacity to enjoy life, again because they have had so much practice. As a generation, they may have more talent for recreation than any in history. And this is not meant unkindly. It gives them great resilience and the ability to set aside for a while problems that might ravage their parents. So even their escapism has its value. Most of all, their sense of specialness gives them a hidden layer of ego strength. They may crack or run away when the world does not treat them as they expect, but they are not done for. That sense of their own worth—no matter how tattered it is—enables them to rebound and grow up . . . just a little later.

There are, however, two specific and, I hope, final bail-outs that parents might make. Young adults seem to do very well with therapy. Many whom I interviewed managed to turn their lives around after getting professional help, and this was especially true for dependency problems. Dependent young people, by virtue of their problem, can't pay for their own therapy. It seems that parents have to pick up this one last bill to break the cycle.

Another possible last bill is health insurance. Health insurance carriers have not acknowledged the prolonged adolescence of our children. Most cover dependent children until they are nineteen, unless they are full-time students, who are covered until twenty-three. At that time, they should be on their own, with jobs that carry their own policies. However, they aren't, and parents worry what they will do if something happens to their blithely healthy children, who leave school, go back to school, take jobs and quit them with dizzying speed. The parents try to keep track of their insurance status, but the kids feel immortal and don't care.

So I would also suggest that parents buy themselves peace of mind, if they can afford it, and present their children with a major medical policy. It shouldn't be a comprehensive policy that takes care of every doctor visit. Just disaster insurance. It makes a nice birthday present.

On the other hand, if I ran a medical insurance company, I would offer a policy that covers the policy holder's young adult children until they are thirty or so. It would be good for business and little risk. As far as I can tell, there is a providence that watches over them and protects them from illness. Perhaps it is the vitamins and good food their indulgent parents provided years earlier.

Meanwhile, the jury is still out on these slow-growing children we have raised. It is just possible that when they finally reach adulthood, they will have done it right. They were not shoved into it by a conveyer belt, as their parents were. They have had time to think, explore, experiment. Perhaps they will come up at thirty or so, knowing who they are, and they won't have mid-life crises. It is a pretty thought.